A&D

art & display

The Book of American Trade Marks

Edited by
David E. Carter

Art Direction Book Company
19 West 44 Street New York, New York 10036

ART DIRECTION BOOK COMPANY
19 West 44th Street
New York, New York 10036
212/354-0450

1st Printing November 1972
2nd Printing March 1973
3rd Printing June 1973
4th Printing October 1973
5th Printing December 1974
6th Printing June 1975
7th Printing June 1976
8th Printing June 1977
9th Printing October 1978

Library of Congress Catalog Card Number: 72-76493
International Standard Book Number: 0-910158-27-4
ISBN for Standing Orders for this Series: 0-910158-38-X

Introduction

Some time in the late 1950s or early 1960s, a graphic revolution started. An unprecedented number of companies decided to update their corporate symbol.

There is no single answer as to what caused this revolution. Part of the reason was the great number of mergers and acquisitions in the past 10-15 years. Thousands of companies are merging every year. More often than not, the resulting company emerges with a new corporate name — and a new corporate symbol.

Another partial explanation is that, for some reason, companies became more image conscious. Corporate symbols that had been created many years before looked out of step with the times. Many companies made the decision to update their image.

This book is an attempt to show some of the significant trade marks, logotypes, and corporate symbols that now exist in the United States. The contents of this book are meant to reflect the sweeping changes which have taken place in corporate symbol design. The nearly 1,000 corporate symbols included in this book are all considered by the editor to be outstanding examples of contemporary design.

It is readily apparent that this book does not include every good corporate symbol in the United States. (There are certainly more than 992 good marks now in existence.) For this reason, and because of enthusiastic response to the idea of this book, a Volume 2 of The Book of American Trade Marks is now in the early stages of preparation.

Persons wishing to submit marks to be considered for inclusion may mail them to Art Direction Book Company, 19 West 44th Street, New York, New York 10036.

Marks will not be returned, but all material will be acknowledged.

Many of the marks included in this book are registered trade marks, and may not be reproduced without the permission of the owner of the mark.

I would like to thank the many designers and owners of trade marks who have given permission for material to be included in this book.

I would also like to give special thanks to Roger S. Dyer, who assisted in all phases of this project (which has taken more than three years), and to A.T. Turnbull of Ohio University, and to Bob McKinney and Dave Brumfield of Chapman Printing Co., for assistance in pre-press production of the book.

For my mother, who made everything possible, and for my wife, whose patience and understanding made this book possible.

1

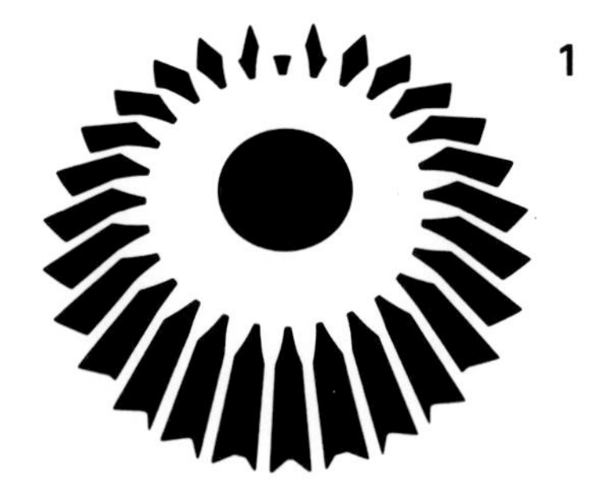

2

GATX

3

4

5

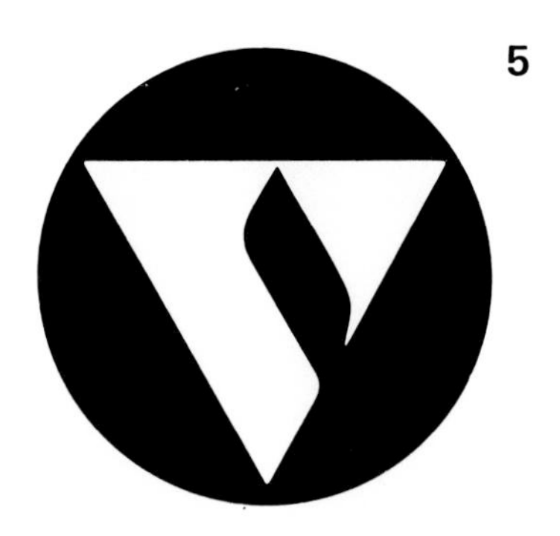

6

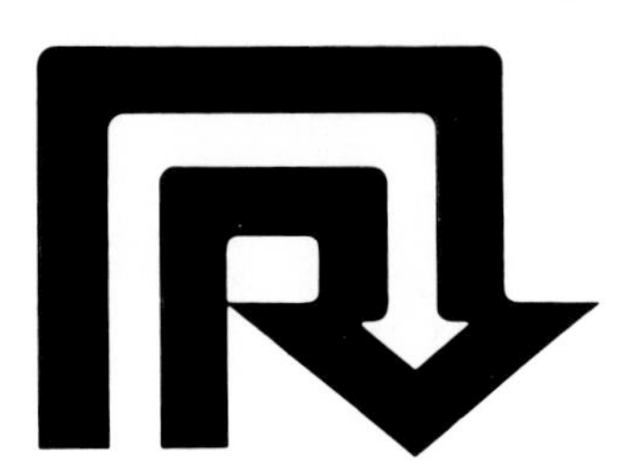

7

8

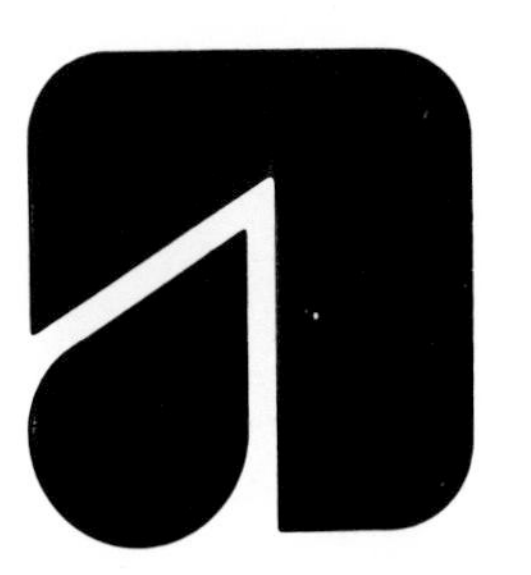

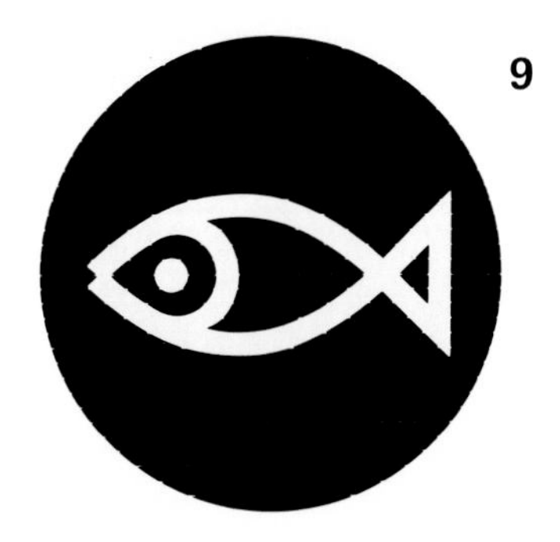

9

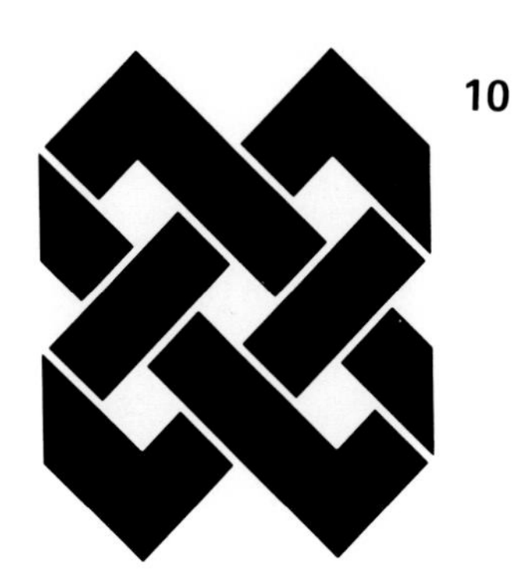

10

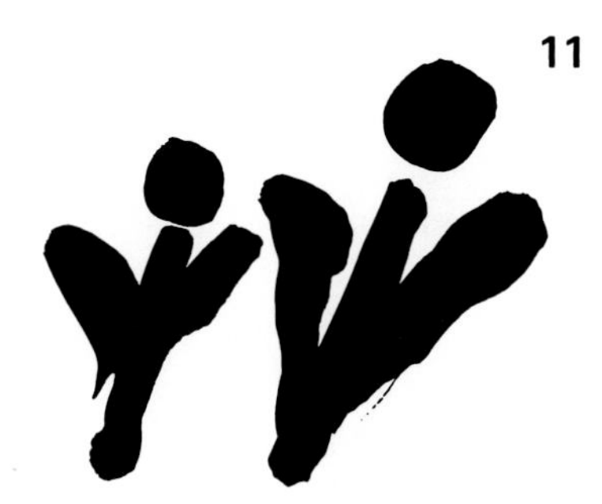

11

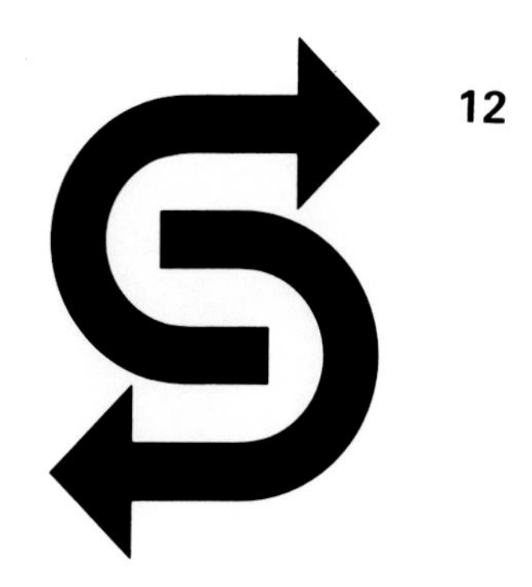

12

1 Perfection Gear Company
Chicago

2 GATX
Chicago

3 Camp Rafa-El
Marin Jewish Community Center

4 Salesvertising Art
Denver

5 Varo, Inc.
Garland, Texas

6 Redactron Corporation
Hauppauge, New York

7 Recognition Equipment, Inc.
Dallas

8 Acheson Colloids Co.
Port Huron, Michigan

9 New England Aquarium
Boston

10 United Banks of Colorado
Denver

11 White House Conference on Youth
Washington

12 Seatrain Lines
New York City

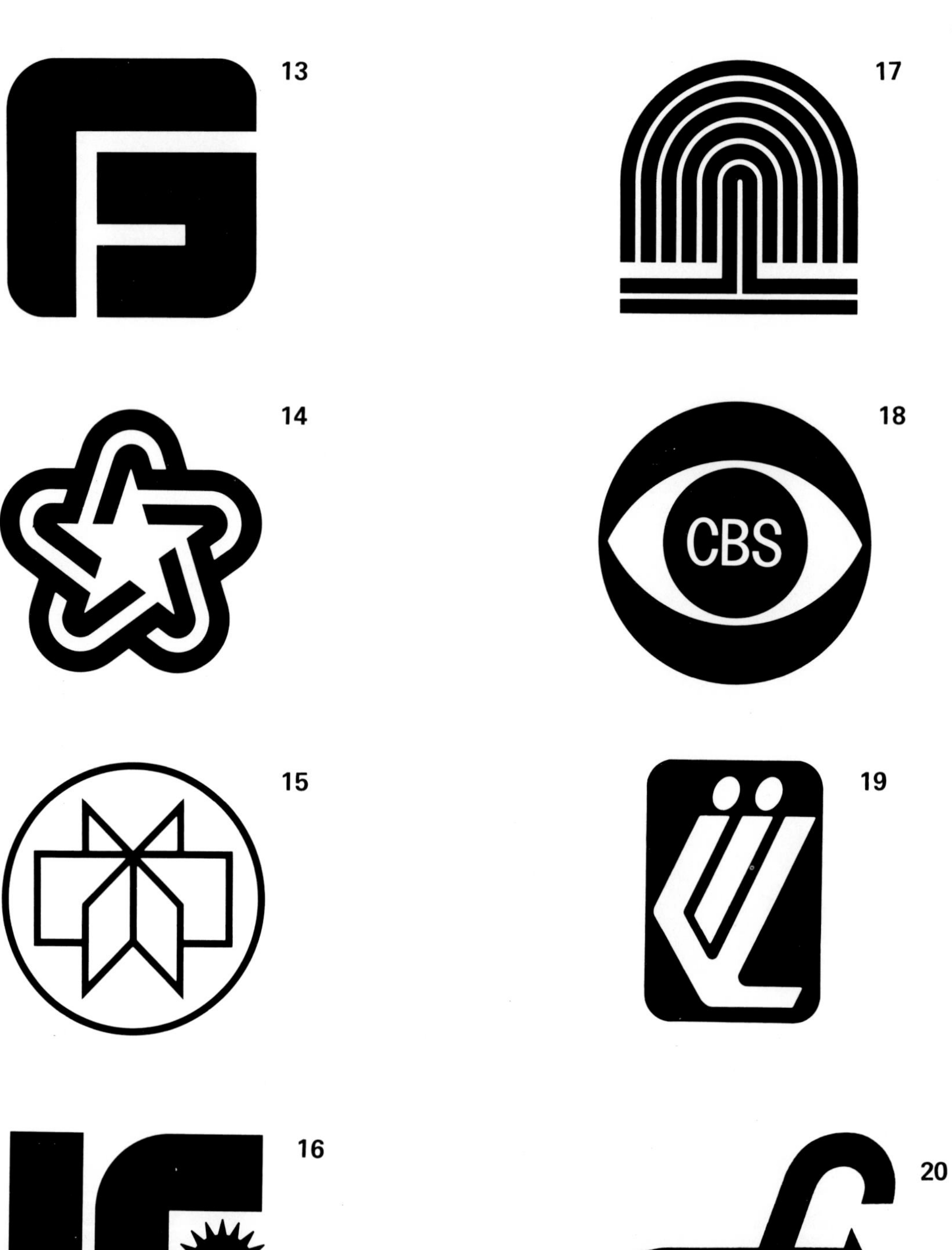
13
17
14
18
CBS
15
19

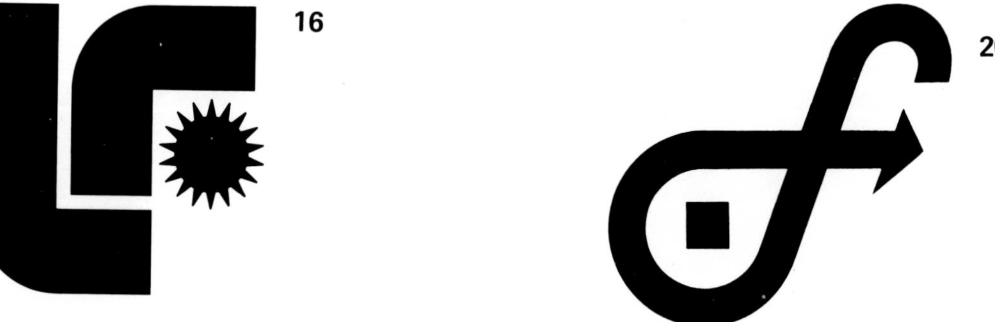
16
20

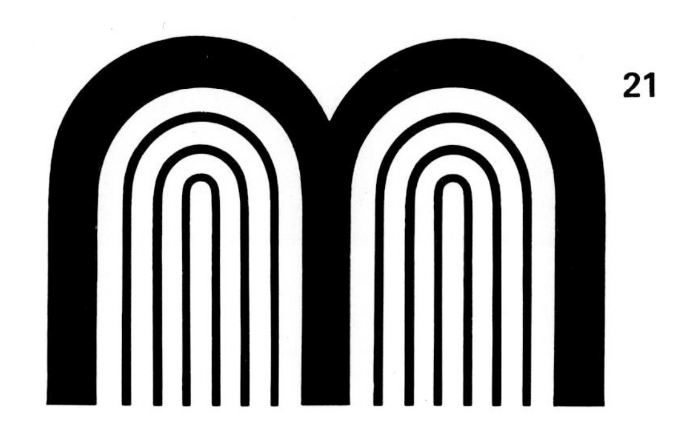

21

22

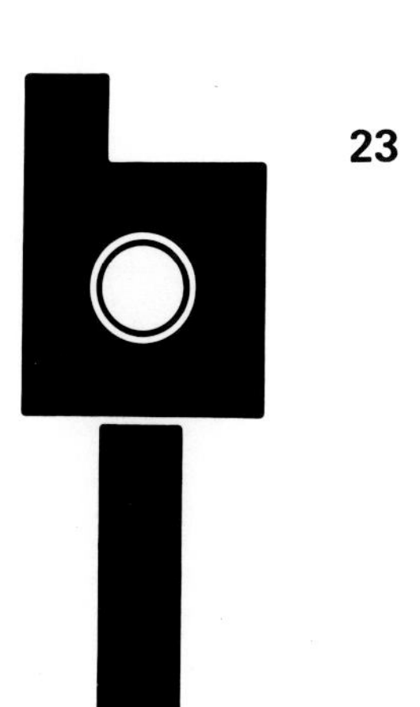

23

24

13 The General Fireproofing Co.
Youngstown, Ohio

14 American Revolution Bicentennial Comm.
Washington, D.C.

15 New York State University of Buffalo
Buffalo

16 Lake Forest National Bank
Lake Forest, Illinois

17 Willow Creek Apartments
Lake Forest, Illinois

18 CBS
New York City

19 Imperial International Learning
Kankakee, Illinois

20 Follett Educational Corp.
Chicago

21 Marcal Paper Mills, Inc.

22 Citizens National Bank
Bowling Green, Kentucky

23 Blakeslee-Lane Photography
Baltimore

24 Beverly Hills Tennis Club
Beverly Hills, California

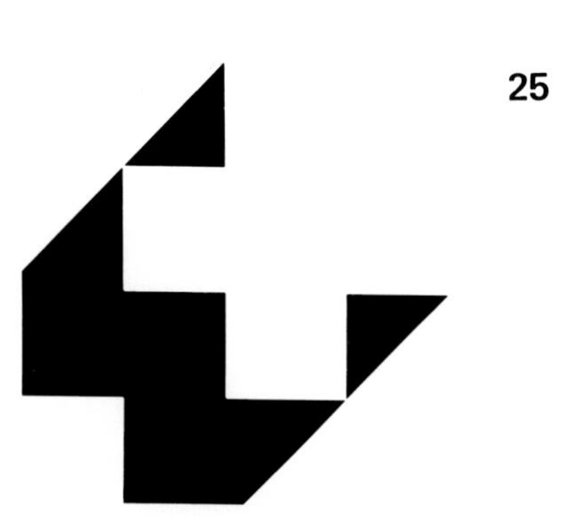
25

26

27

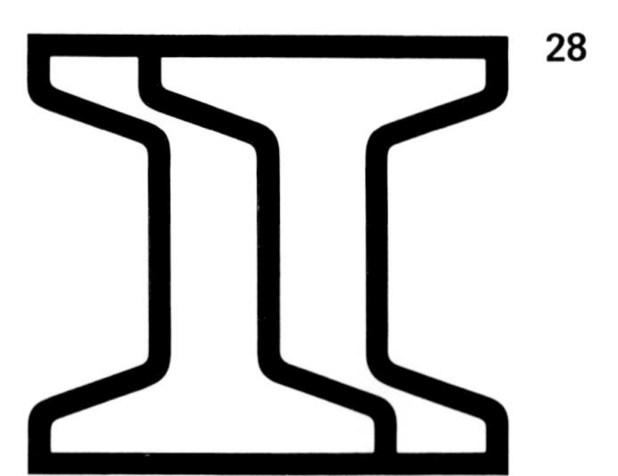
28

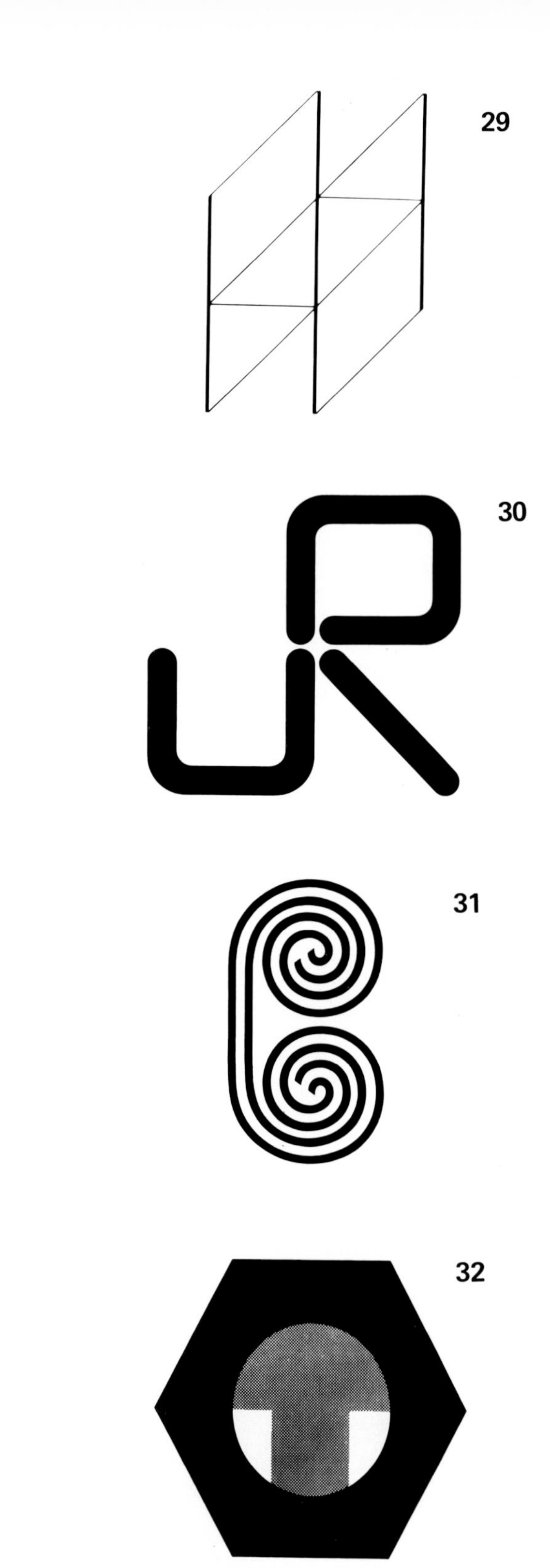
29

30

31

32

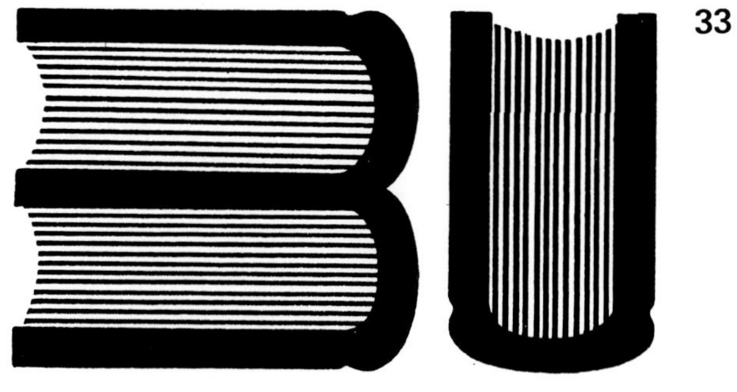

33

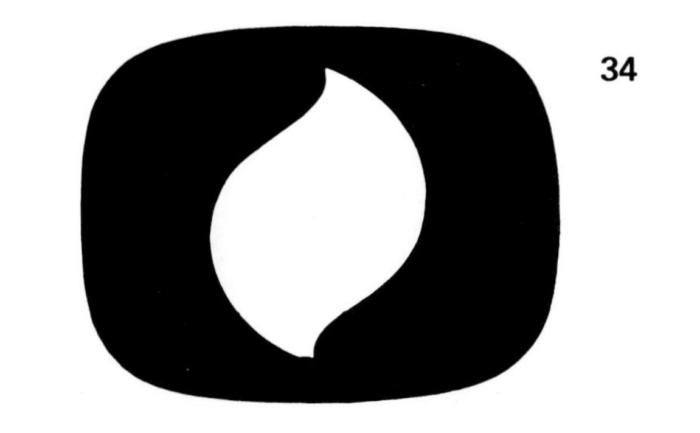

34

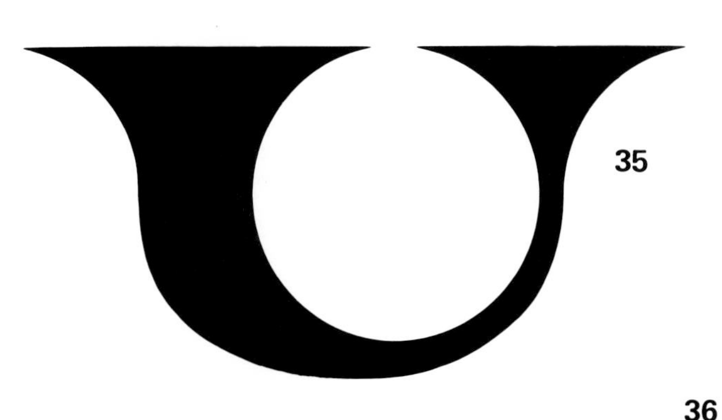

35

36

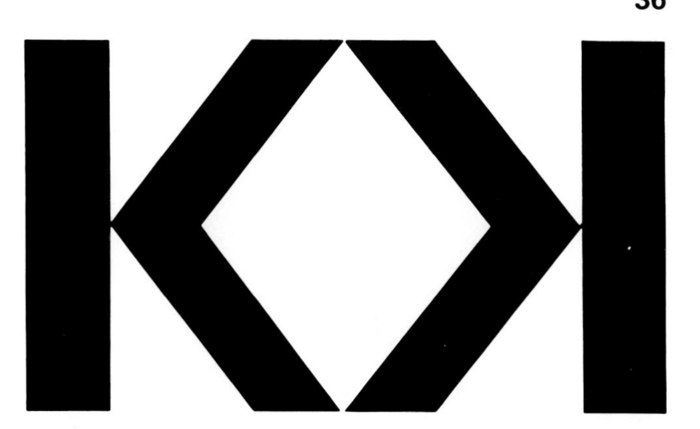

25 Beekman Downtown Hospital
New York City

26 Cooper Tool Co.
Denver

27 Titan Fastners
Roslyn, New York

28 Isramet Trading Corporation
Greenvale, New York

29 Howell Design Associates
Providence, Rhode Island

30 Janet Rosenblum, Inc.
New York City

31 Phili-tec Division
Western World Electronics Corp.
New York City

32 Tern Contracting Corporation
Brooklyn

33 Books Unlimited
Sarasota, Florida

34 Torrid Oven, Inc.
Buffalo, New York

35 Uniworld Export Corporation
New York City

36 Kasparians, Inc.
Los Angeles

37

38

39

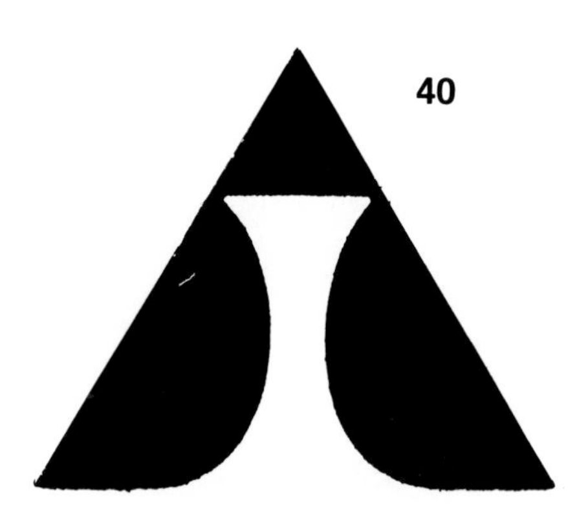
40

41

42

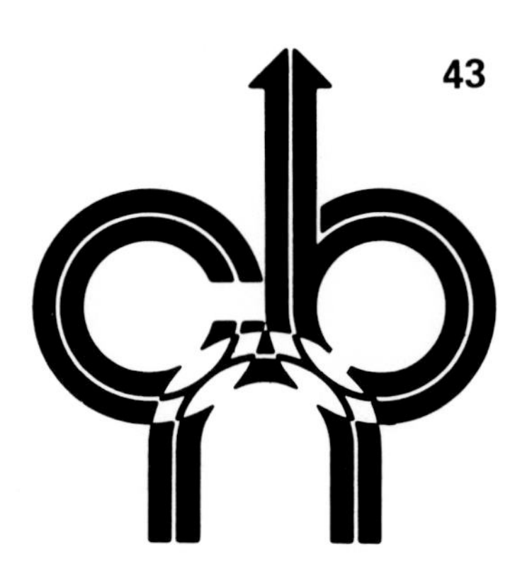
43

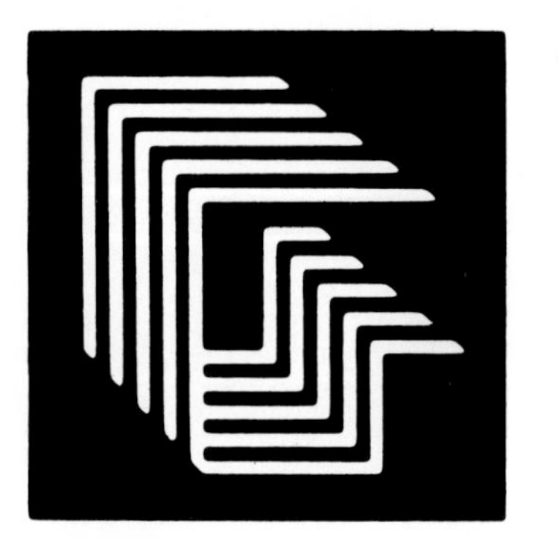
44

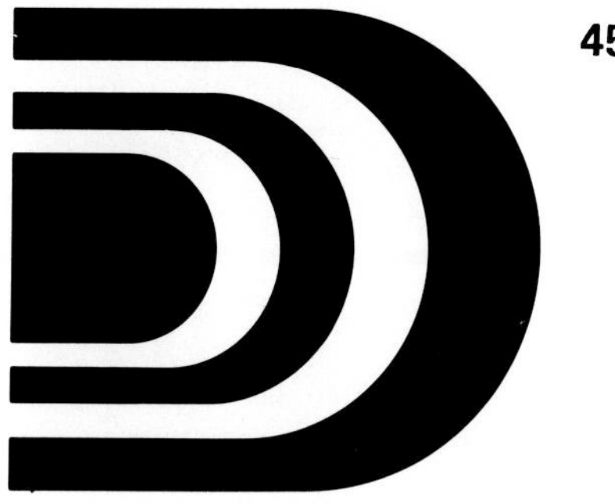

45

46

47

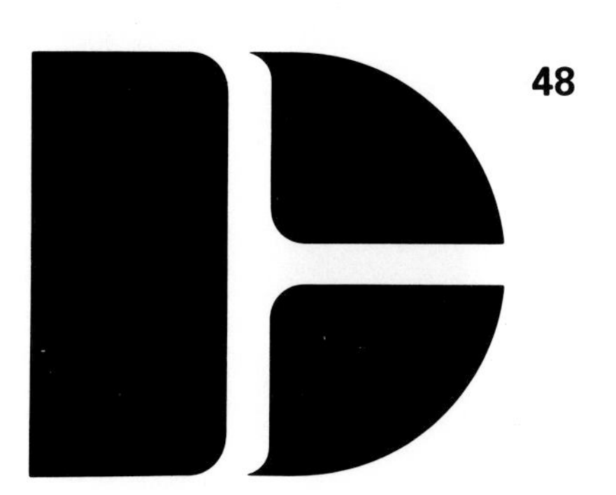

48

37 Franklin Town
Philadelphia

38 Capitol Records
Hollywood

39 Vibrodyne, Inc.
Dayton, Ohio

40 Intertechnique
Dover, New Jersey

41 Envirotech Corporation
Menlo Park, California

42 Ink, Inc.
Lakewood, Colorado

43 City National Bank
Austin, Texas

44 W.D. Gradison & Company
Cincinnati

45 Delaware Management Co., Inc.
Philadelphia

46 Decatur Income Fund
Philadelphia

47 Delta Trend Fund
Philadelphia

48 Delaware Fund
Philadelphia

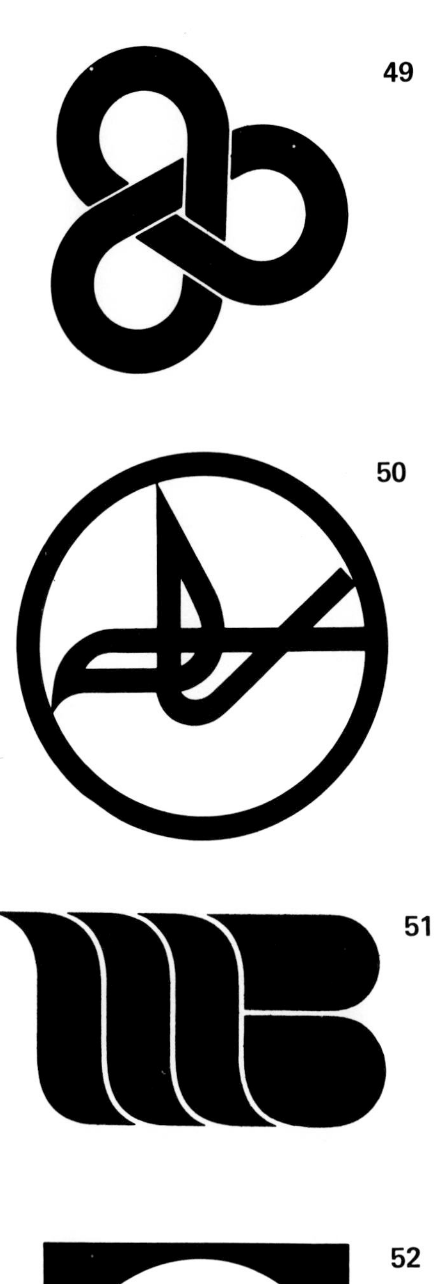

49

50

51

52

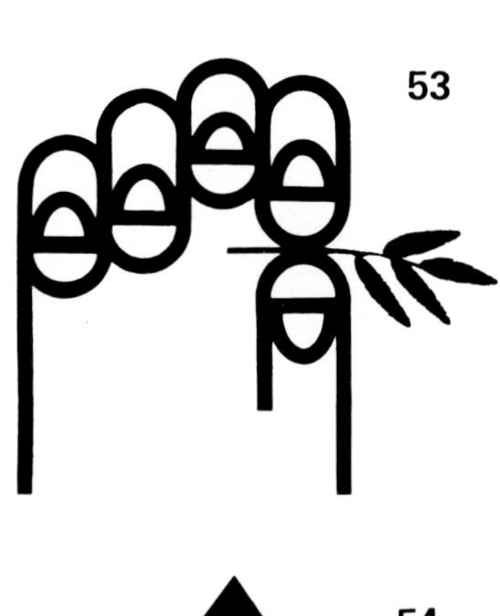

53

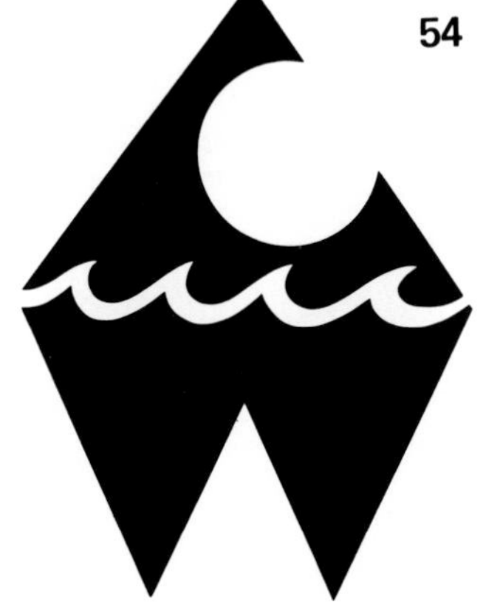

54

55

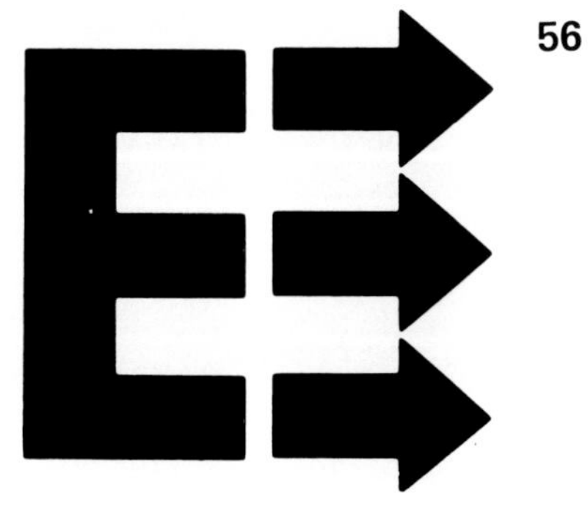

56

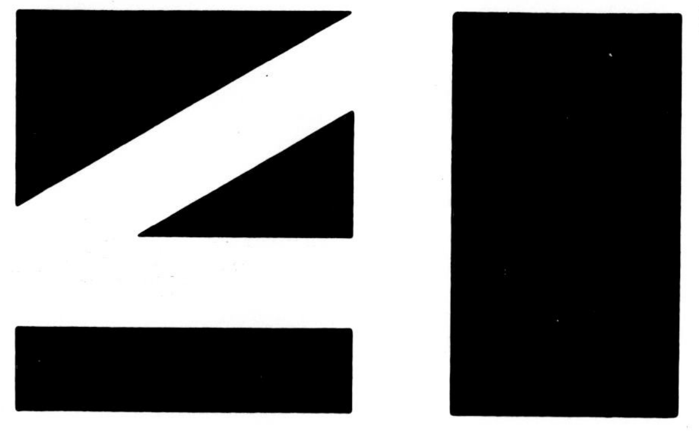

57

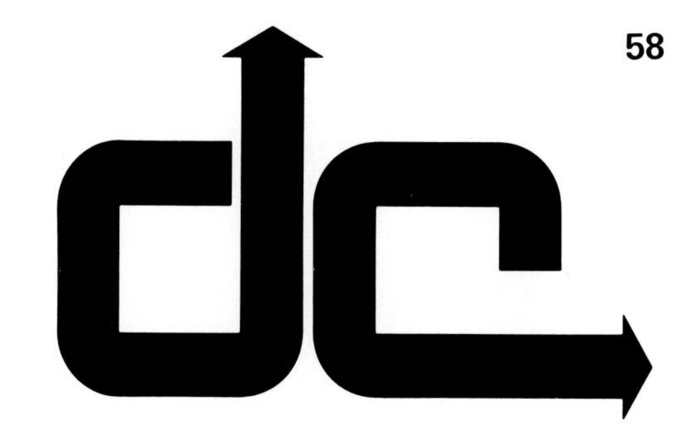

58

59

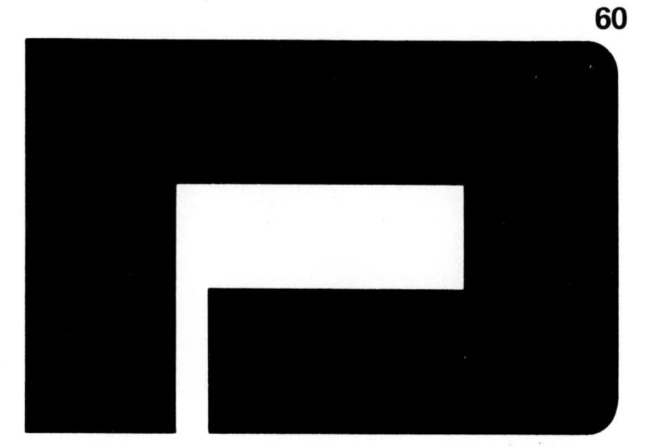

60

49 MPB Corporation
Keene, New Hampshire

50 John Birdsall Creative Service Assoc.
Los Angeles

51 Marker-Berry Graphics
San Francisco

52 Gallmeyer & Livingston Co.
Grand Rapids, Michigan

53 Peace Corps
Washington

54 Canadian Waters, Inc.
Ely, Minnesota

55 Public Service Indiana
Plainfield, Indiana

56 Emhart Corporation
Hartford, Connecticut

57 Fourth National Bank
Tulsa, Oklahoma

58 The Decker Clark Corporation

59 International Minerals & Chemicals
Chicago

60 The Platt Bros. & Co.
Waterbury, Connecticut

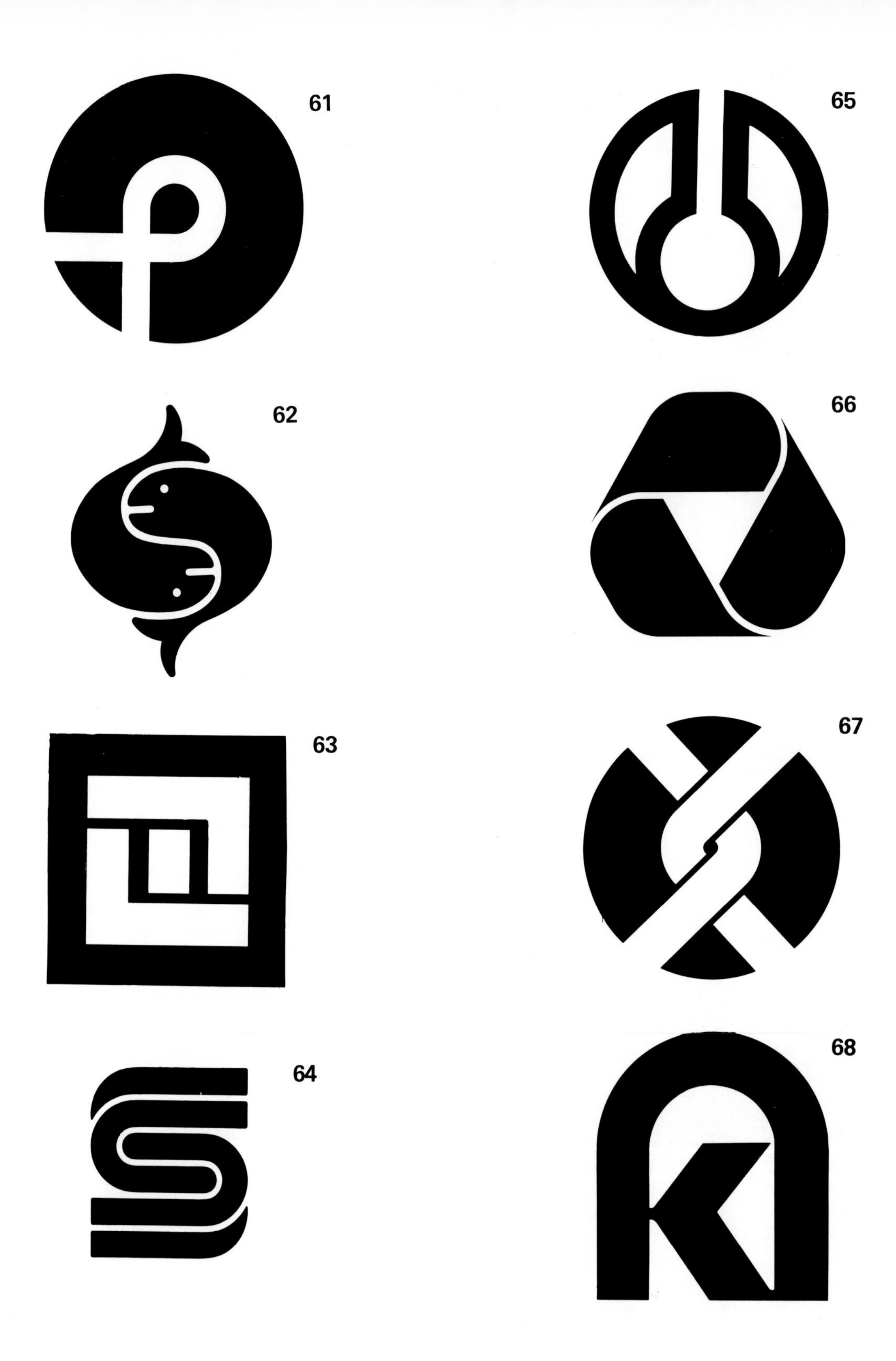
61
62
63
64
65
66
67
68

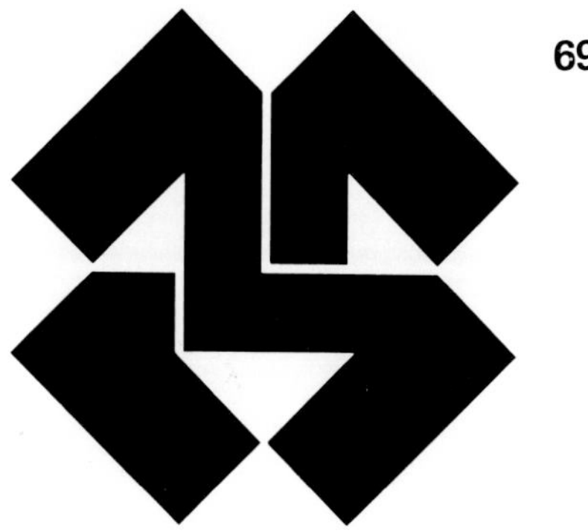

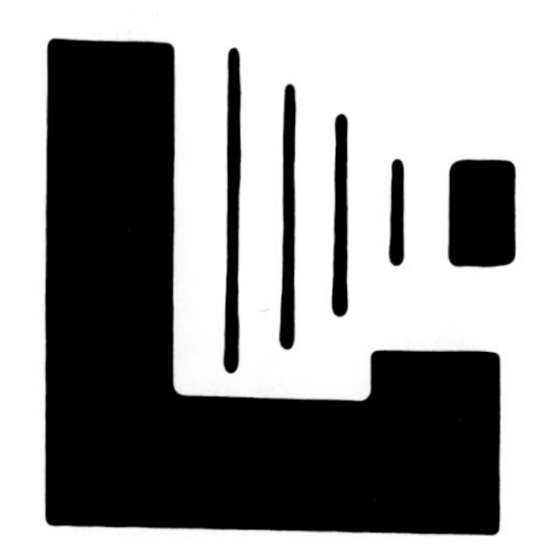

71

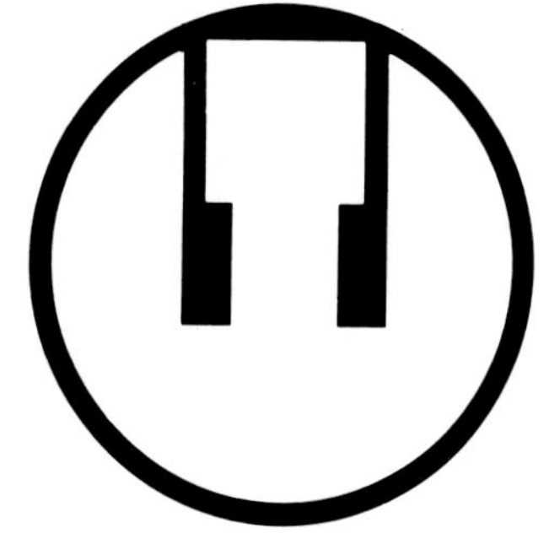

72

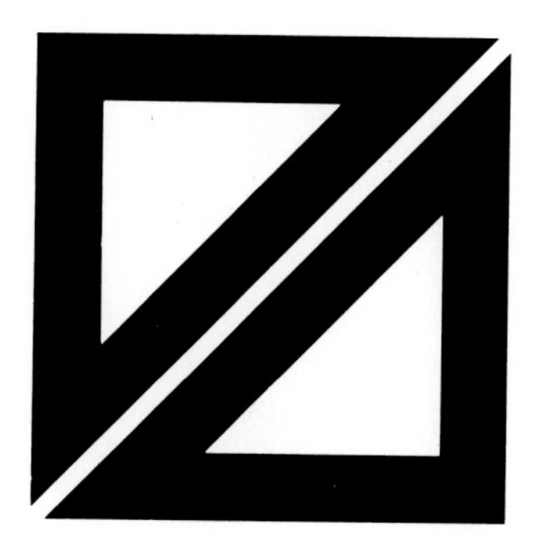

61 Pembroke's
Salt Lake City, Utah

62 Aquaria, Inc.
Los Angeles

63 Franklin Interiors
Pittsburgh

64 Security First National Bank
Los Angeles

65 International Applied Science Laboratory
Hempstead, L.I., New York

66 Innerspace Environments, Inc.
San Francisco

67 American Protection Industries
Los Angeles

68 Keepper Nagel, Inc.
Lake Forest, Illinois

69 Morris Museum of Arts & Sciences
Morristown, N. J.

70 Jim Lucas Photography
Oklahoma City, Oklahoma

71 Pacific Electrical
Gardena, California

72 View Seal
Container Corporation of America
New York City

73
74
75
76

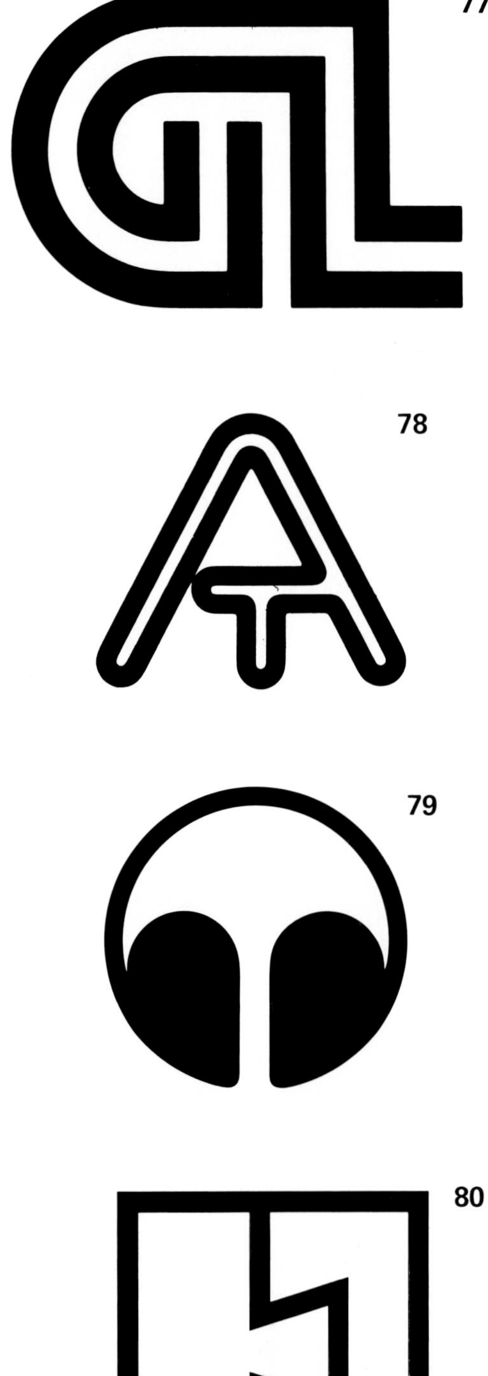
77
78
79
80

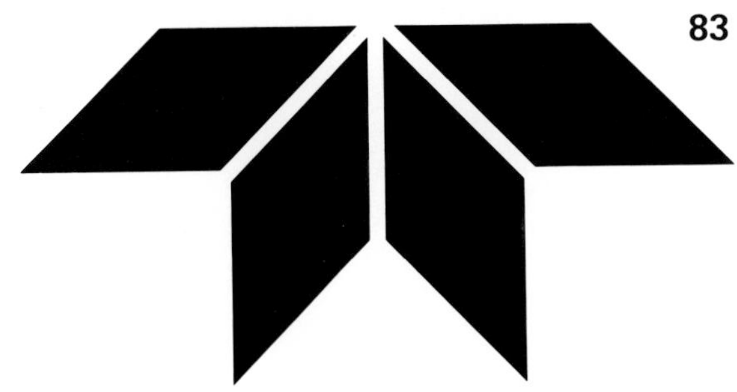

84

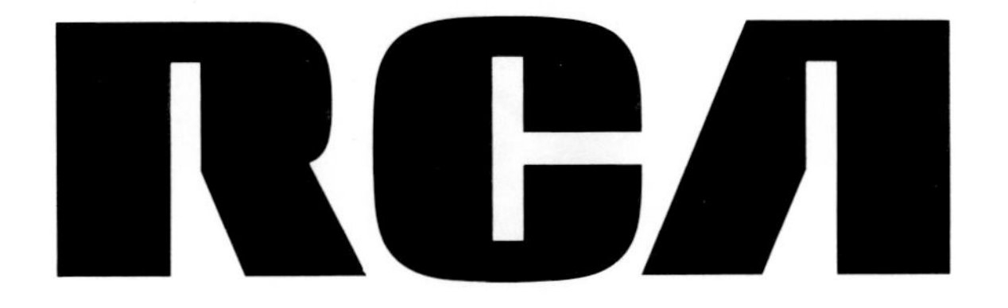

73 M.C. Canfield Sons, Quality Solder
Union, New Jersey

74 Lee Myles Assoc., Inc., Advertising
New York City

75 Lee Myles Assoc., Inc., Printing
New York City

76 Carrier Envelope Co.
Chicago

77 General Learning Corporation
New York City

78 American Tube and Controls Inc.
West Warwick, Rhode Island

79 First National Bank in Palm Beach
Palm Beach, Florida

80 Foothill General Corporation
Century City, California

81 Technical Exhibits Corporation
Subsidiary of Model Builders, Inc.
Chicago

82 Carefree Services
Denver

83 Teledyne, Inc.
Los Angeles

84 RCA
New York City

85

86

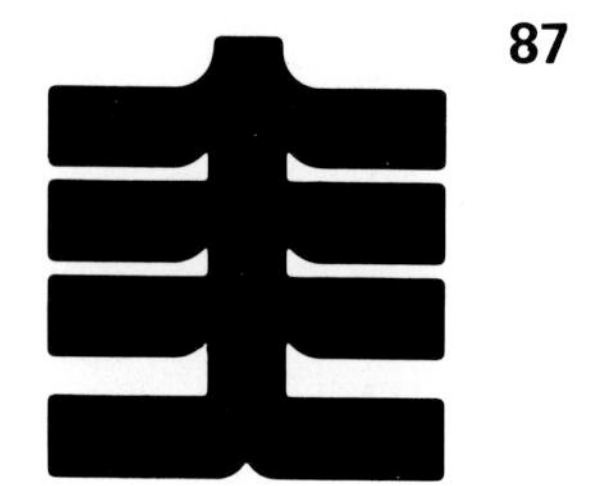

87

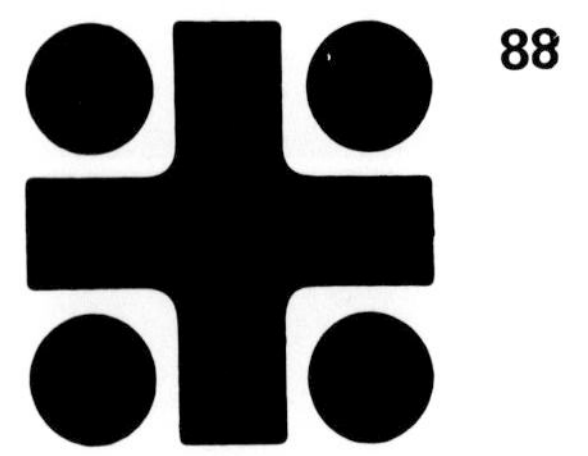

88

89

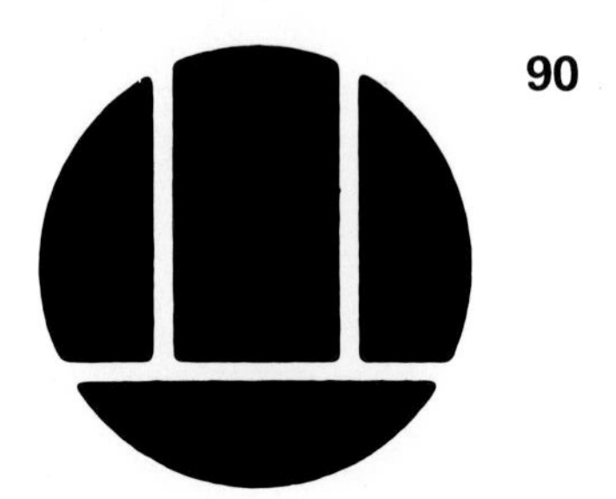

90

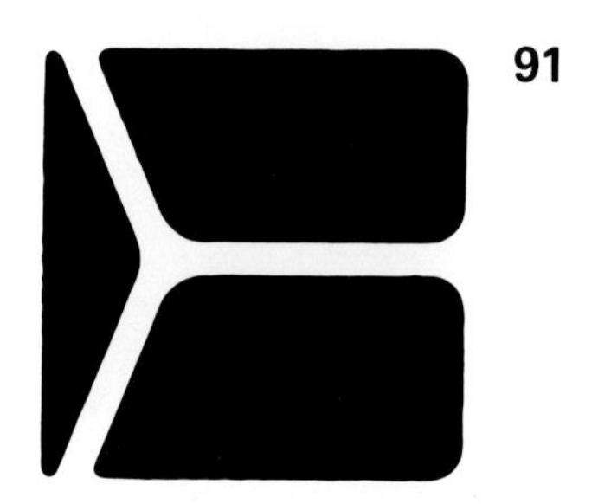

91

92

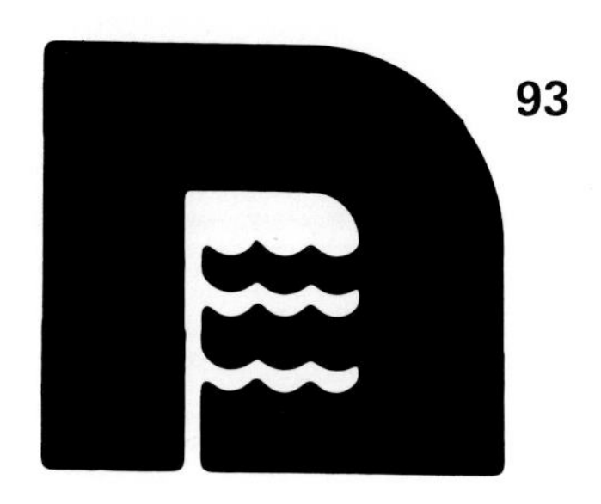
93

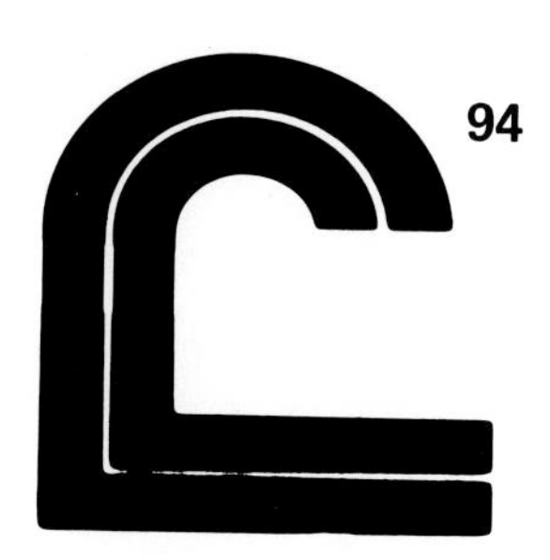
94

95

96

85 Penguin Industries, Inc.
Parkesburg, Pennsylvania

86 Hoppe's, a Division of
Penguin Industries, Inc.
Parkesburg, Pennsylvania

87 Redwood Bank
San Rafael, California

88 Typagraph Corporation
San Diego, California

89 Holiday Airlines
Los Angeles

90 Merchants Bank of Allentown
Allentown, Pennsylvania

91 Bianco Manufacturing Co.
St. Louis

92 United Engineers & Contractors, Inc.
Philadelphia

93 Nor-Lake, Inc.
Hudson, Wisconsin

94 The Larwin Group, Inc.
Beverly Hills, California

95 Ohio National Bank
Columbus, Ohio

96 Norman L. Mayell & Associates
Chicago

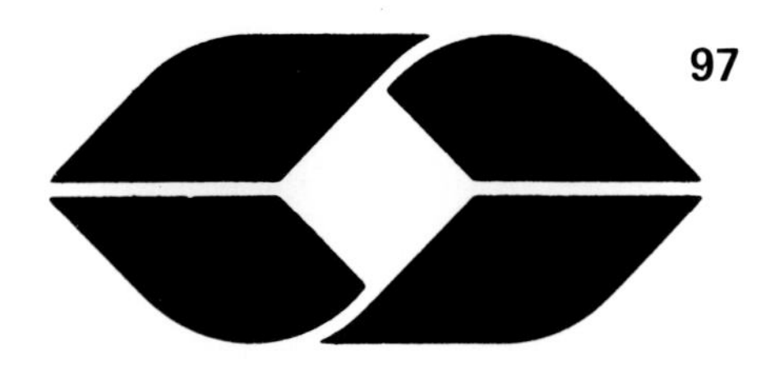

97

98

99

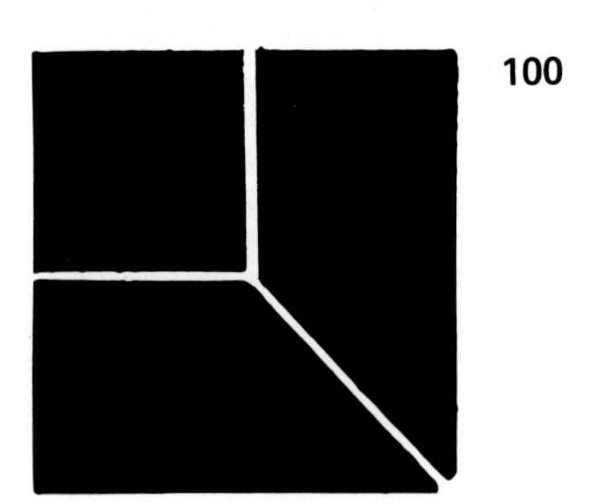

100

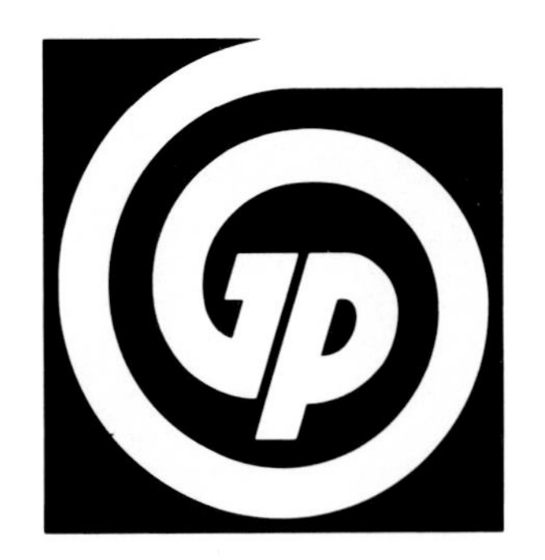

101

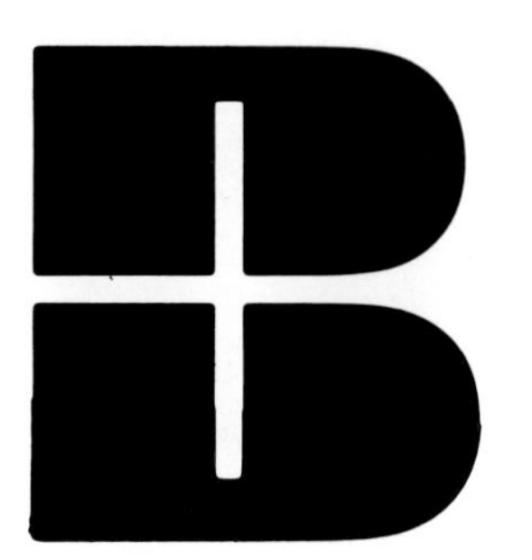

102

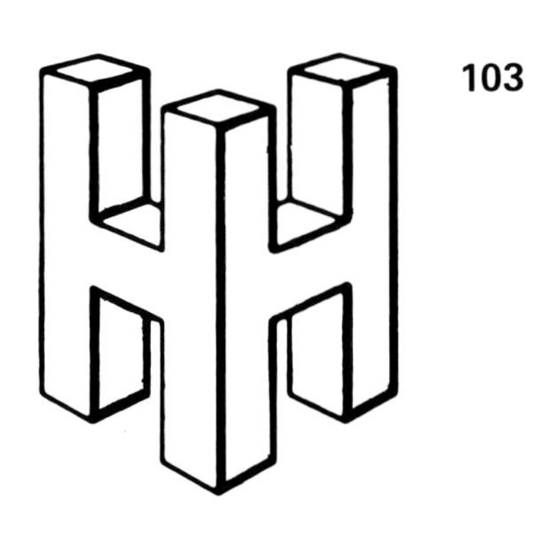

103

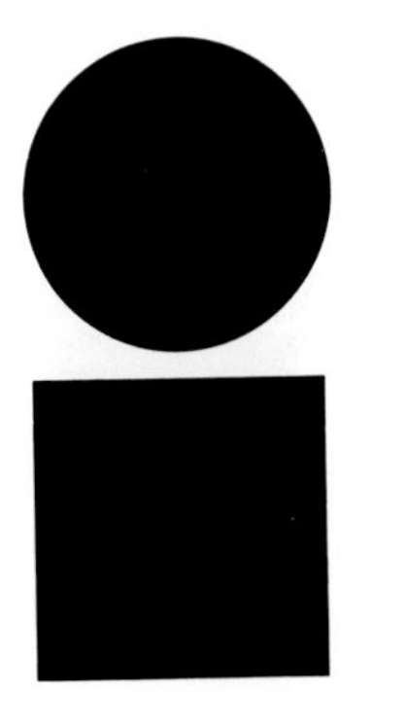

104

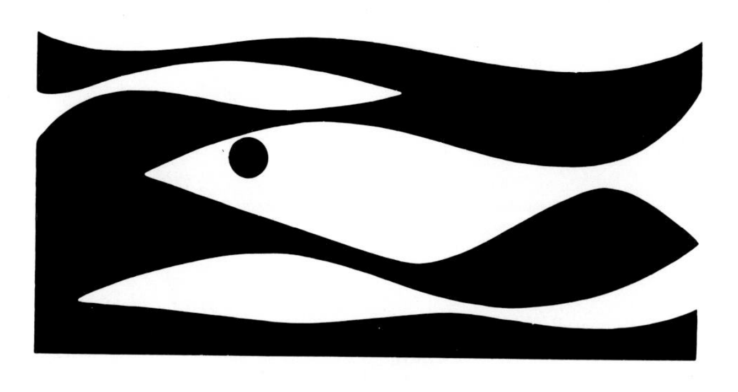

105

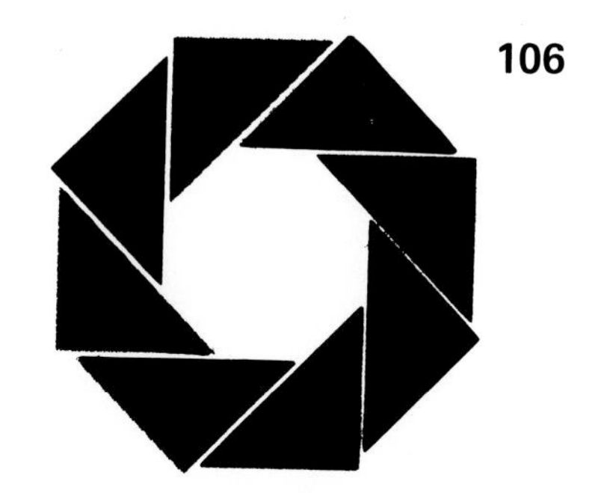

106

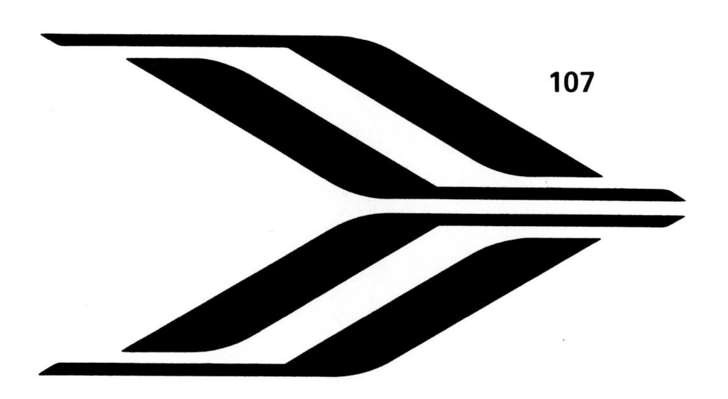

107

108

97 Equity Funding Corp. of America
Los Angeles

98 Air Products and Chemicals, Inc.
Allentown, Pennsylvania

99 Southern Natural Gas Co.
Birmingham, Alabama

100 College/University Corporation
Indianapolis

101 Goulds Pumps
Seneca Falls, New York

102 Buffalo Savings Bank
Buffalo, New York

103 Hartford Hospital
Hartford, Connecticut

104 Imaginetics, Inc.
White Plains, New York

105 Tropical Air Pump Mfg. Corp.
New York City

106 Color Service, Inc.
Monterey Park, California

107 Aerostar, Ted Smith
Aircraft Co., Inc.
Van Nuys, California

108 The Carborundum Co.
Niagara Falls, New York

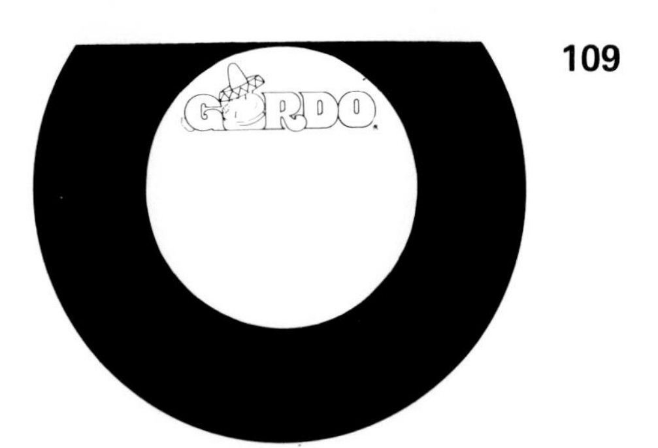

109

110

111

112

113

114

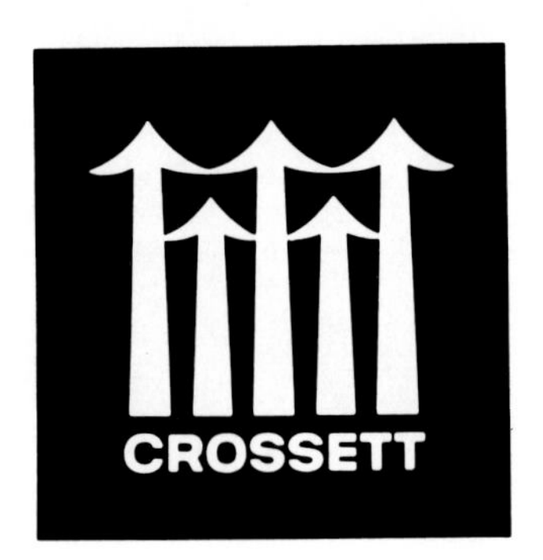

115

116

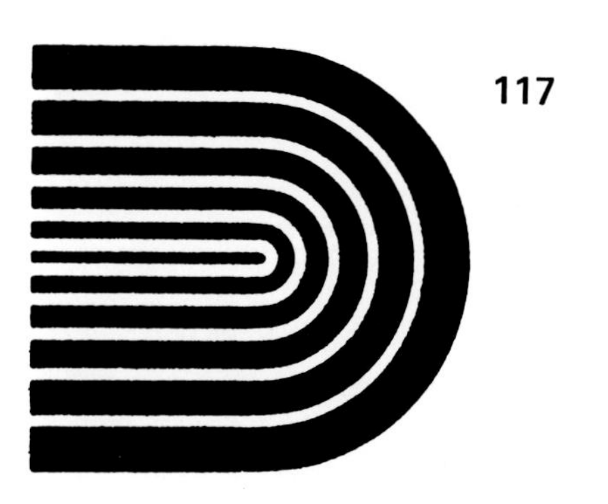

117

118

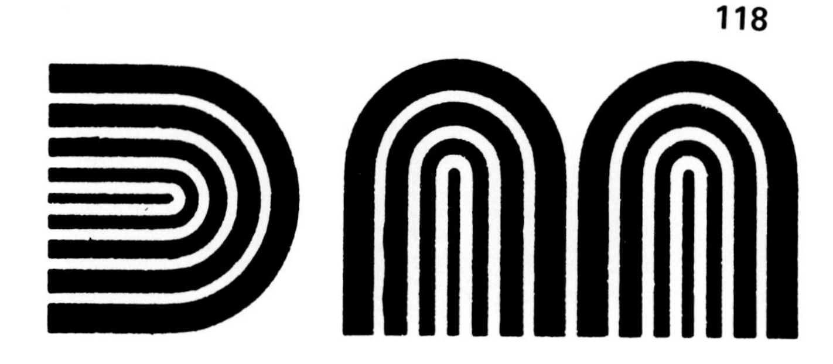

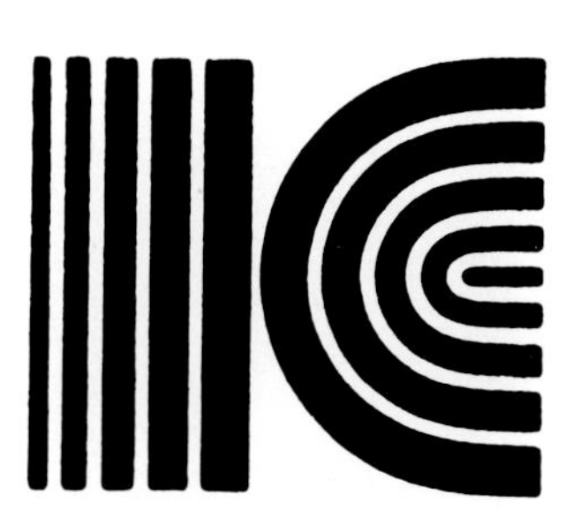

119

120

109 Gordo Records
Los Angeles

110 Atlantic Richfield Co.
New York City

111 Ekco Products, Inc.
Wheeling, Illinois

112 The Durst Organization
New York City

113 Problematics
Waltham, Massachusetts

114 Pollota & Sommers,
General Contractors
Palisades Park, New Jersey

115 The Crossett Company
Crossett, Arkansas

116 Heatilator Fireplaces
Vega Industries
Syracuse, New York

117 Ducommun Incorporated
Los Angeles

118 Ducommun Metals & Supply Co.
Los Angeles

119 Kierulff Electronics, Inc.
Los Angeles

120 Super-Temp Co.
Santa Fe Springs, California

121

122

123

125

126

127

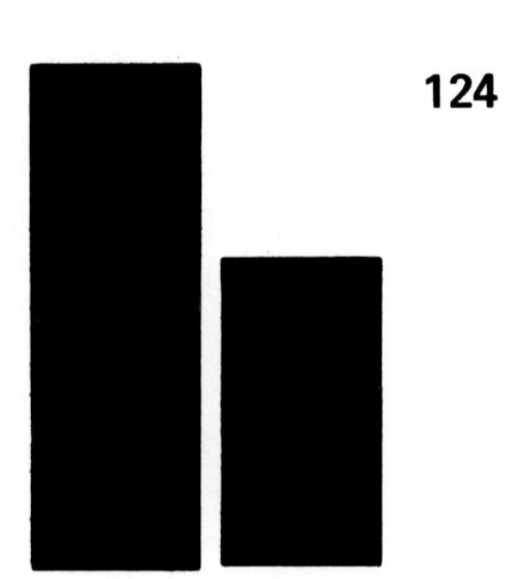

124

128

129

130

131

132

121 Sun Newspapers
Edina, Minnesota

122 Valentine Pulp & Paper Co.
Lockport, Louisiana

123 Jeppesen & Co.
Denver

124 Hooker Chemical Corp.
New York City

125 Beverly Hills Bancorp
Beverly Hills, California

126 Ajax Magnathermatic Corp.
Warren, Ohio

127 American Sentry Corp.
Beverly Hills, California

128 Information International
Los Angeles

129 Metropolitan Wire Goods Corp.
Wilkes-Barre, Pennsylvania

130 Jacks 4
Thousand Oaks, California

131 Aspen Skiing Corp.
Aspen Colorado

132 Central Penn National Bank
Philadelphia

133
134
135
136
137
138
139
140

141

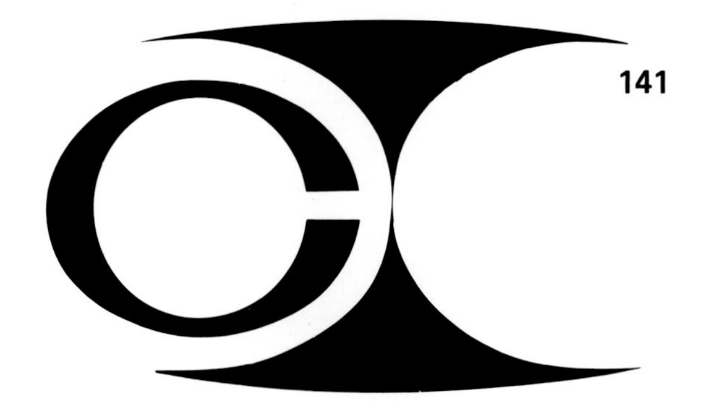

142

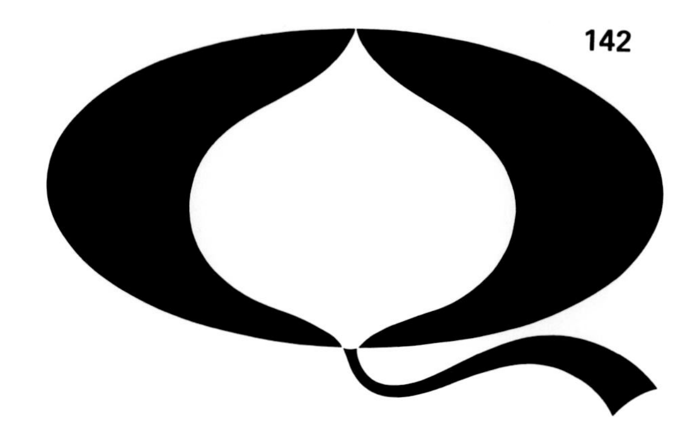

143

144

133 Bankers Trust
New York City

134 Lawter Chemicals, Inc.
Chicago

135 Toyo Printing Co.
Los Angeles

136 Merchants Insurance Group
Buffalo, New York

137 Cascade Electric
Tacoma, Washington

138 Advance Mortgage Corp.
Southfield, Michigan

139 Johnson Foils, Inc.
Springfield, Massachusetts

140 Cascade Airways
Spokane, Washington

141 California Products Corp.
Cambridge, Massachusetts

142 Quality Cheese & Spice
Somerville, Massachusetts

143 Massachusetts Bank & Trust
Brockton, Massachusetts

144 First National Bank
Dayton, Ohio

145

149

146

150

147

151

148

152

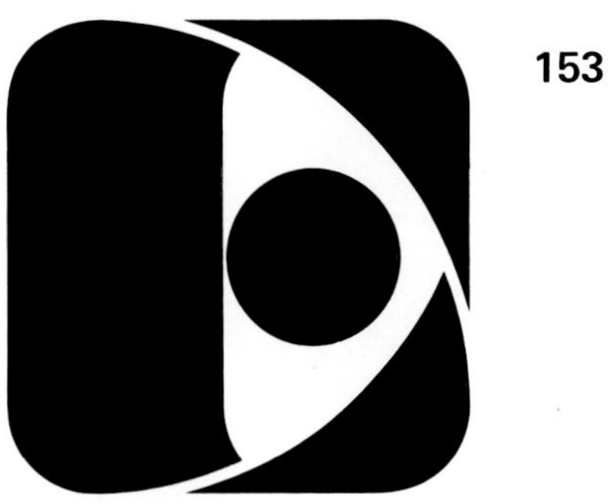

153

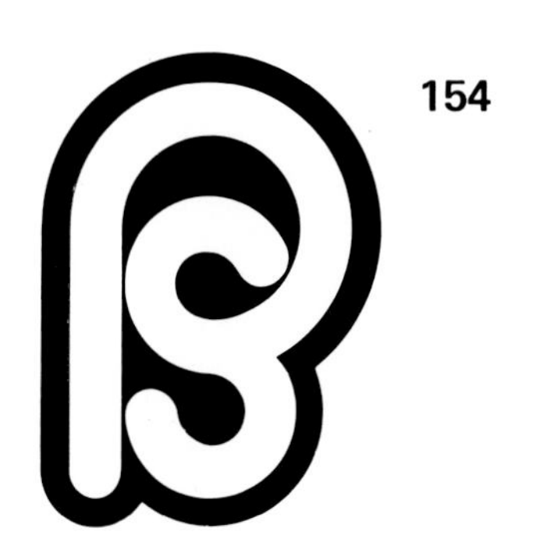

154

155

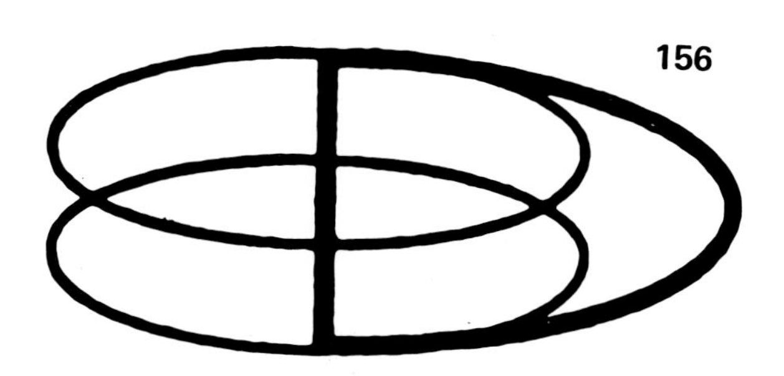

156

145 Finn Industries
Chicago

146 Federal Compress & Warehouse Co.
Memphis, Tennessee

147 Pioneer Electronics USA Corp.
Farmingdale, New York

148 Hancock-Gross
Philadelphia

149 New York Aquarium

150 Hardwood House
Rochester, New York

151 Spicer Divisions
Dana Corp.
Toledo, Ohio

152 Richmond Research Corp.
Richmond Hill, New York

153 Scientific Resources Corp.
Philadelphia

154 Porcelain Studio
San Francisco

155 The Seiberling Tire & Rubber Co.
Akron, Ohio

156 Dickenson Publishing Co., Inc.
Encino, California

157

158

159

161

162

163

160

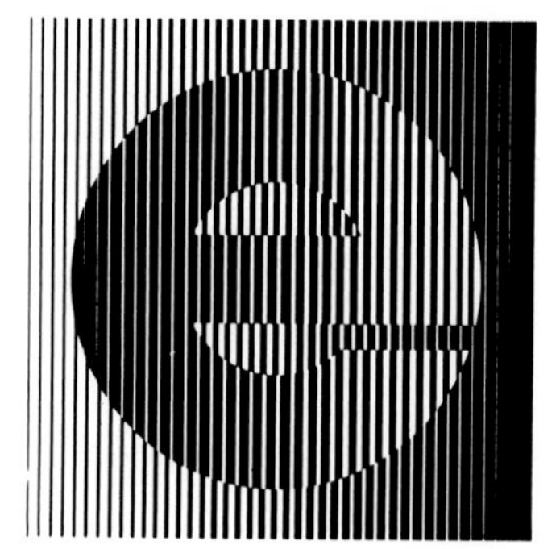

164

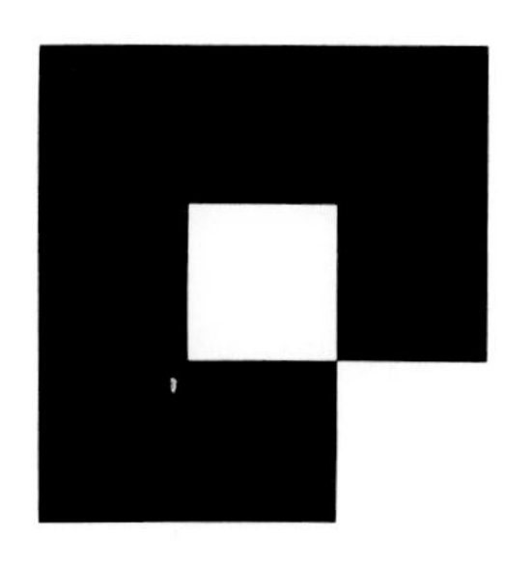

165

166

167

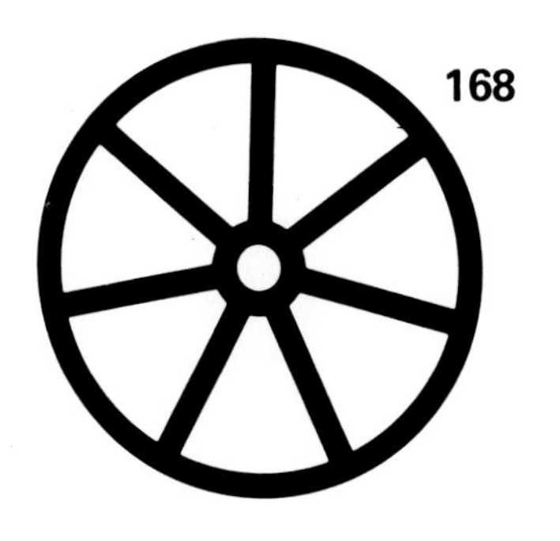

168

157 G. Leblanc Corp.
Kenosha, Wisconsin

158 Springer-Verlag New York, Inc.
New York City

159 American Journal of Nursing
New York City

160 Loft's Candy Co.
Long Island City, New York

161 The Twentieth Century Fund
New York City

162 Bank of the Commonwealth
Norfolk, Virginia

163 Industrial Design Collaborative
Brooklyn

164 Eisert Racing Enterprises, Inc.
Costa Mesa, California

165 Rochester Institute of Technology
Rochester, New York

166 Lone Star Industries, Inc.
Greenwich, Connecticut

167 Snowbird, Ltd.
Alta, Utah

168 Northwest Bancorporation
Minneapolis

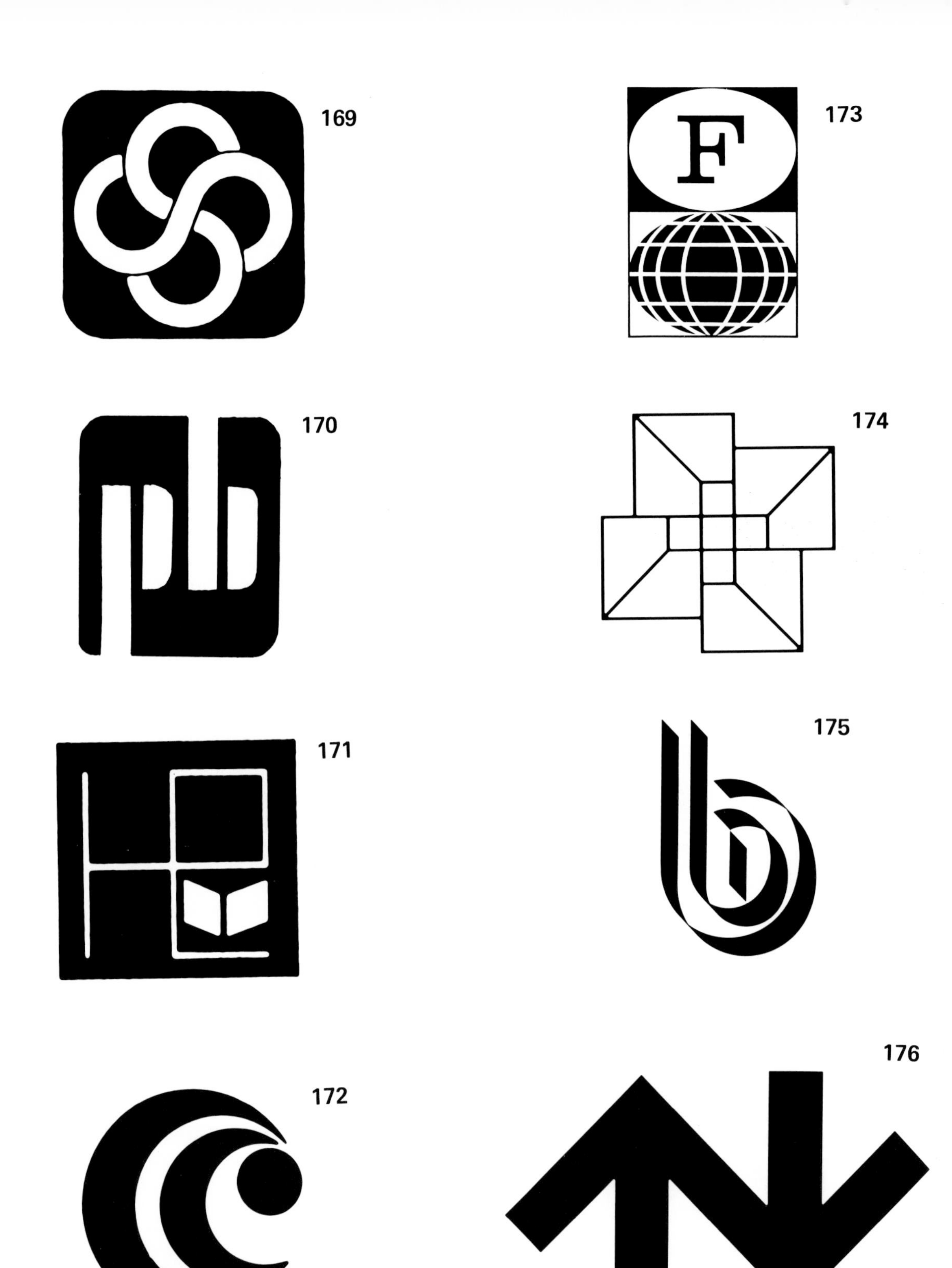
169
173
F
170
174
171
175
172
176

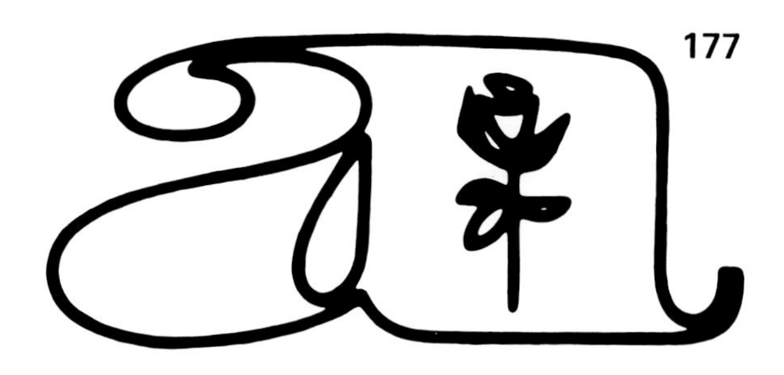

177

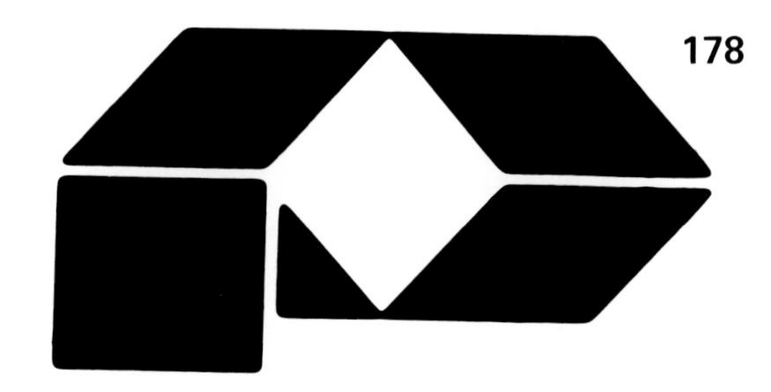

178

179

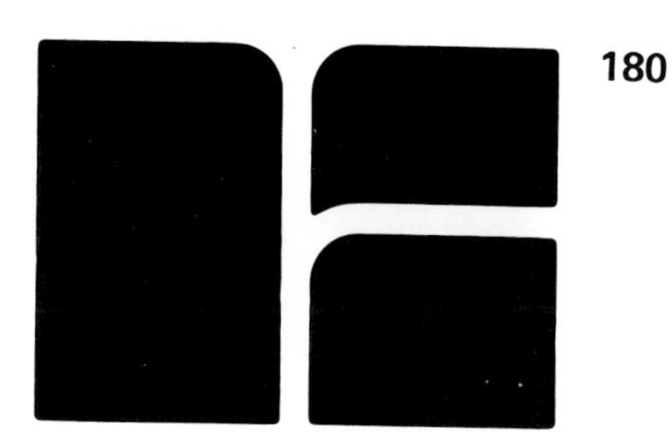

180

169 Oakley Tube Corp.
Englewood, Colorado

170 Peoples Bank of Western Pennsylvania
New Castle, Pennsylvania

171 Hartford Public Library
Hartford, Connecticut

172 Conwed Corp.
St. Paul, Minnesota

173 Follett Corporation
Chicago

174 Omniplan
Dallas

175 Brammer's Business Interiors
Memphis, Tennessee

176 National Elevator

177 American Greetings Corporation
Cleveland

178 Prudent Publishing Co.
Englewood Cliffs, New Jersey

179 Matheson Gas Products
Milwaukee

180 W.H. Freeman and Co., Publishers
San Francisco

181
182
183
184
185
186
187
188

189

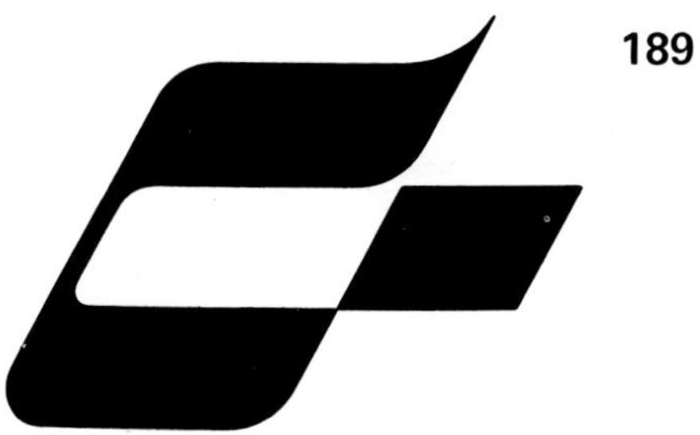

190

191

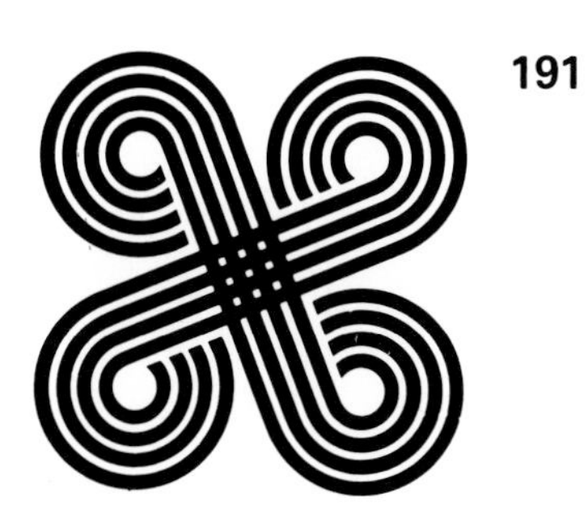

192

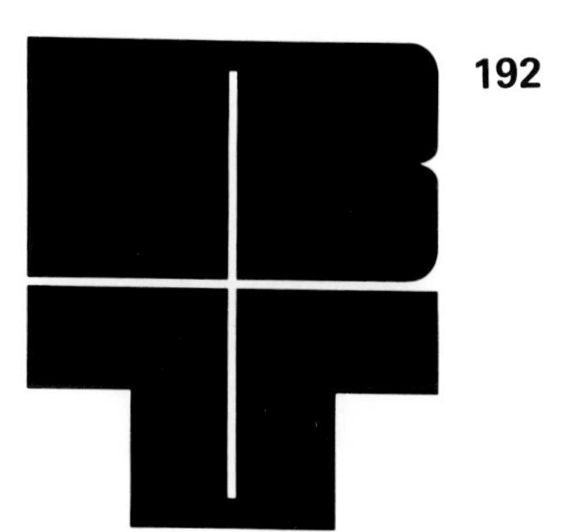

181 Jefferson National Bank
Lynchburg, Virginia

182 Delray Dunes Golf & Country Club
Delray Beach, Florida

183 Corpus Christi Bank & Trust
Corpus Christi, Texas

184 First National Bank
Hot Springs, Arkansas

185 Lawry's Foods, Inc.
Los Angeles

186 Photographic Display Laboratories
St. Paul, Minnesota

187 Baseler Photo Marketing Co., Inc.

188 The Continental Bank
Chicago

189 Gillette Tolitries
Boston

190 Huntly Gaming Company
Beverly Hills, California

191 Klopman Mills
New York City

192 Burns & Towne
Malden, Massachusetts

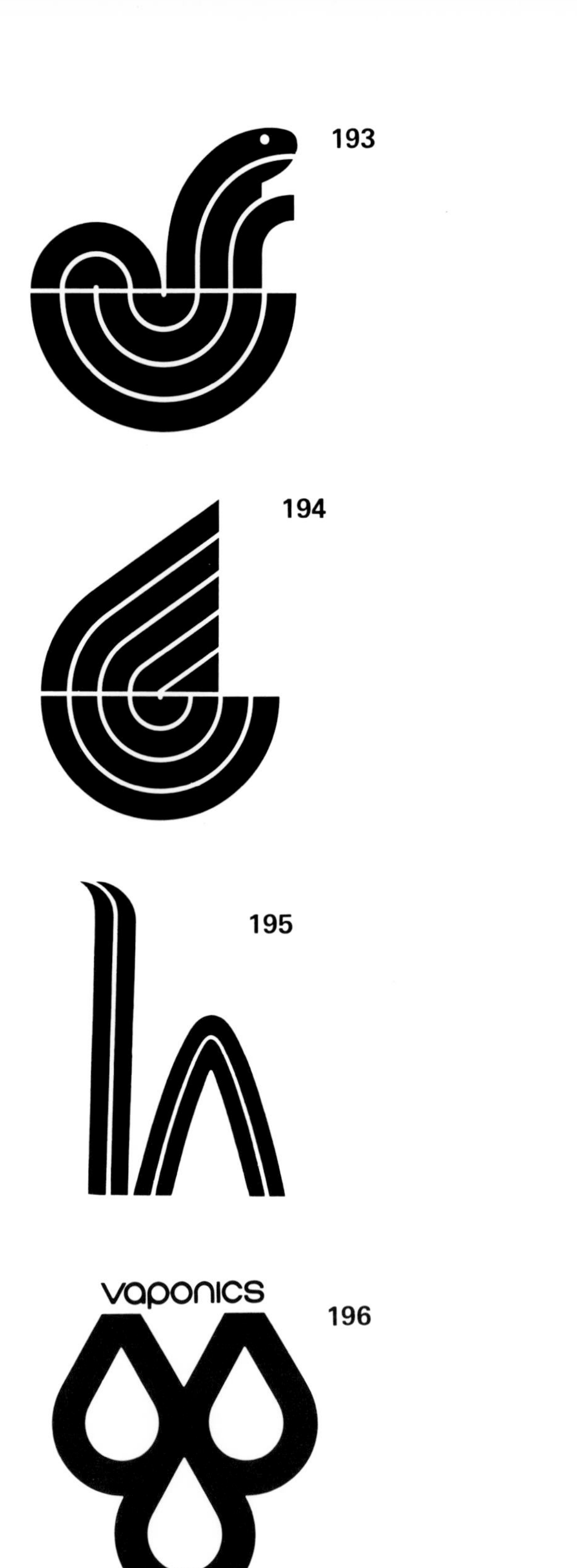
193
194
195
vaponics
196

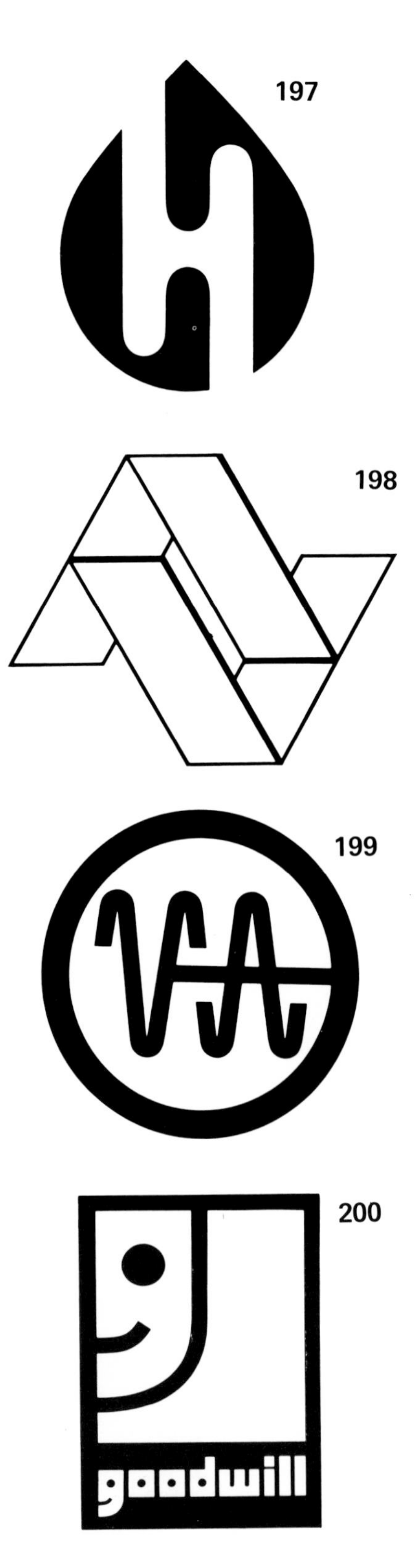
197
198
199
200
goodwill

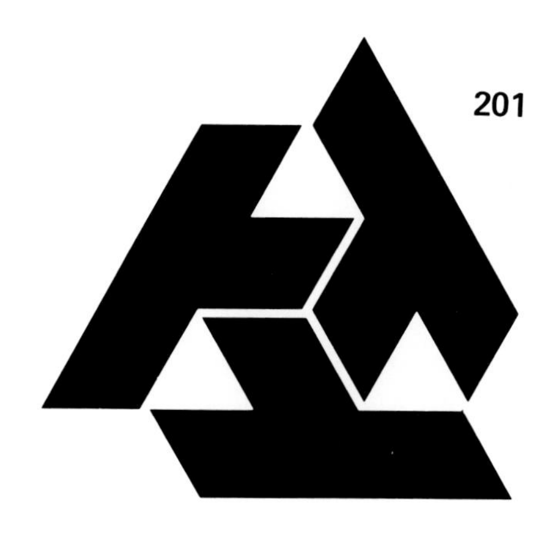

201

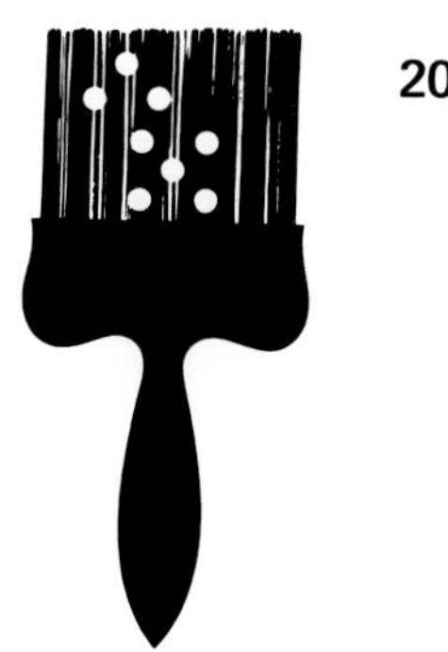

202

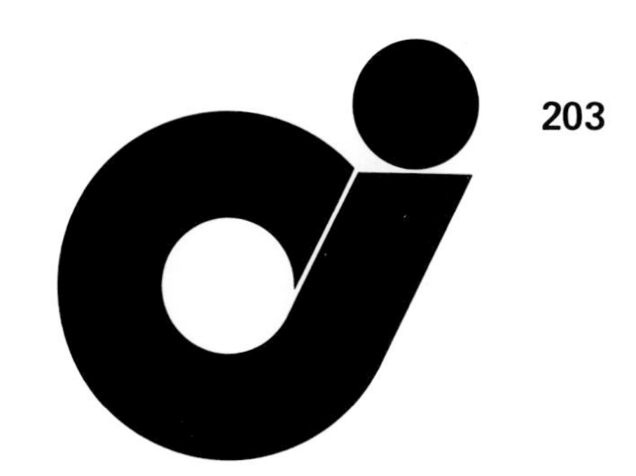

203

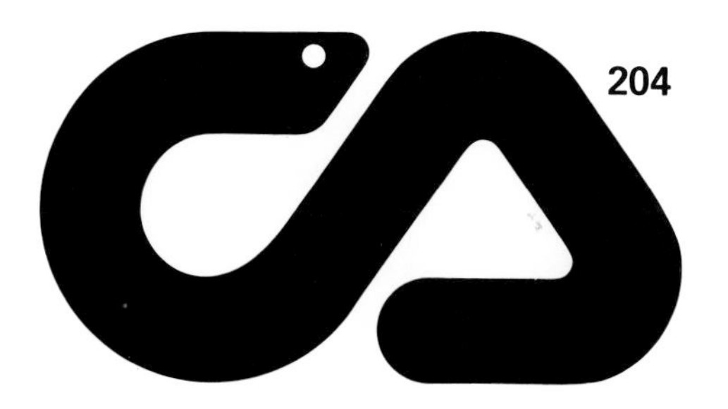

204

193 Beaver Cove
Greenville, Maine

194 Beaver Cove Marina
Greenville, Maine

195 Haystack Ski Area
Vermont

196 Vaponics
Dedham, Massachusetts

197 Houghton Chemical Corp.
Boston

198 Architectural Design Assoc.
Providence, Rhode Island

199 Varian
Palo Alto, California

200 Goodwill Industries
Boston

201 Turbo Train Transportation
U.S. Dept. of Transportation
Washington

202 Martin Senour Paints
Chicago

203 Corporate Identities
Division of Gray & Rogers
Philadelphia

204 Clay-Adams
Parsippany, New Jersey

205

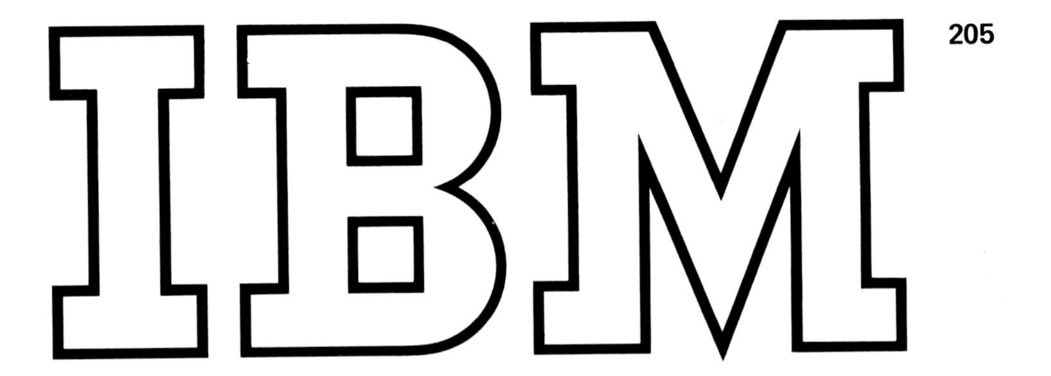

206

207

208

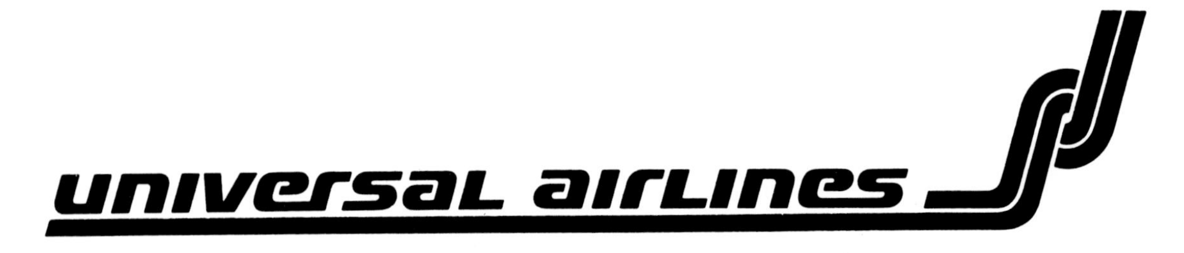

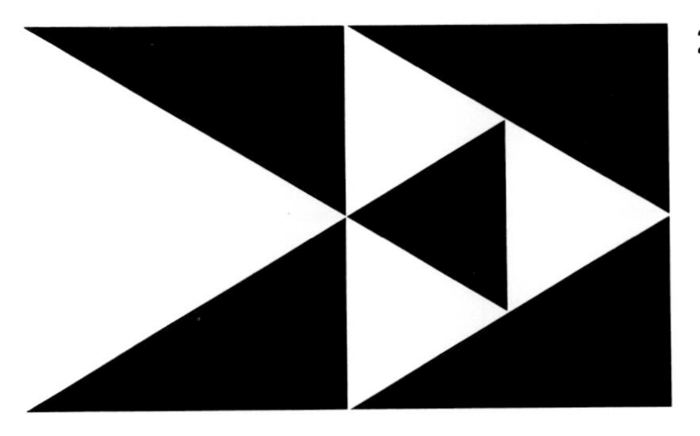

209

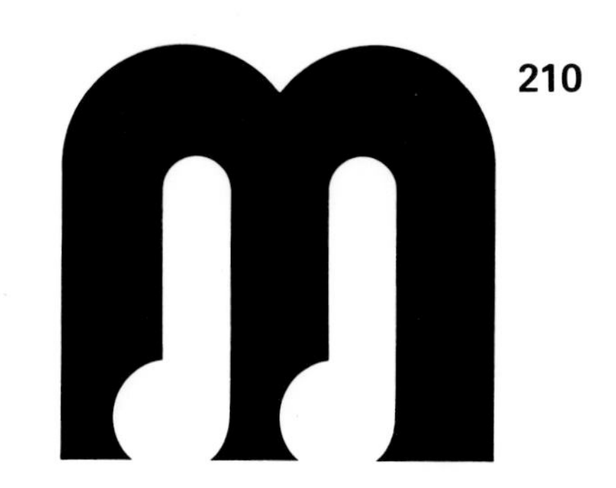

210

205 IBM
New York City

206 Sperry Rand Corp.
New York City

207 Pennwalt Corp.
Philadelphia

208 Universal Airlines
New York City

209 Edgewood Furniture Co., Inc.
New York City

210 Manhattan School of Music
New York City

211 Middle South Services Inc.
New Orleans,

212 Eidophor Inc.
Division of CIBA

211

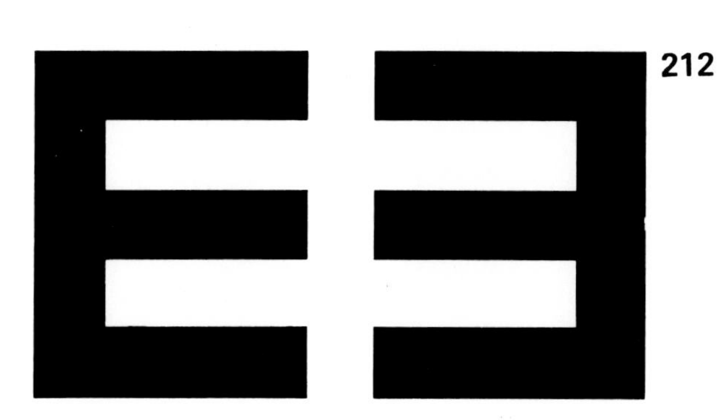

212

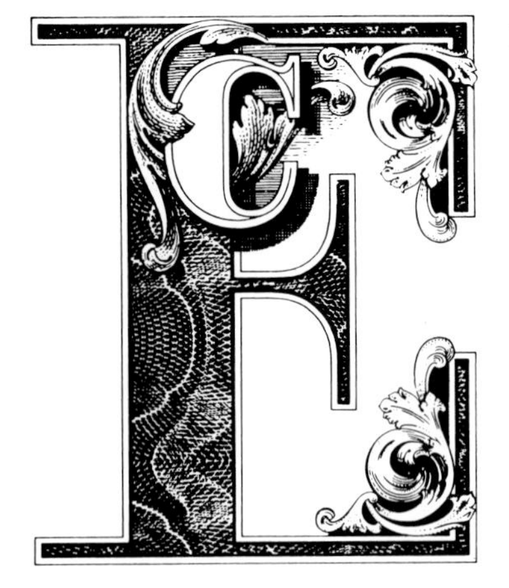

213

214

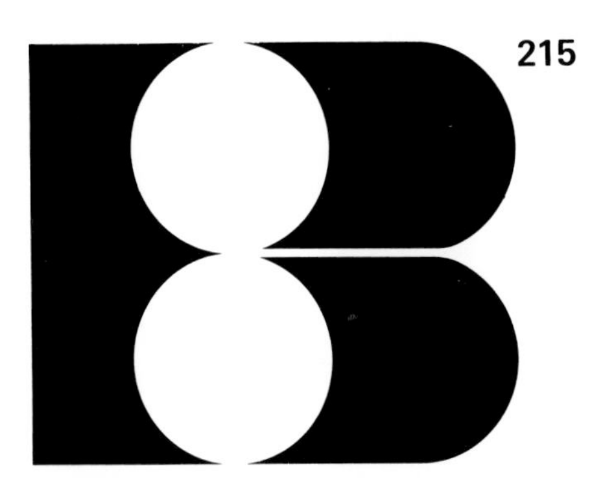

215

216

217

218

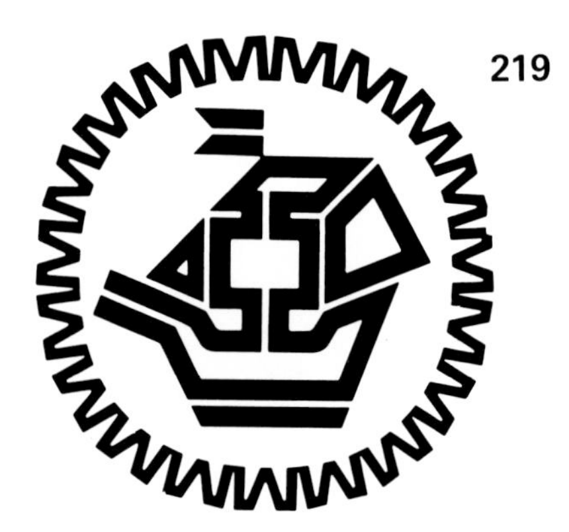

219

220

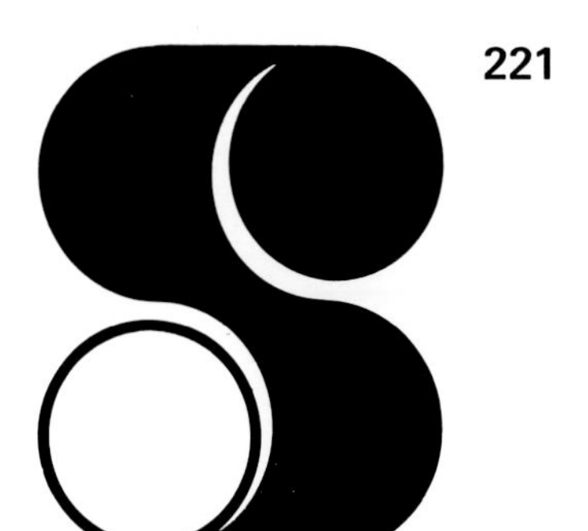

221

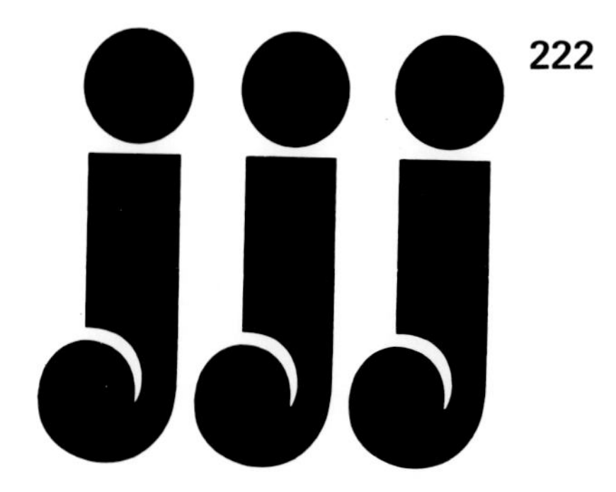

222

223

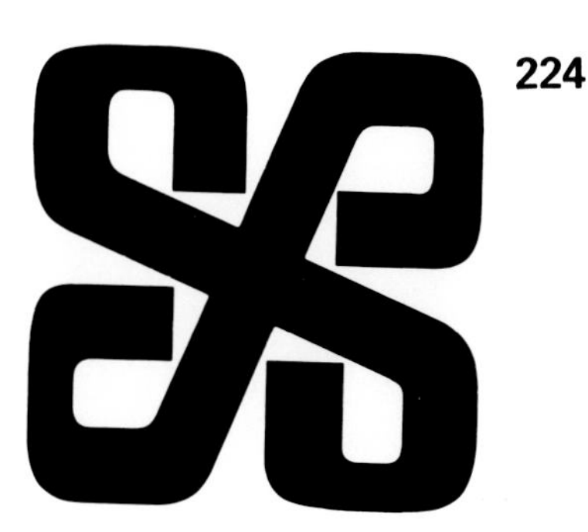

224

213 Creative Equity Corp.
Redondo Beach, California

214 National Council of Negro Women

215 Bryant Press
New York City

216 Scott Engineering Sciences
Pompano Beach, Florida

217 Burlington Northern
St. Paul, Minnesota

218 Fain's Floor Covering
Providence, Rhode Island

219 Marine Midland Bank
New York City

220 Montessori Family Centre
Boston

221 Sperti Sunlamp Division
Ft. Mitchell, Kentucky

222 Salada Foods
Junket Dessert Tablets
Woodburn, Massachusetts

223 Walter Kidde & Co.
Belleville, New Jersey

224 Sundial Electronic Corp.
Greenvale, L.I., New York

225

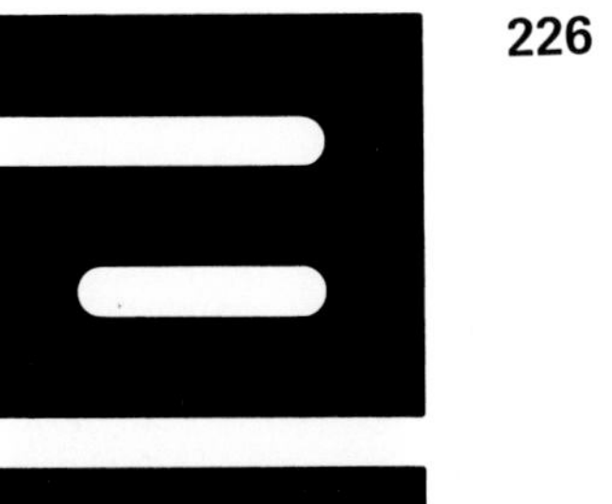

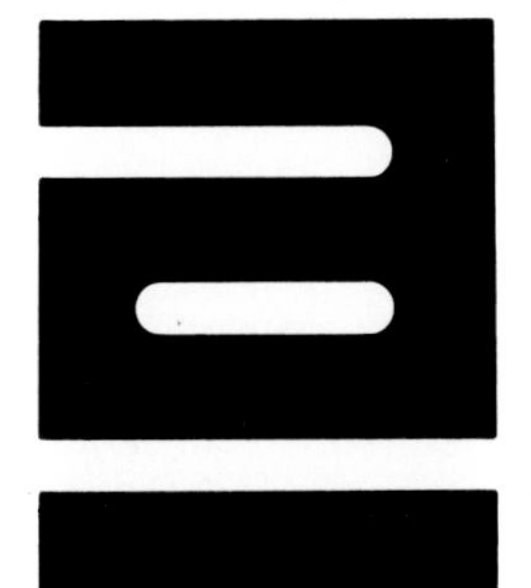

226

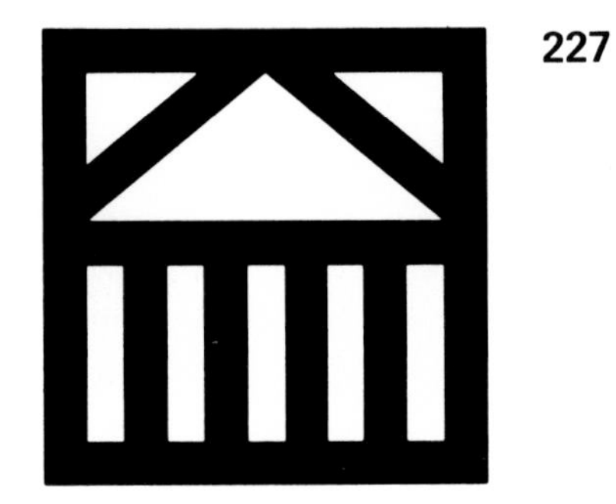

227

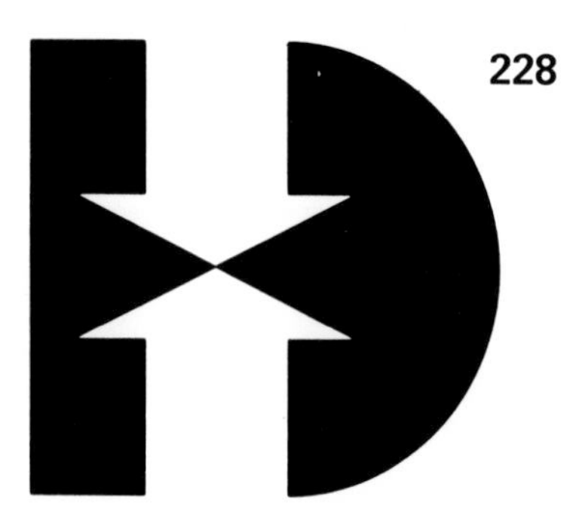

228

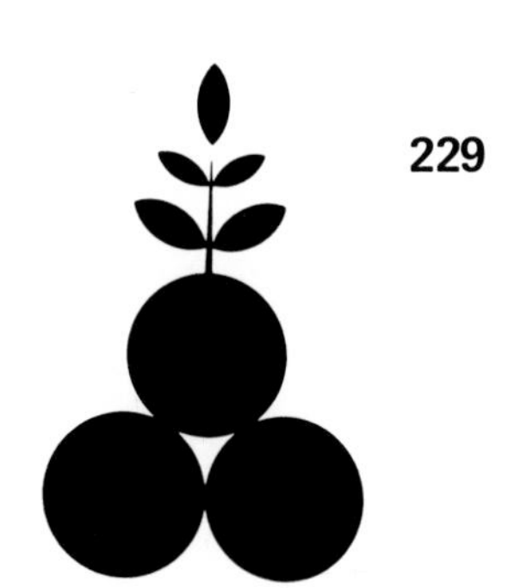

229

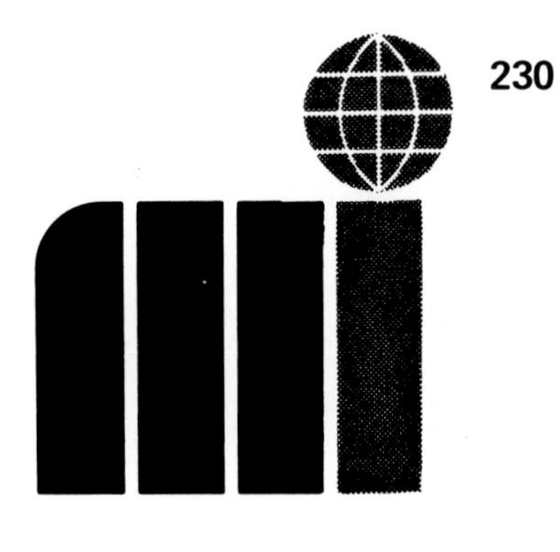

230

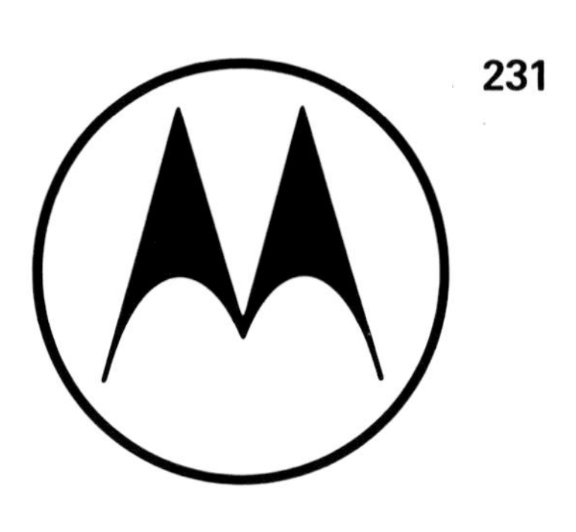

231

232

233

234

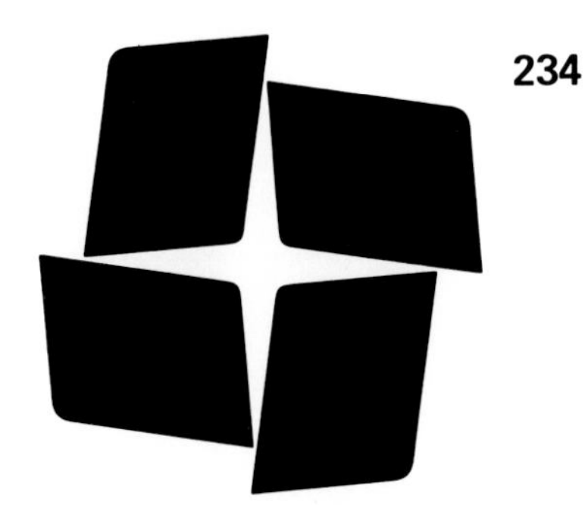

235

236

225 Philadelphia Chapter, AIA
Philadelphia

226 Allied Casting Corp.
Philadelphia

227 Erfft Associates, Inc.
Philadelphia

228 Dynastructures, Inc.
Philadelphia

229 Gettysburg Urban Renewal
Gettysburg, Pennsylvania

230 Mayfran, Inc.
Cleveland

231 Motorola, Inc.
Chicago

232 New York Life Insurance Co.
New York City

233 Citizens Fidelity Bank
Louisville

234 First National Bank of Minneapolis
Minneapolis

235 Gelman Instrument Co.
Ann Arbor, Michigan

236 Facit-Oohner, Inc.
Secaucus, New Jersey

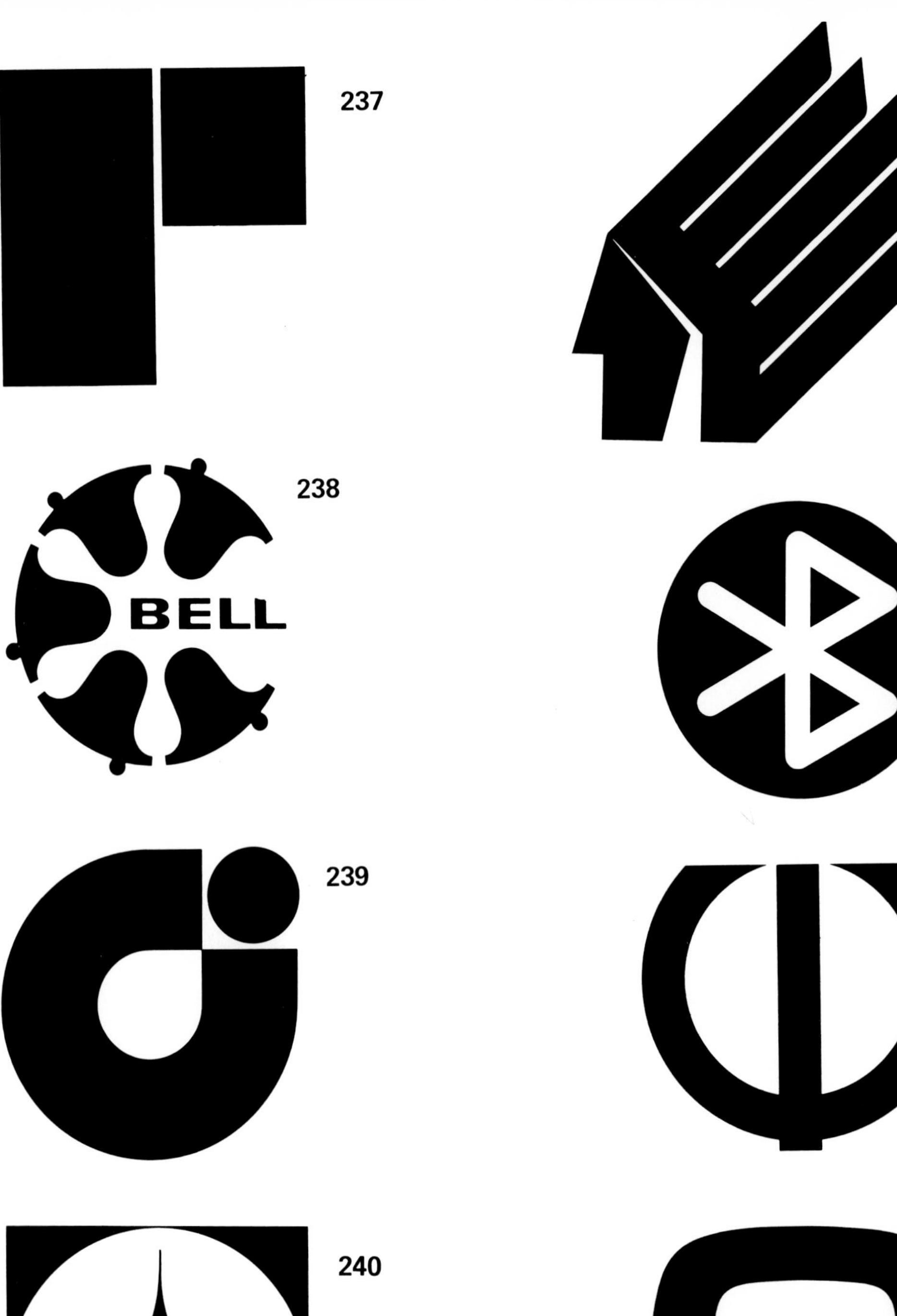

237

238

239

241

242

243

240

244

245

246

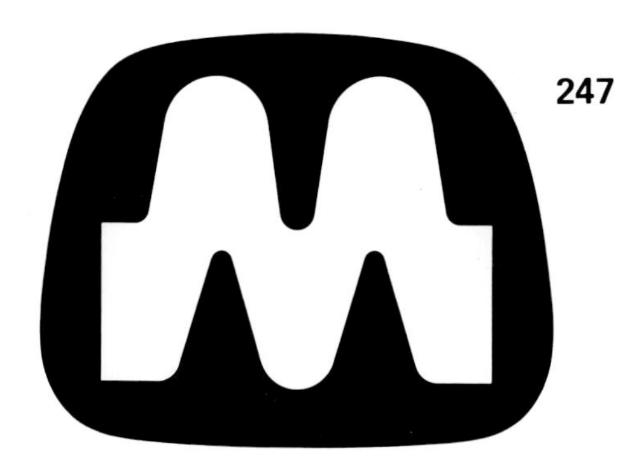

247

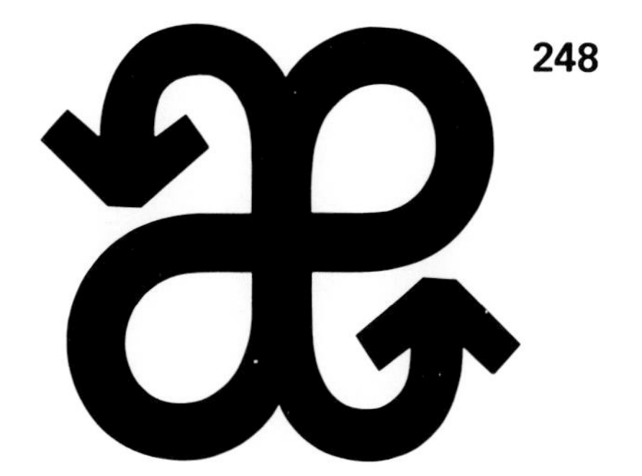

248

237 Roth Office Environments
Dayton, Ohio

238 Bell Brand Foods
Division of Sunshine Biscuits, Inc.
Los Angeles

239 Cordon International Corporation
West Los Angeles

240 The Exolon Co.
Tonawanda, New York

241 Industrious Agricolas
Calexico, California

242 Beaunit Corporation
New York City

243 Webb and Company
Richmond, Virginia

244 Ohmite Manufacturing Co.
Skokie, Illinois

245 Arapahoe Earth Movers
Englewood, Colorado

246 Alcan Corporation
Cleveland

247 Memphis Area Chamber of Commerce
Memphis, Tennessee

248 American-Exporter
New York City

249

250

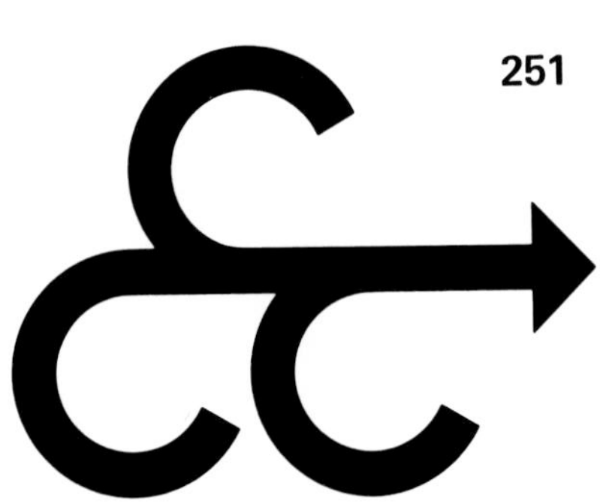

251

252

253

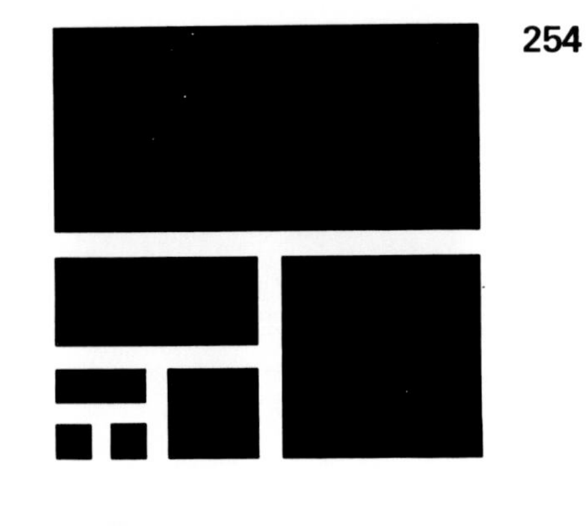

254

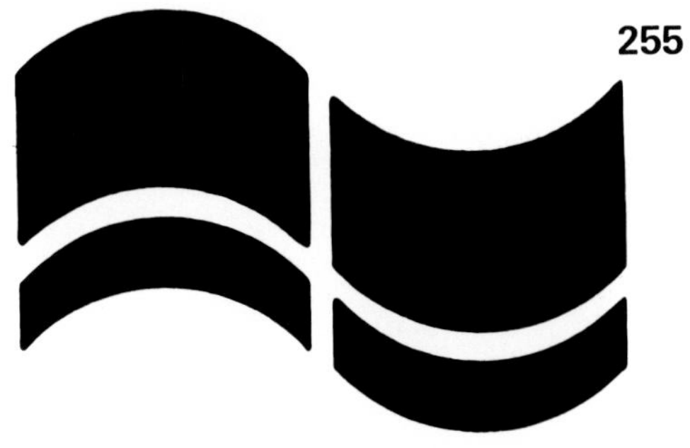

255

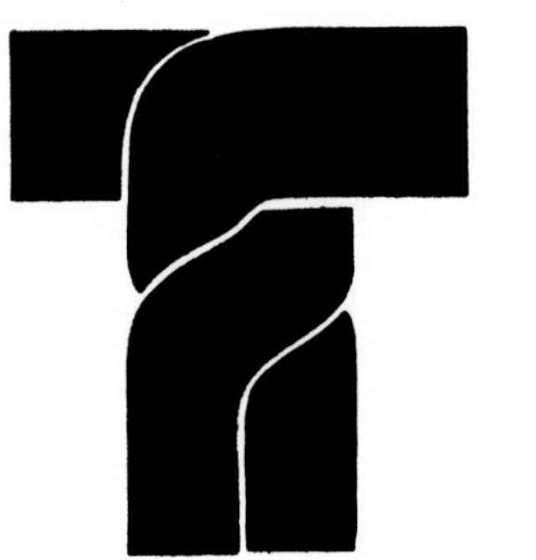

256

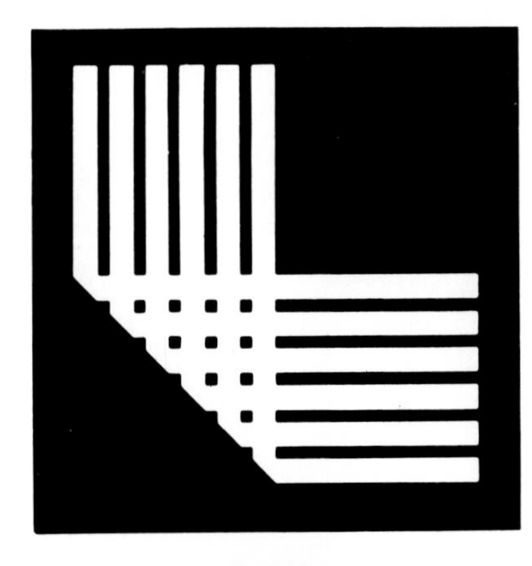

257

258

259

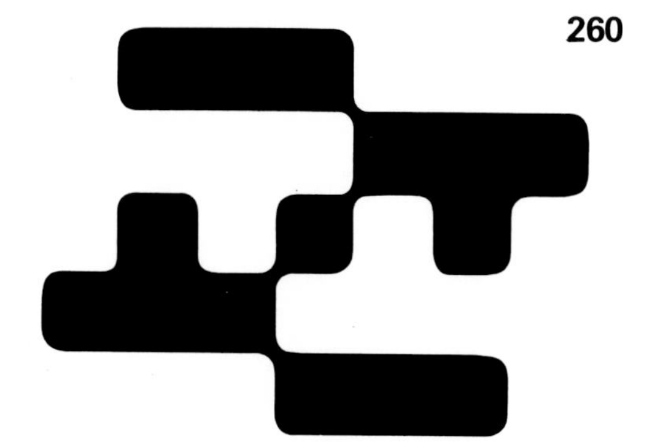

260

249 Florissant Land Development
Denver, Colorado

250 Rancho San Diego
San Diego

251 Corporate Communications Co., Inc.
Los Angeles

252 Marshall Industries
San Marino, California

253 House of Fabrics, Inc.
Sun Valley, California

254 The Titan Group, Inc.
Louisville, Kentucky

255 Clarksville Theatre
Clarksville, Indiana

256 Together, Inc.
Memphis, Tennessee

257 Larson Enterprises, Inc.
Los Angeles

258 Virginia Commonwealth Univ.
Richmond, Virginia

259 Tubeco Pipe Mfg. Corp.
Brooklyn

260 Triad Offset, Inc.
New York City

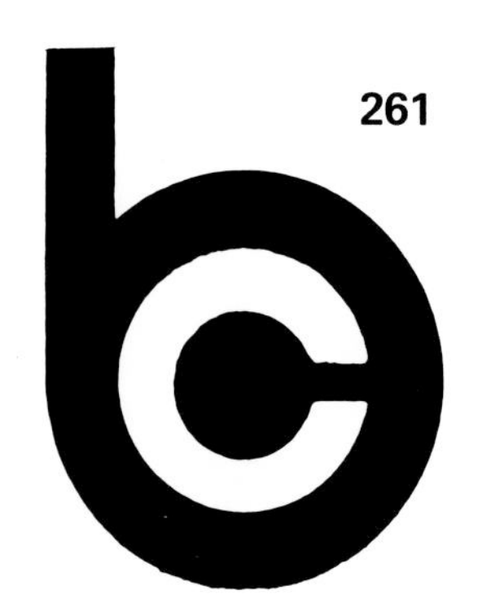
261

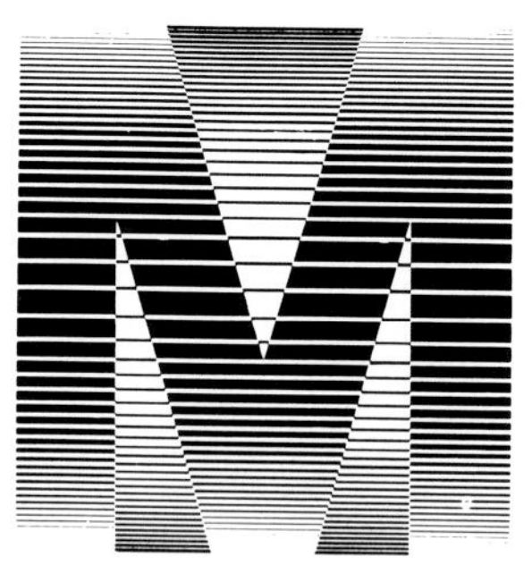
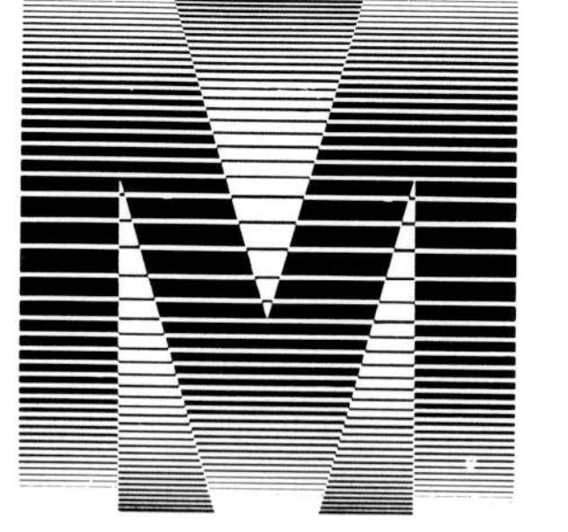
262

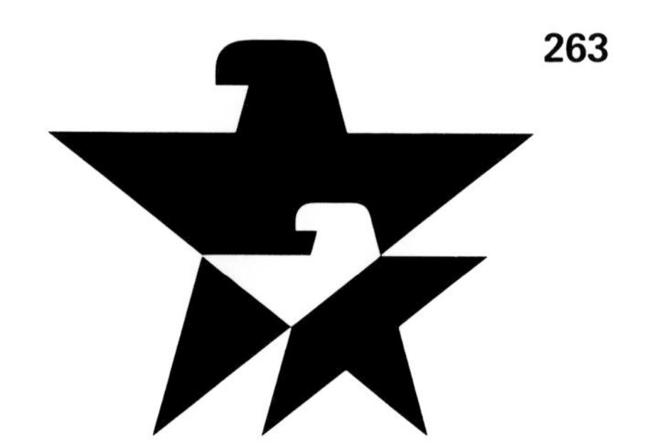
263

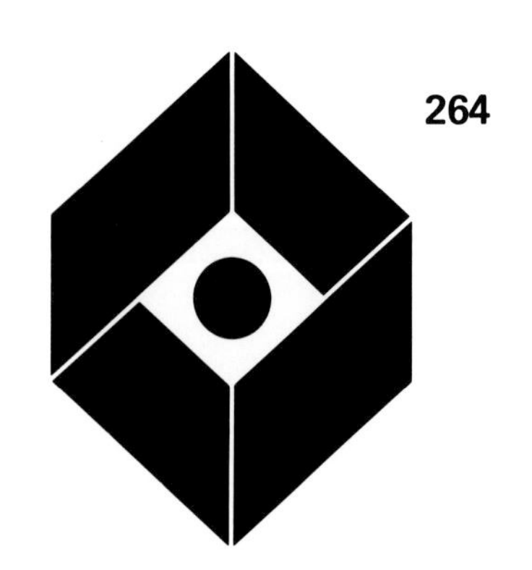
264

265

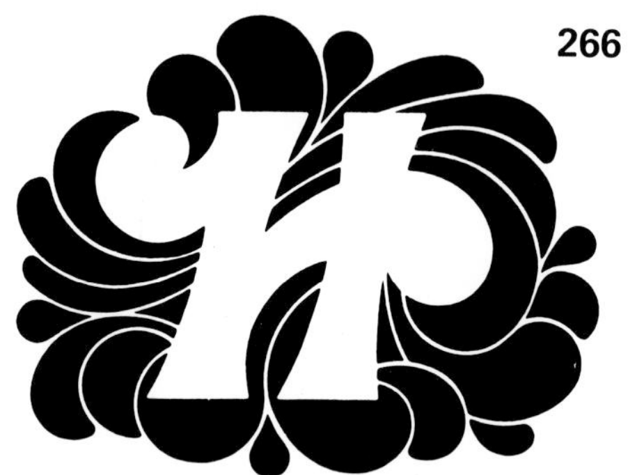
266

267

268

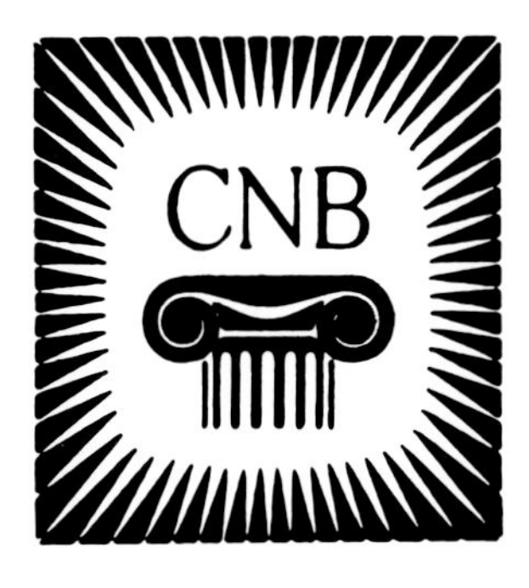

269

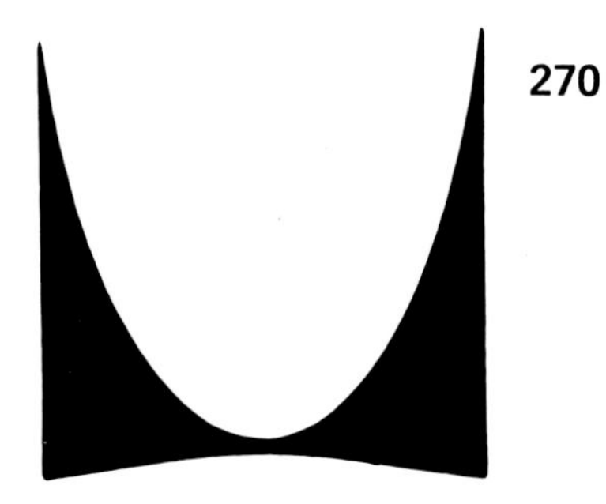

270

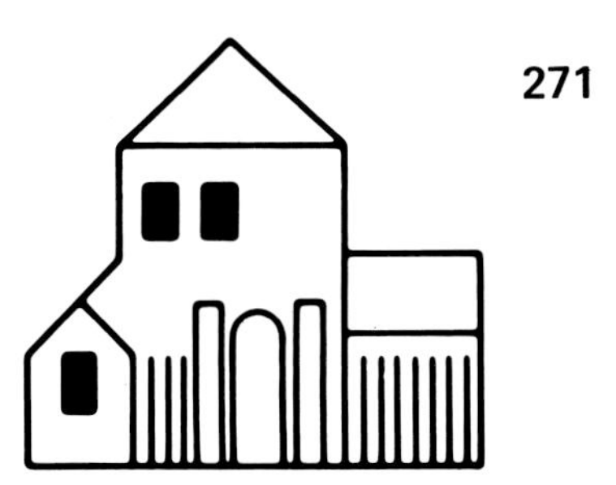

271

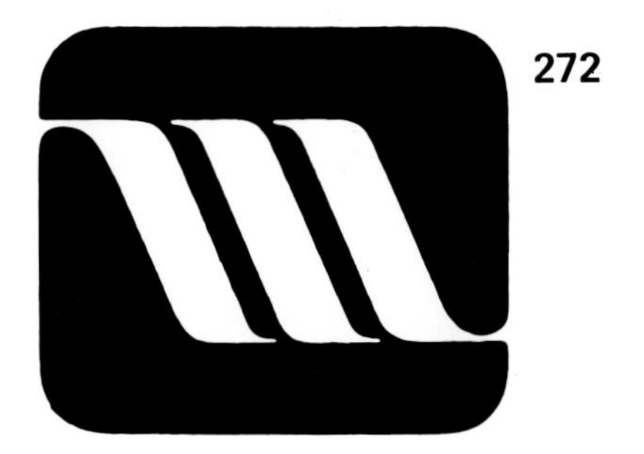

272

261 Beam-Cast, Inc.
Buffalo, New York

262 Malacandra Productions

263 American Republic Insurance Co.
Des Moines, Iowa

264 Main Place
Dallas

265 Community Relations Center
Boulder, Colorado

266 Hawaiian Wines, Inc.
Fresno, California

267 The Small Circle of Friends
Palo Alto, California

268 Welsh-Hannafin, Inc.
Philadelphia

269 Colorado National Bank
Denver

270 Herman Miller Inc.
Zeeland, Michigan

271 Random House
New York City

272 The Maytag Co.
Newton, Iowa

273

277

274

278

275

279

276

Arkansas

280

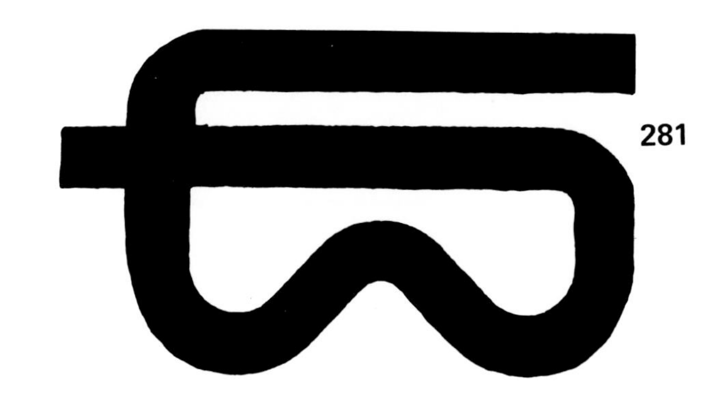

281

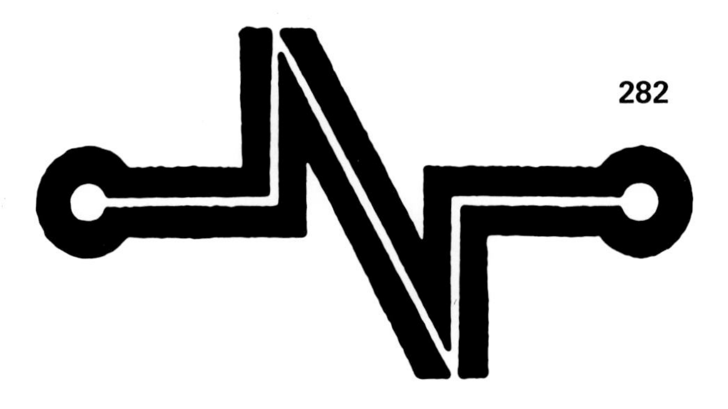

282

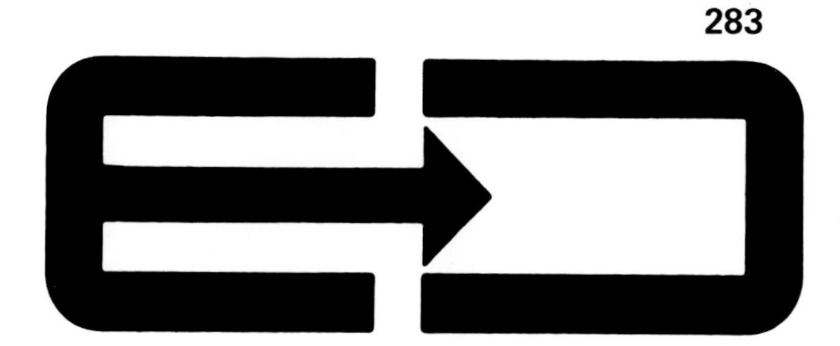

283

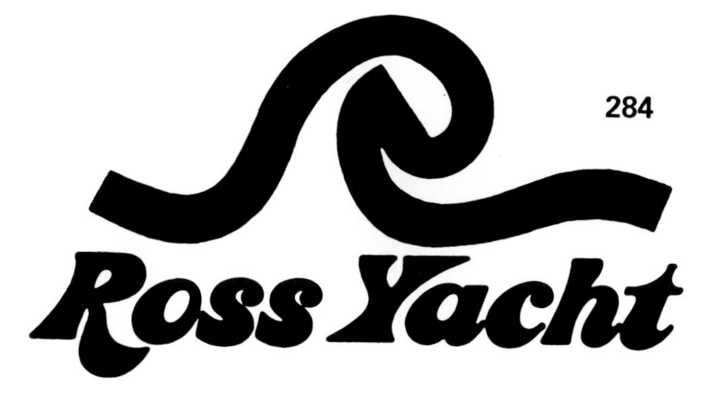

284

273 Architectural Pottery
Los Angeles

274 Panelgraphic Corporation
Caldwell, New Jersey

275 Aragon, International, Inc.
Boulder, Colorado

276 Arkansas Industrial Development Comm.
Little Rock

277 Brite Industries
Providence, Rhode Island

278 R & D Thiel
Palatine, Illinois

279 International Instant Archery Assn.

280 B. R. Starnes Company

281 Flex-Weld, Inc.
Bartlett, Illinois

282 Ohio Safety Systems, Inc.
Cincinnati

283 East Dayton Tool & Die Co.
Dayton, Ohio

284 Ross Yacht
Clearwater, Florida

285

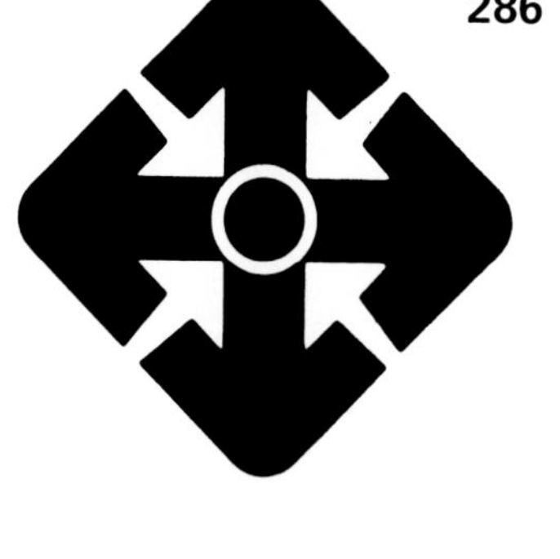

286

287

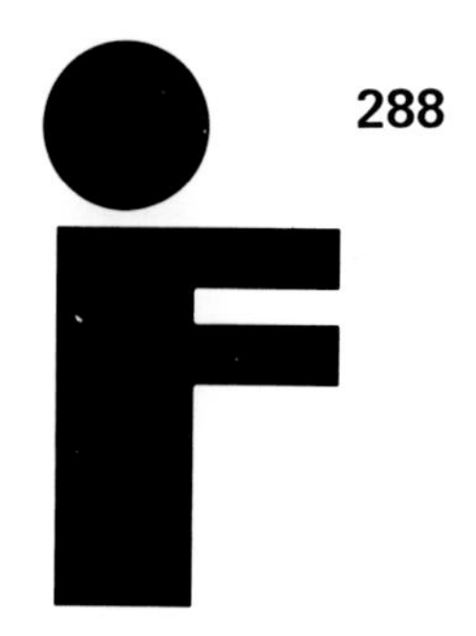

288

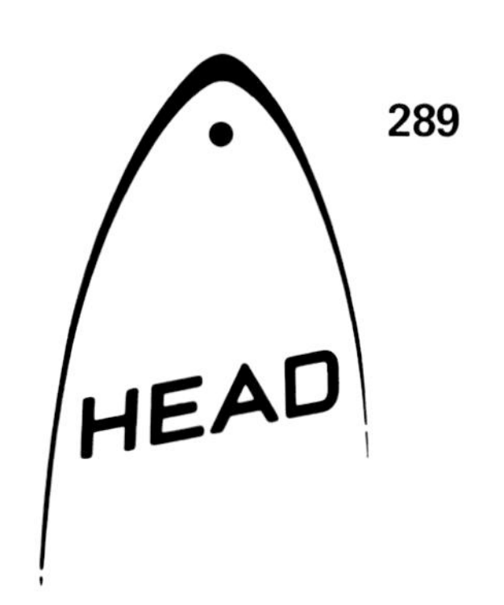

289

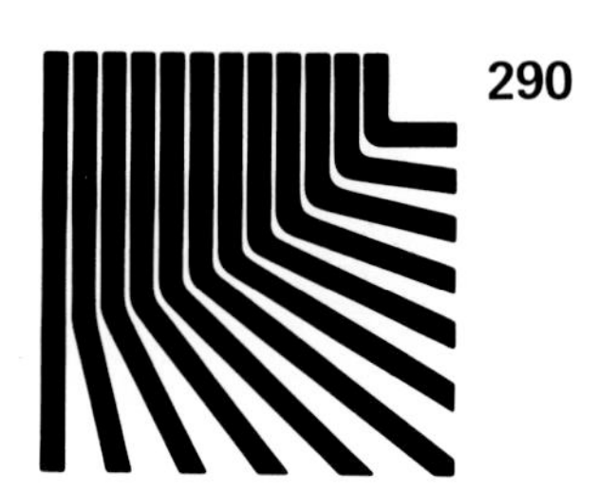

290

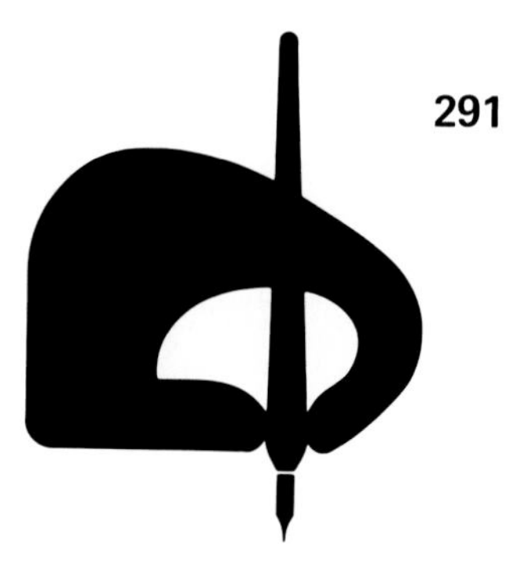

291

292

293

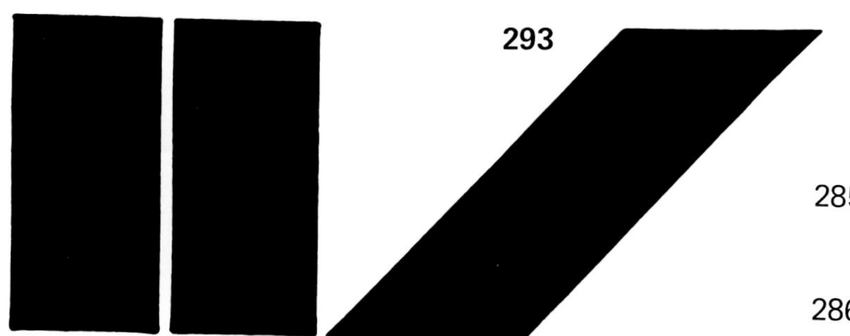

294

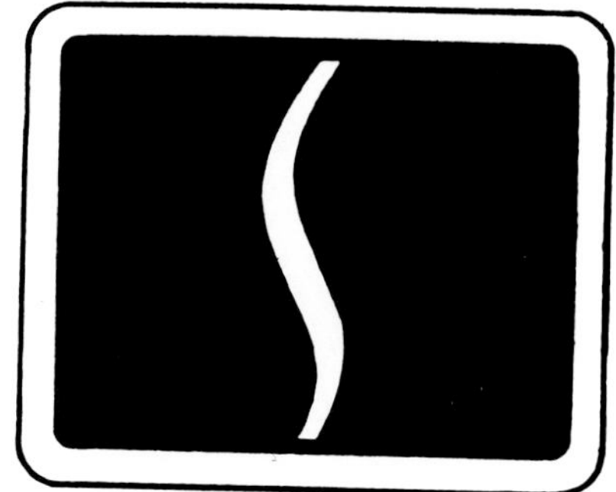

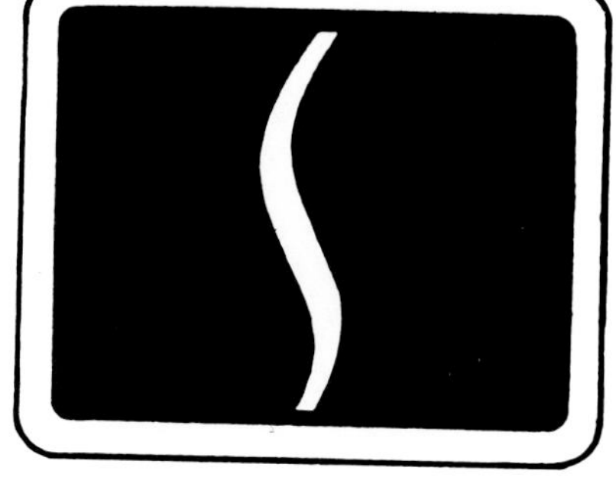

295

296

Lord & Burnham

285 Parker Machine, Inc.
North Adams, Massachusetts

286 White Lines
Oxford, Ohio

287 Fuller-O'Brien Corporation
Menlo Park, California

288 Inter-Faith Task Force
Littleton, Colorado

289 Head Ski Co., Inc.
Timonium, Maryland

290 Logistics Systems, Inc.
Cambridge, Massachusetts

291 The Graphics Studio
Los Angeles

292 Weinschel Engineering
Gaithersburg, Maryland

293 Four-Phase Systems, Inc.
Cupertine, California

294 Sherer-Gillett Co.
Marshall, Michigan

295 Applied Logic Corp.

296 Lord & Burnham
Irvington-on-Hudson, New York

297

298

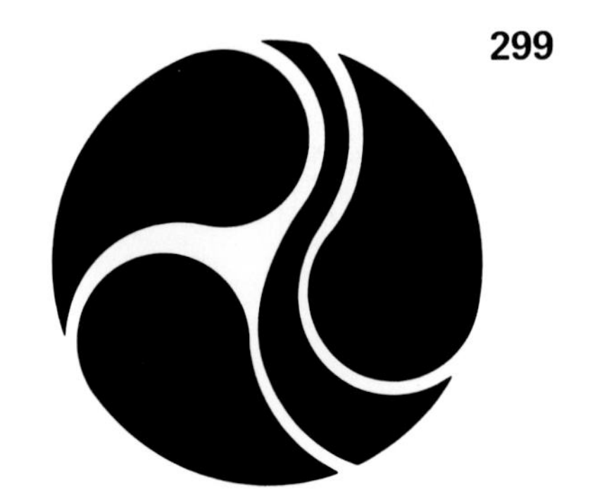

299

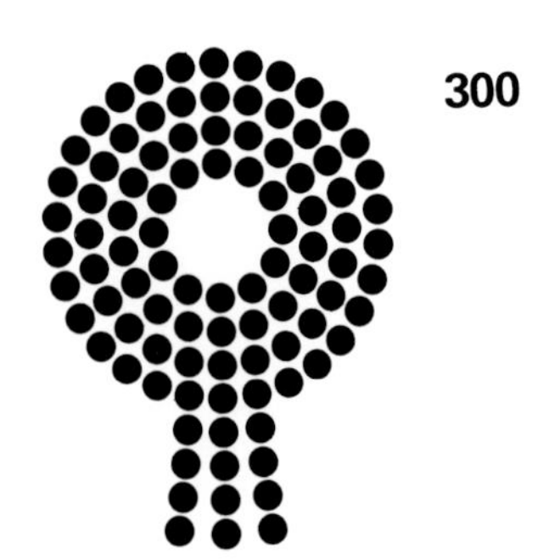

300

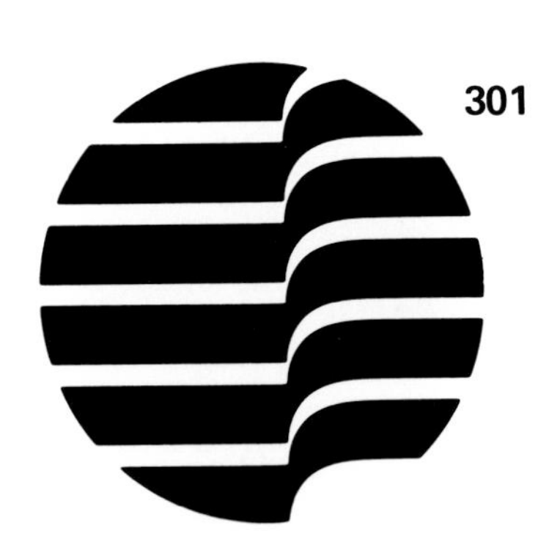

301

302

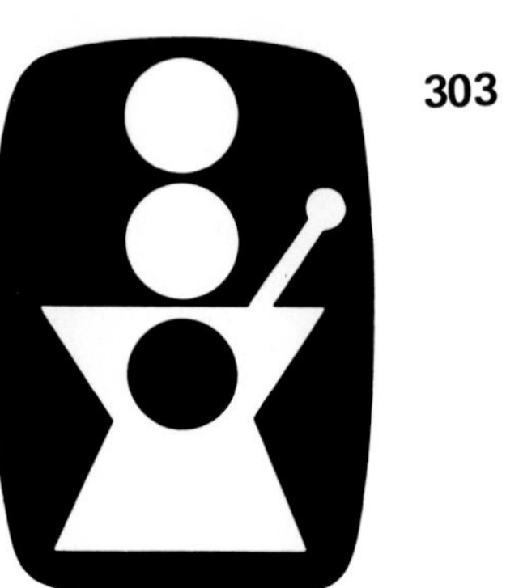

303

304

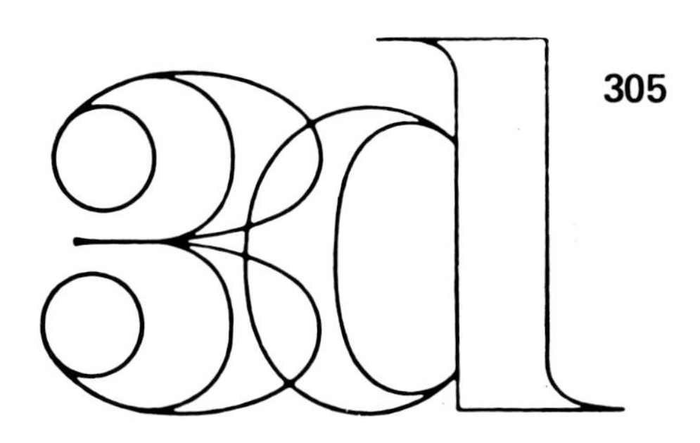

305

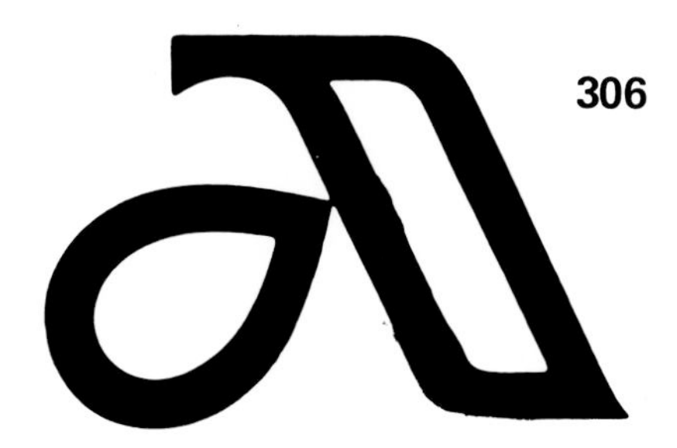

306

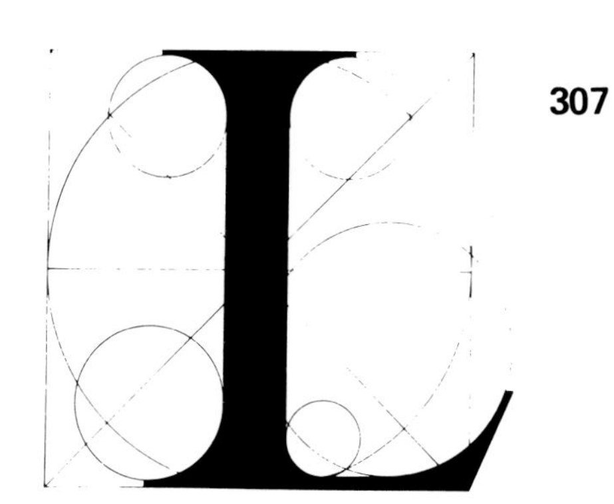

307

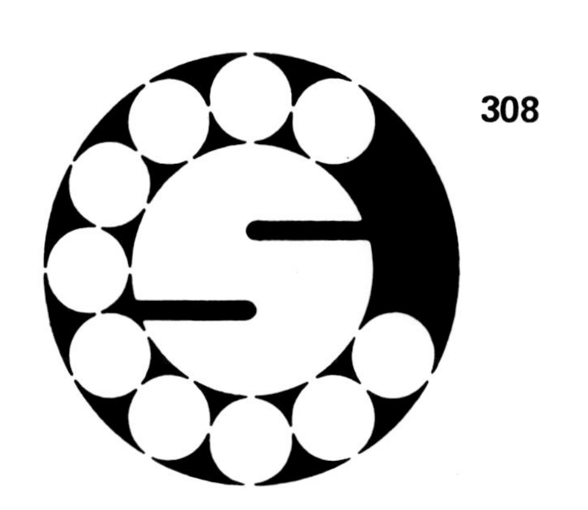

308

297 Brown-Foreman Distillers Corp.
Louisville, Kentucky

298 Philadelphia Diagnostic & Rehabilitation Serv.
Philadelphia

299 Pennsylvania, New Jersey & Delaware
Committee of Governors
Philadelphia

300 Lutheran Fraternal Organizations
Appleton, Wisconsin

301 South Carolina National Bank
Columbia, South Carolina

302 Stop and Shop
Boston

303 Medi Mart
Bosotn

304 Fun Stop
Boston

305 Third Dimension Studio
Wichita, Kansas

306 Asgrow Seed Company
Orange, Connecticut

307 Letterforms
New York City

308 Sterling Answer Service
Wilton, Connecticut

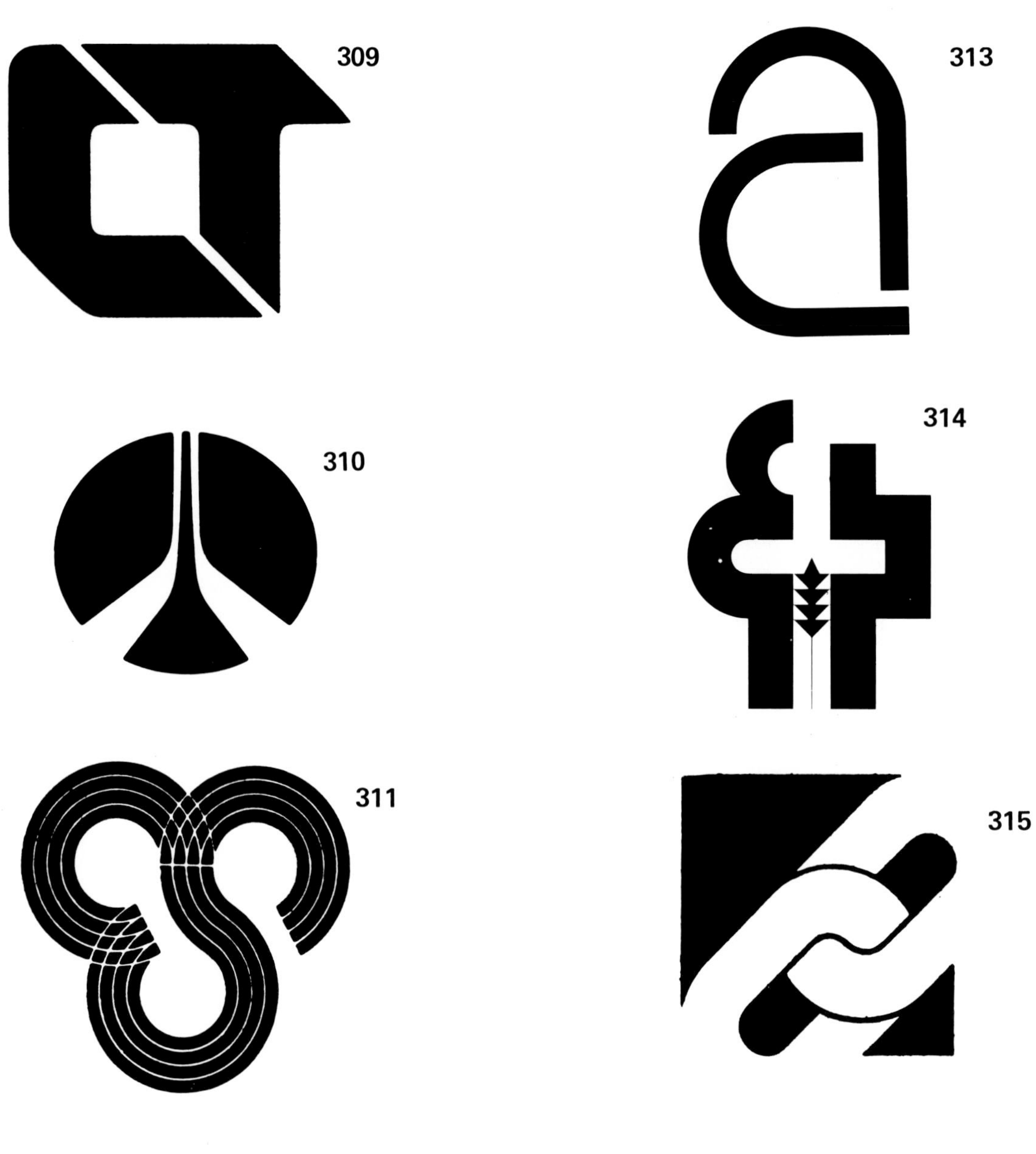

309 310 311 313 314 315

312 316

317

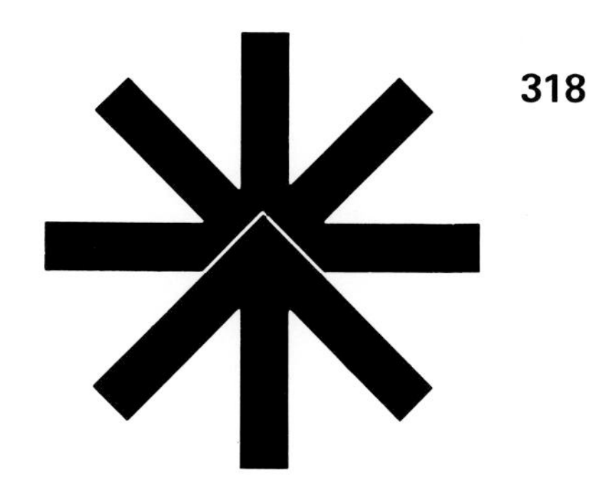

318

319

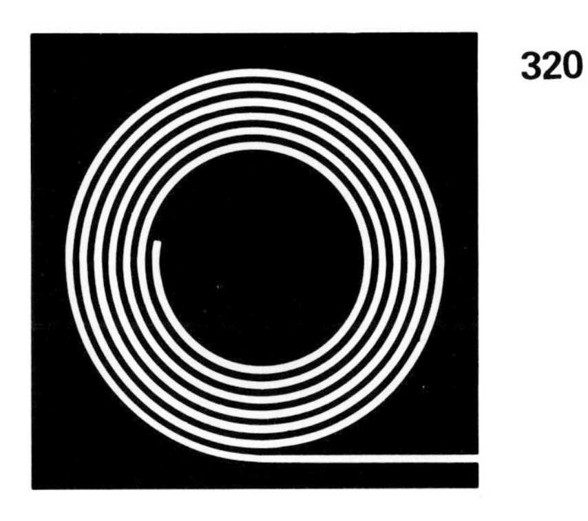

320

309 Cleveland Trust
Cleveland, Ohio

310 North American Rockwell
Pittsburgh

311 Charles Schnier Development Co.
Bloomfield, Connecticut

312 Gravely Corporation
Clemmons, North Carolina

313 The Aluminum Association
New York City

314 Agricultural Missions, Inc.
New York City

315 Broward Bancshares, Inc.
Ft. Lauderdale, Florida

316 Makaha Inn
Waianae, Oahu, Hawaii

317 Boles Aero, Inc.
Sun Valley, California

318 Merchandise Display, Inc.
Dayton, Ohio

319 Cleveland Institute of Art
Cleveland

320 Washington Steel Co.
Washington, Pennsylvania

321
322
323
324
326
327
328
U.S. DEPARTMENT OF THE INTERIOR

325

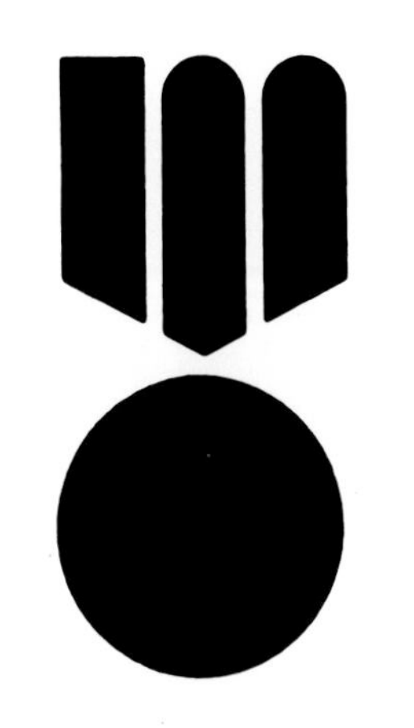

329

330

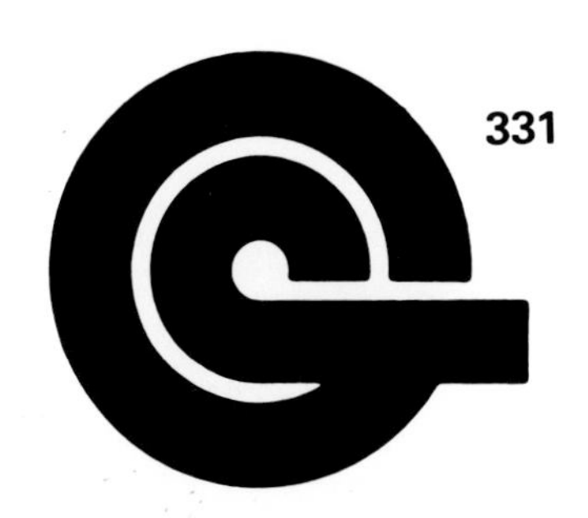

331

332

321 Associated Spring Co.
Briston, Connecticut

322 New York School of Interior Design
New York City

323 Helbros Watches
New York City

324 Western International Hotels
Seattle, Washington

325 SMC Industries, Inc.
Chattanooga, Tennessee

326 Swedcast Division
Swedlow, Inc.
Florence, Kentucky

327 American International Bank
New York City

328 U.S. Department of the Interior
Washington, D. C.

329 Medalist Industries
Milwaukee

330 Carlton Screw Mfg. Co.
Northfield, Illinois

331 Graphic Communications
Little Rock, Arkansas

332 Laco Signs, Inc.
Libertyville, Illinois

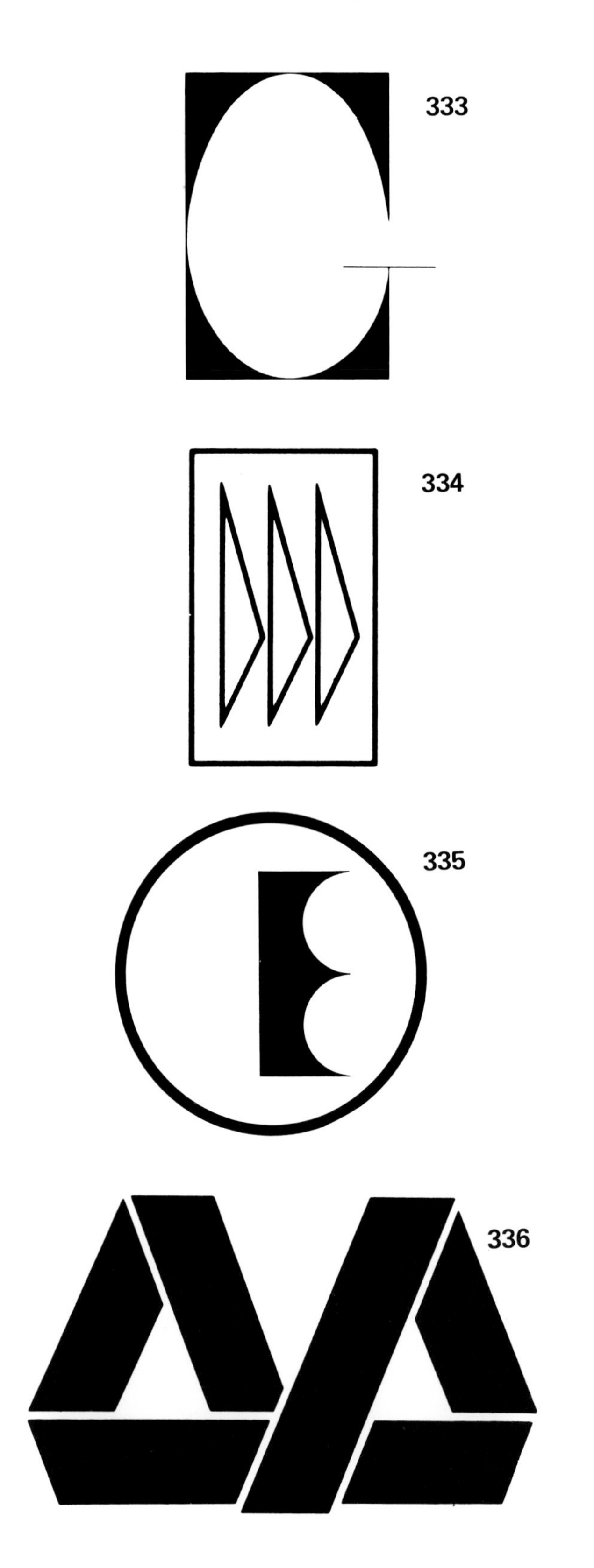
333
334
335
336

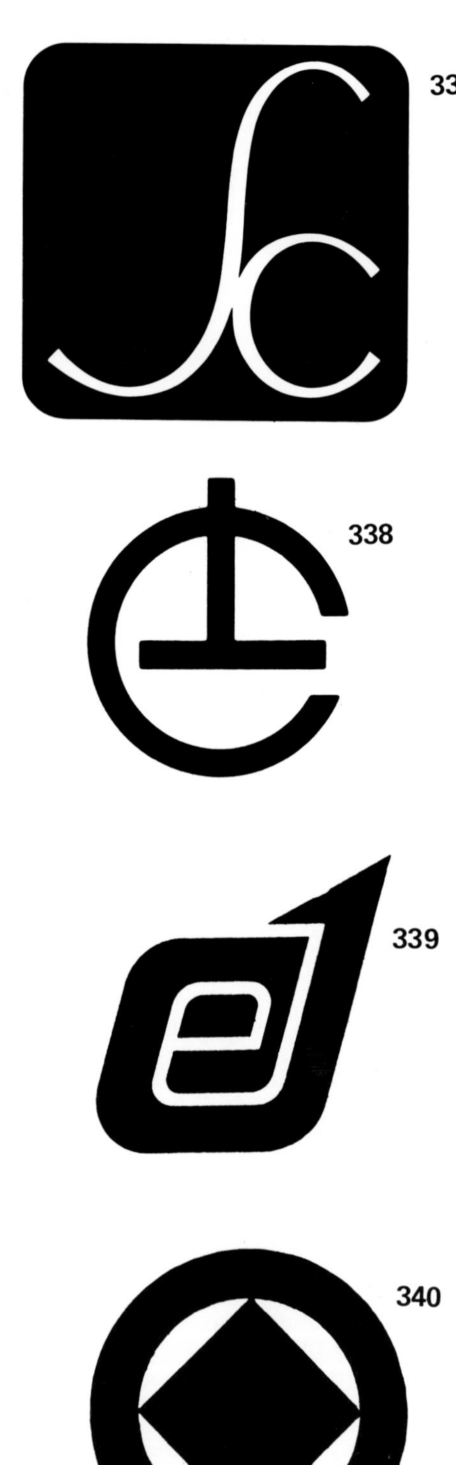
337
338
339
340

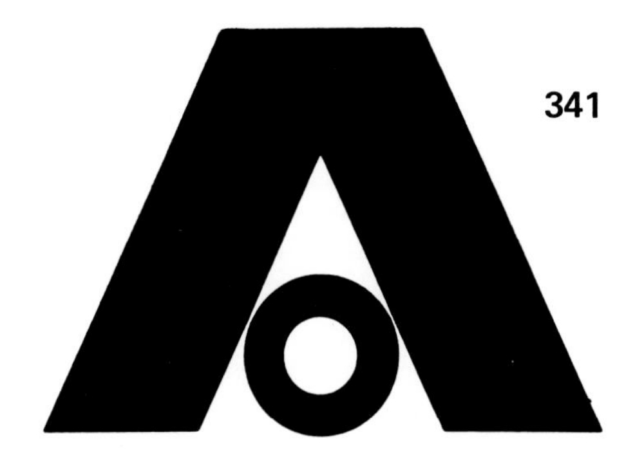

341

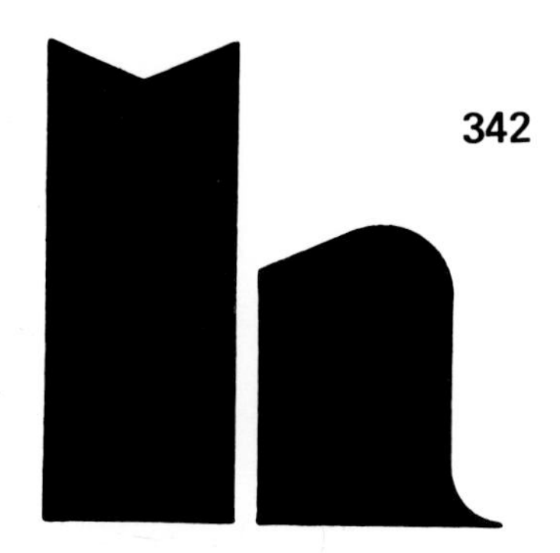

342

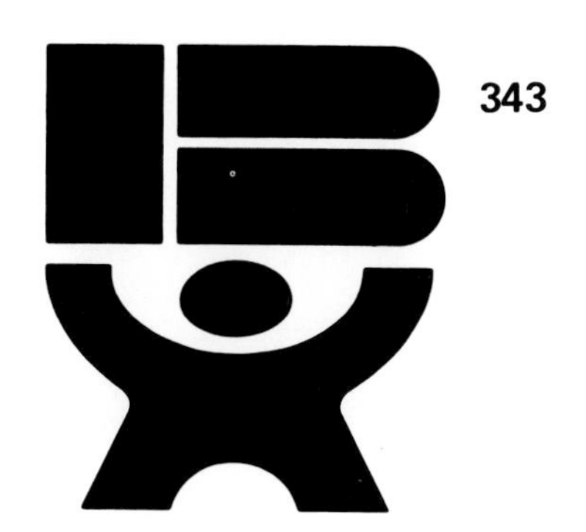

343

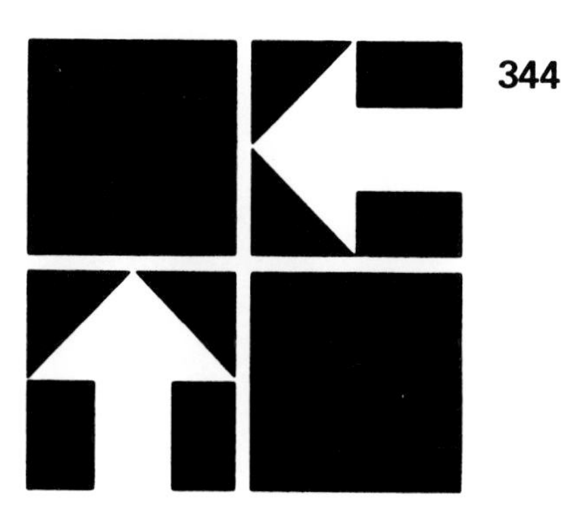

344

333 Poultry Guild
Moorefield, West Virginia

334 Planning Research

335 The Barden Corporation
Danbury, Connecticut

336 Moore Business Forms
Niagara Falls, New York

337 Sculpture Collectors, Ltd.
New York City

338 J.L. Clark
Rockford, Illinois

339 Economic Development Corp. of
San Diego County

340 Bronwill Scientific Inc.
Rochester, New York

341 American Cast Iron Pipe Co.
Birmingham, Alabama

342 Hankscraft
Reedsburg, Wisconsin

343 Behlen Mfg. Co.
Columbus, Nebraska

344 Land Search Corporation
Seattle, Washington

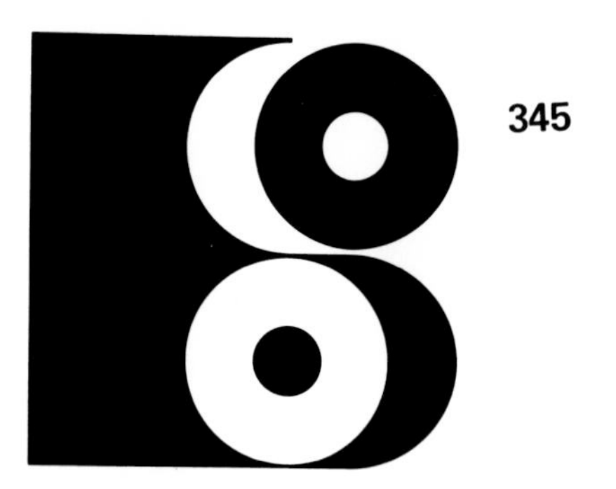
345

346

BURNS
347

New England Farms
348

349

350

351

352

357

358

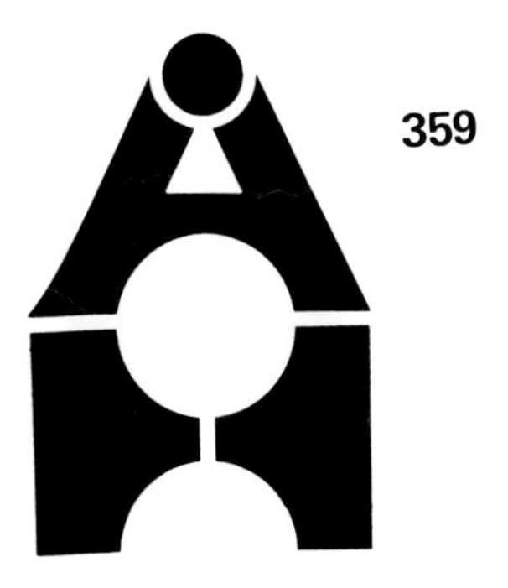
359

360

361

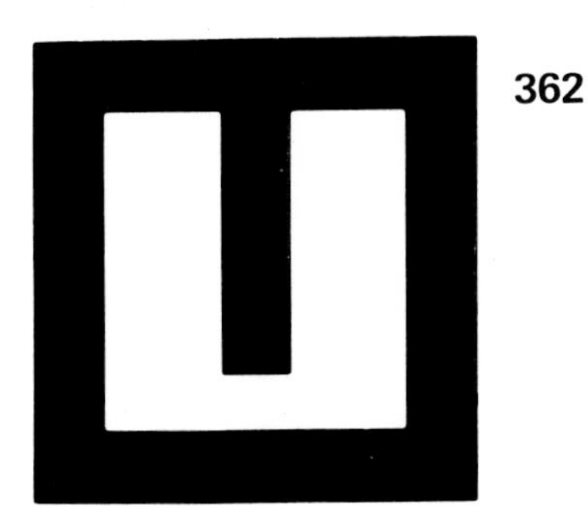
362

363

364

353

354

355

KENDALL

356

345 Bay State Abrasives

346 Goren Foods Co.
Boston

347 William J. Burns Detective Age

348 New England Farms
Arlington, Massachusetts

349 Tax Man
Cambridge, Massachusetts

350 Sunnyside Products, Inc.
Chicago

351 C.A. Norgren Co.
Littleton, Colorado

352 House of Ronnie, Inc.
New York City

353 EG&G
Bedford, Massachusetts

354 Anzio (movie)

355 The Kendall Co.
New York City

356 Living Marine Resources, Inc.
San Diego

365

366

367

368

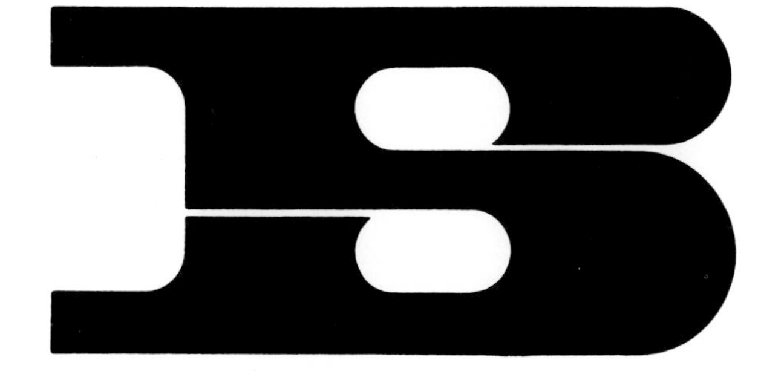

357 Presbyterian Hospital Center
Albuquerque, New Mexico

358 Mountain Sports
Boulder, Colorado

359 Ajax Hardware Corp.
City of Industry, California

360 Strathmore Paper Co.
West Springfield, Massachusetts

361 Mister Donut
Westwood, Massachusetts

362 United Bank & Trust Co.
Hartford, Connecticut

363 Willamette Industries, Inc.
Albany, Oregon

364 Nancy Martin Public Relations
Los Angeles

365 Maine Savings Bank
Portland, Maine

366 Aero Bankers
Denver, Colorado

367 LaChoy Food Products
Div. of Beatrice Foods Co.

368 Brennan & Sloane Construction Co.

369

370

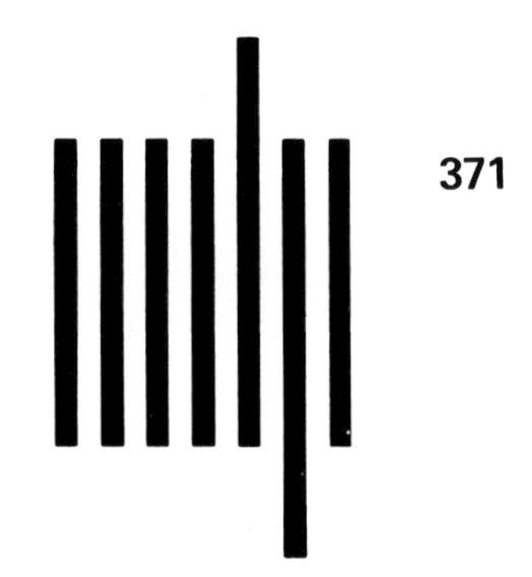
371

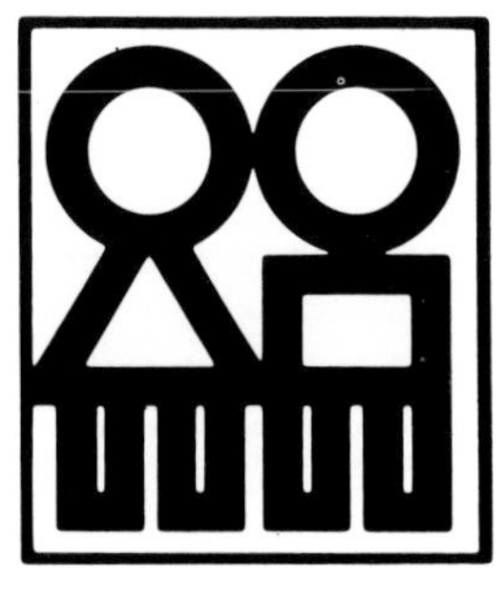
372

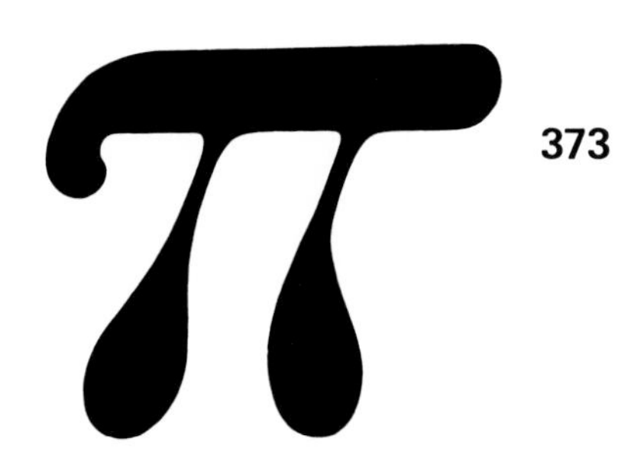
373

374

375

376

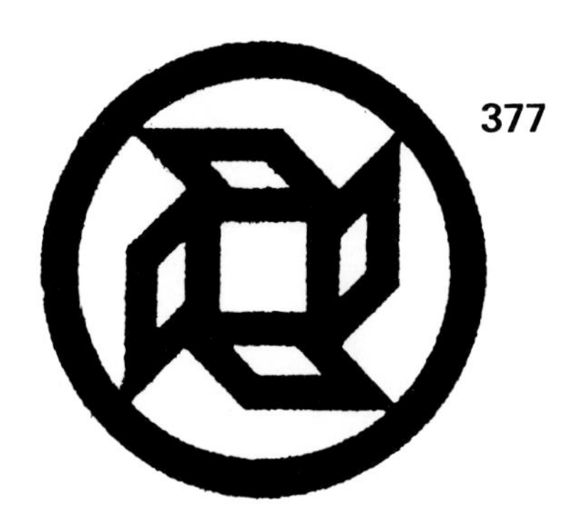

377

369 Culligan, Inc.
Northbrook, Illinois

370 Central Soya
Ft. Wayne, Indiana

371 MIT Press
Cambridge, Massachusetts

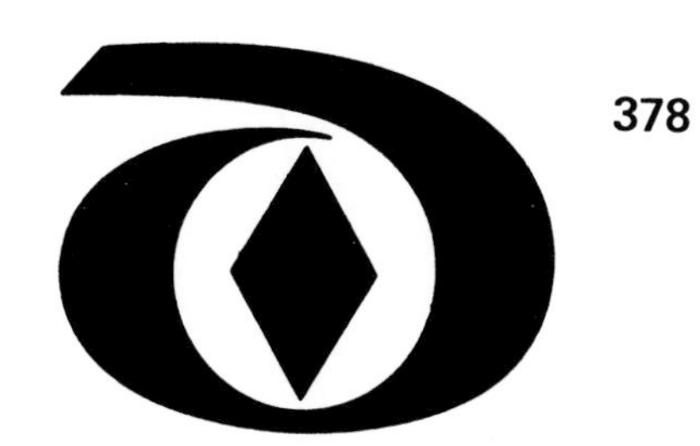

378

372 Foster Parents Plan, Inc.
New York City

373 Pyttronic Inc.
Harrisburg, Pennsylvania

374 Applied Power Industries, Inc.
Milwaukee

375 Computer Products
Ft. Lauderdale, Florida

379

376 NBC
New York City

377 Royal Continental Box Co.
Chicago

378 Diamond Shamrock Corp.
Cleveland

379 Universal Ultrasonics, Inc.
West Babylon, New York

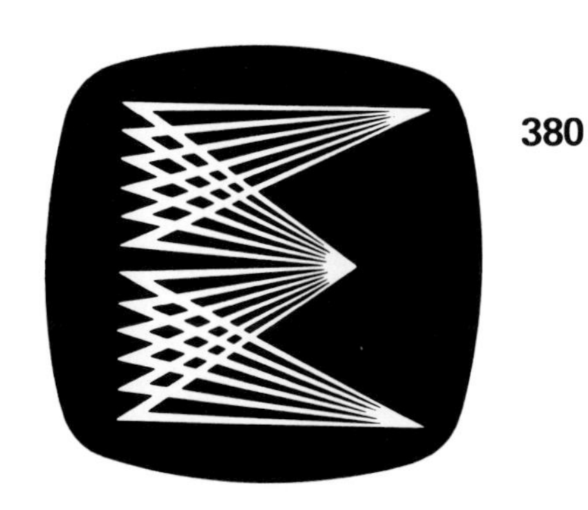

380

380 Edmund Scientific Co.
Barrington, New York

381
385
382
386
383
387

384
388

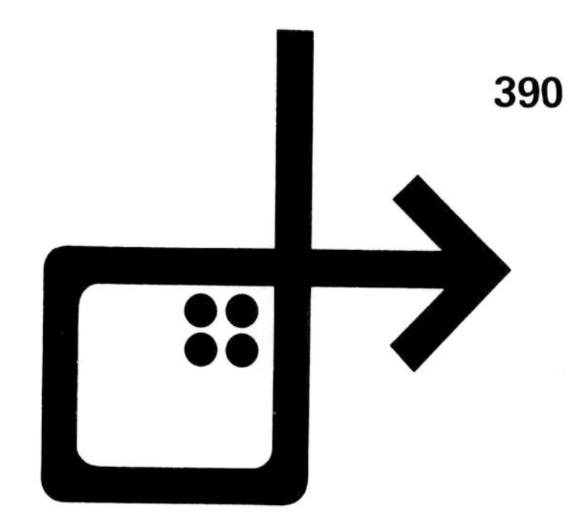

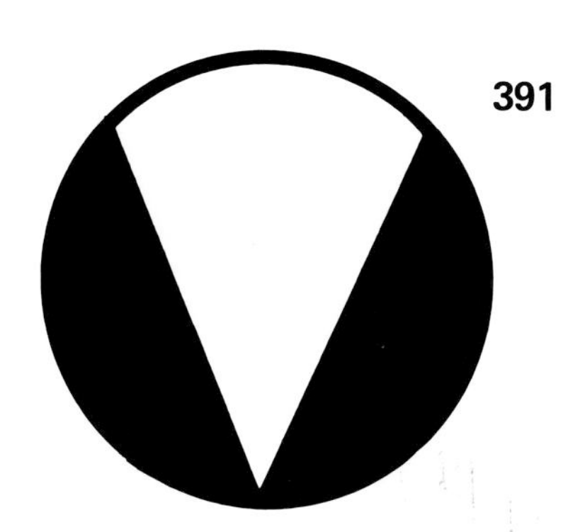

381 American Bankers Association

382 First National Bank in Little Rock
Little Rock, Arkansas

383 Synthane-Taylor Corporation
Valley Forge, Pennsylvania

384 Thompson-Brown Co.

385 World Airways Inc.
Oakland, California

386 The National Bank
St. Petersburg, Florida

387 Bank of Commerce
Milwaukee

388 Ingram Paper Co.
Los Angeles

389 Speekrack, Inc.
Skokie, Illinois

390 Dukane Press
Hollywood, Florida

391 Velsicol Chemical Corp.
Chicago

392 Deere & Company
Moline, Illinois

393

394

395

396

397

398

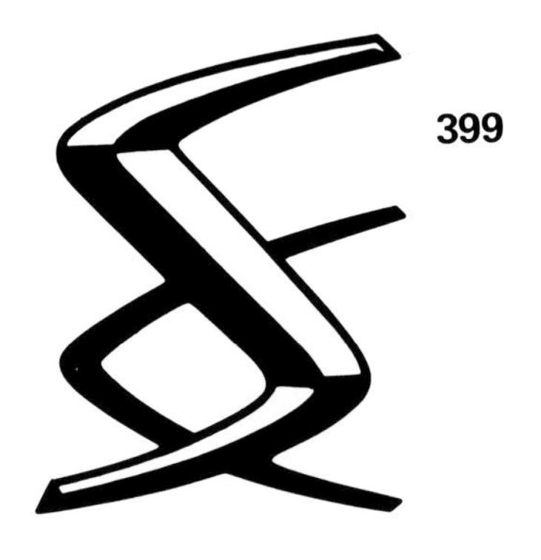

399

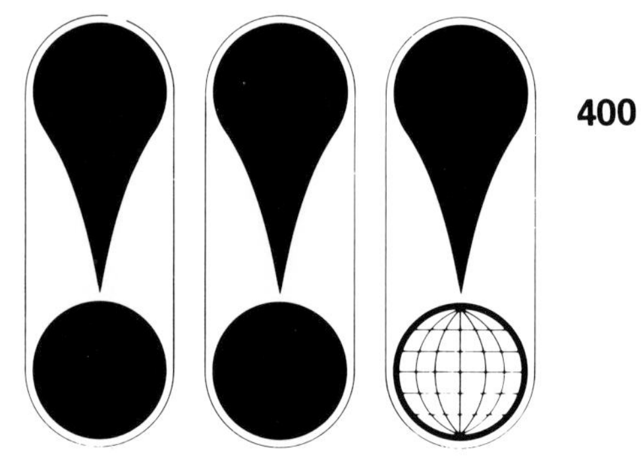

400

401

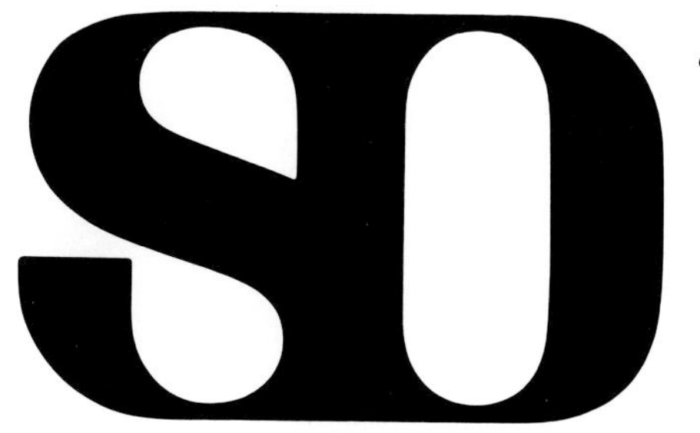

402

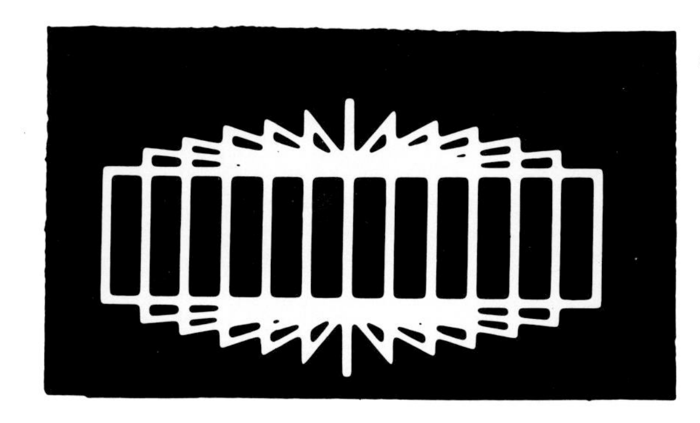

403

404

393 Computer Knowledge Corp.
San Antonio, Texas

394 Clevepak Corp.
New York City

395 Piedmont Minerals Company, Inc.
Greensboro, North Carolina

396 Directional Industries, Inc.
New York City

397 American Institute of Architects
New York City

398 Albright-Knox Art Gallery
Buffalo, New York

399 Superior Coach Corp.
Lima, Ohio

400 LaBow, Haynes Co., Inc.
Seattle, Washington

401 Boothe Resources International, Inc.
Los Angeles

402 Stow-Davis Furniture Co.
Grand Rapids, Michigan

403 Madison Square Garden
New York City

404 Pacific Palm Pools
Latham, New York

405

406

407

408

409

410

INA

411

412

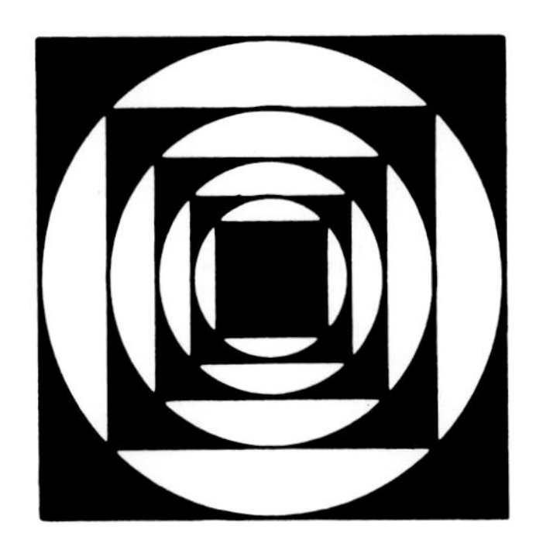

413

414

415

416

405 Moen, a Division of Stanadyne
Elyria, Ohio

406 Foster's Meats
Manchester, New Hampshire

407 Cameron Machine Co.
Dover, New Jersey

408 Sawyer Industries, Inc.
Arcadia, California

409 Halliday & Blalock, Inc.
Louisville, Kentucky

410 Insurance Company of North America
Philadelphia

411 United Yarn Products Co., Inc.
Paterson, New Jersey

412 Pellon Corp.
New York City

413 Charles Industries
Upper Montclair, New Jersey

414 Diehl Pumps Co.
Louisville, Kentucky

415 Self-Development, Inc.
San Jose, California

416 Amplex Mfg. Co.
Philadelphia

417
421
418
422
419
423
420
424

425

426

427

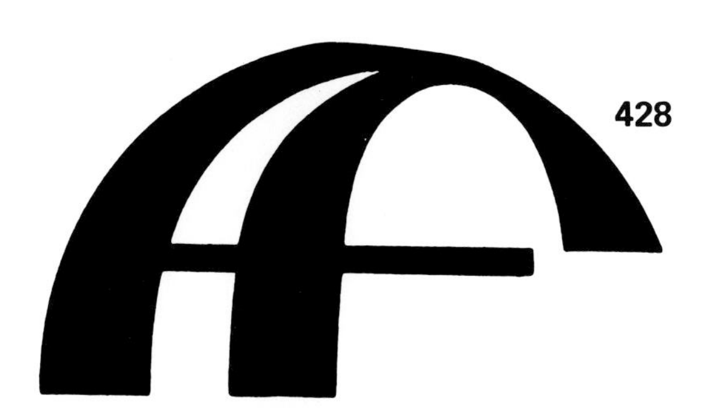

428

417 Screen Gems — Columbia Publications

418 Mount Attitash Association
North Conway, New Hampshire

419 NYU Glee Club
New York City

420 Lauter-Franklin Road Paving
Flatwoods, Kentucky

421 Screen Gems — Columbia Music
New York City

422 Greater Washington Jewish Community Fndn.
Washington, D.C.

423 Girard Bank
Philadelphia

424 J.F. Freeman, Inc.
Los Angeles

425 Maico Hearing Instruments
Minneapolis

426 Northwestern National Life Insurance Co.
Minneapolis

427 Vance, Sanders & Co., Inc.
Boston

428 Form & Function
Philadelphia

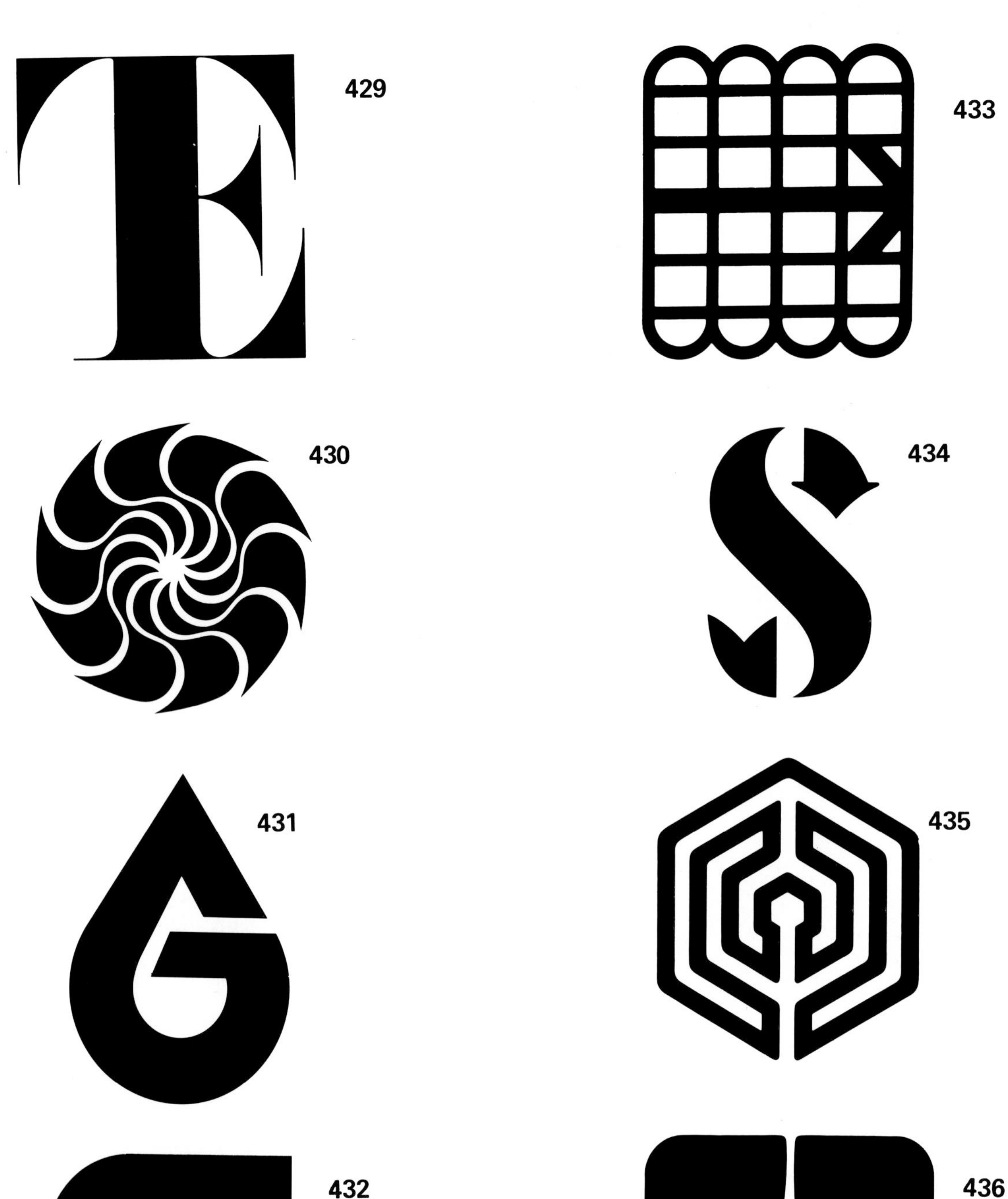

429

433

430

434

431

435

432

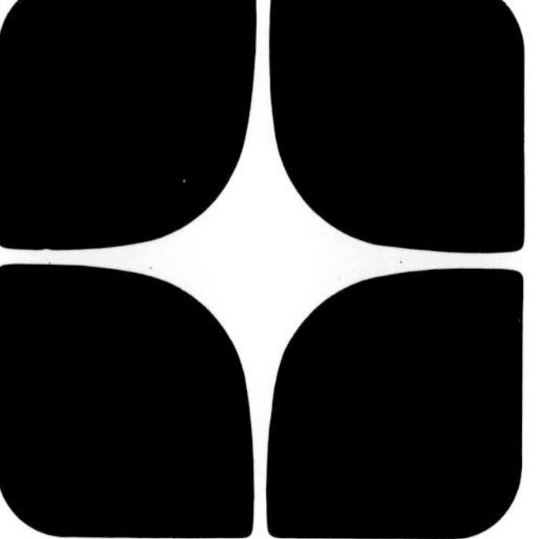

436

438

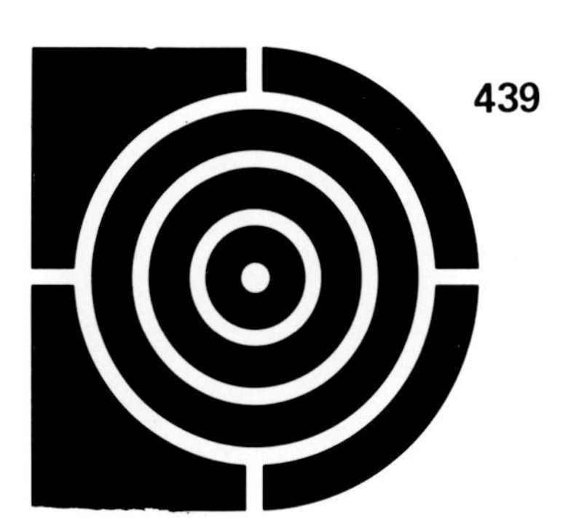

439

440

429 Time Equities Corp.
New York City

430 Newport Center
Newport Beach, California

431 Grayrock Oil & Gas
Dallas

432 Franklin Supply Co.
Denver

433 Government in the Modern World
Macmillan Company
New York City

434 Scubapro Diving Equipment
Los Angeles

435 Polyplan Plastic Products Mfg.
Santa Barbara, California

436 Southern Cross Industries, Inc.
Atlanta

437 First National Bank
Memphis, Tennessee

438 Aircraft Radio Corp.
Boonton, New Jersey

439 The Charles Stark Draper
Laboratory of MIT
Cambridge, Massachusetts

440 Watkins-Johnson Co.
Palo Alto, California

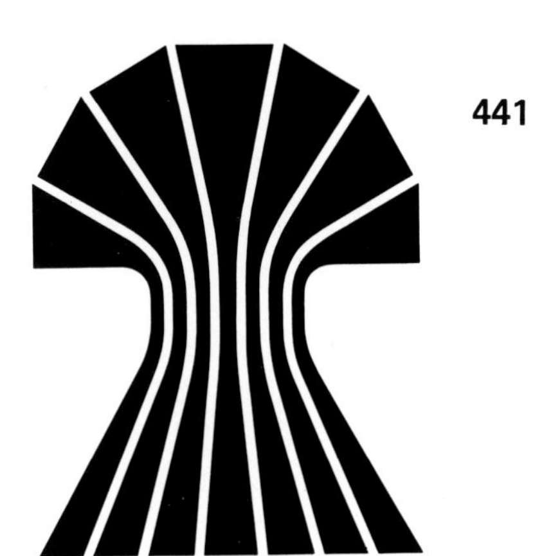

441

442

443

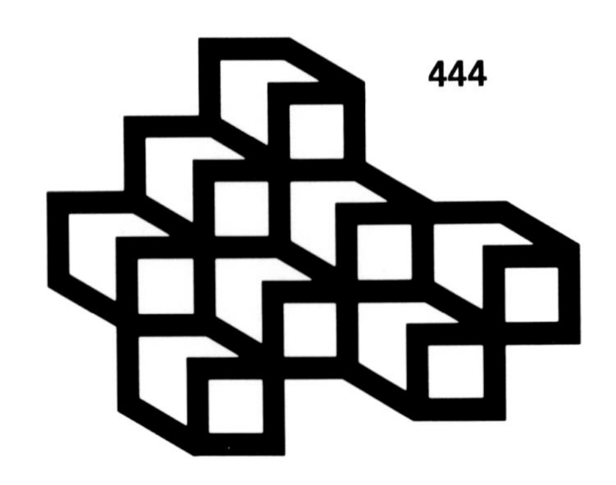

444

445

446

447

448

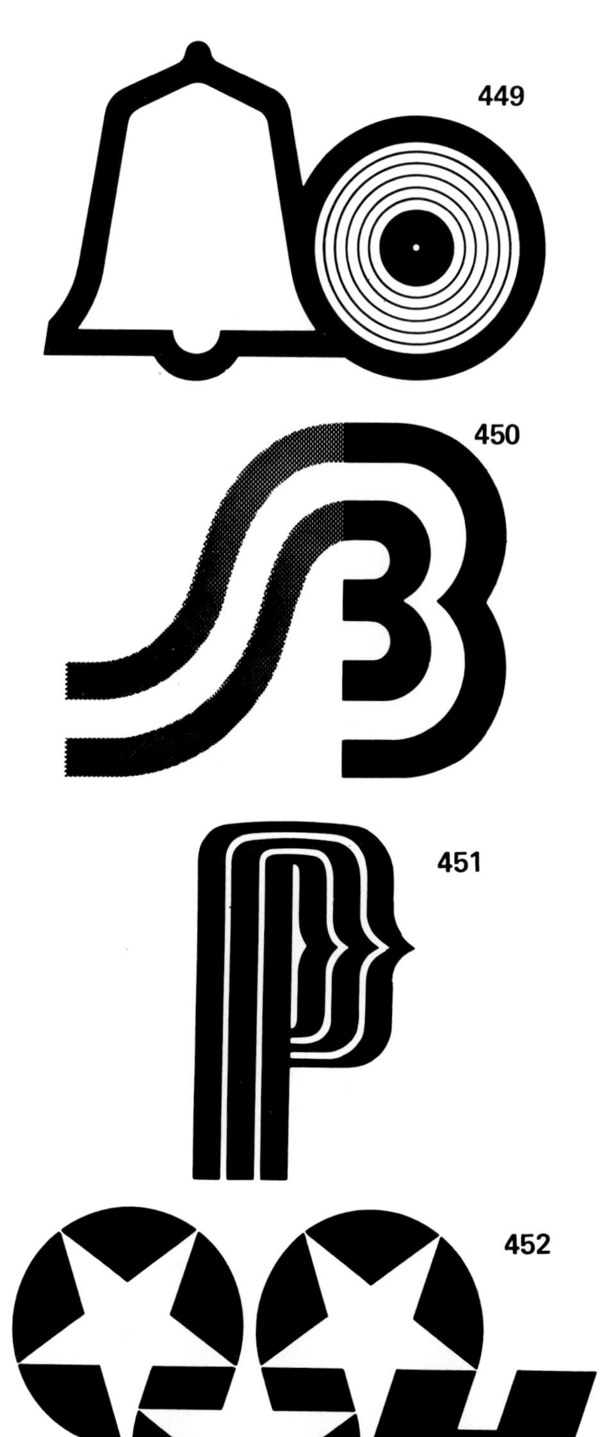

441 Comerco, Inc.
Tacoma, Washington

442 Pacific National Bank of Washington

443 Sun and Powder, Inc.
Sun Valley, Idaho

444 The Community Banks of Washington

445 The American Forest Institute
Washington, D.C.

446 Great Northwest Federal Savings & Loan Assn.

447 Arthur Cox & Sons, Inc.
Pasadena, California

448 Fremerman-Papin, Inc.
Kansas City, Missouri

449 Bell Records
New York City

450 Schorr Brothers
Brooklyn

451 People's Bank
Providence, Rhode Island

452 Hennessey Three Star Industries
Los Angeles

453

454

455

456

457

458

459

460

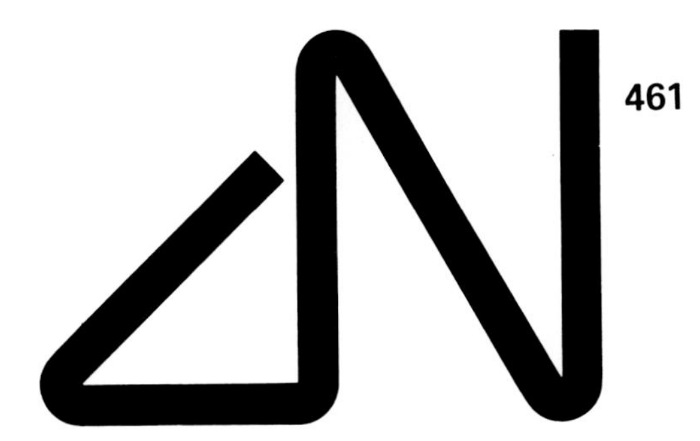
461

462

463

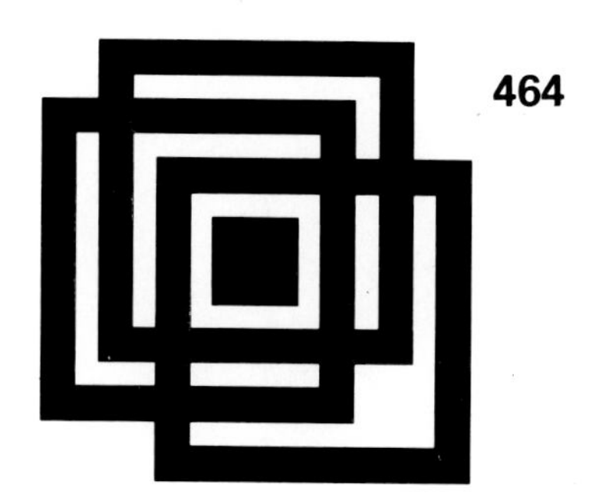
464

453 War/Peace Report, Inc.
New York City

454 Unifair, Inc.
New York City

455 Patient Care Projects Division
Miller & Fink Publishers
Greenwich, Connecticut

456 Innovation House, Inc.
New York City

457 Growth Fund of America, Inc.
Greenwich, Connecticut

458 Income Fund of America, Inc.
Greenwich, Connecticut

459 Farmlands U.S.A.
New Jersey

460 Recreation Industries, Inc.
Los Angeles

461 Data Network Corporation
New York City

462 The Treecrop Company
Oakland

463 Berley Industries, Inc.
Brooklyn

464 The Capital Group, Inc.
Los Angeles

465
469
466
470
467
471
468
472

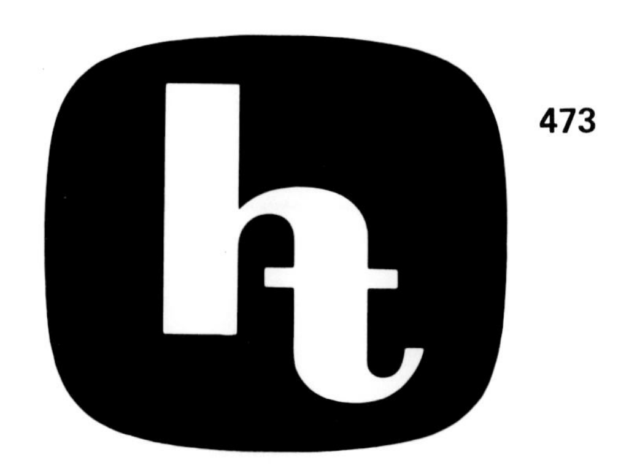
473

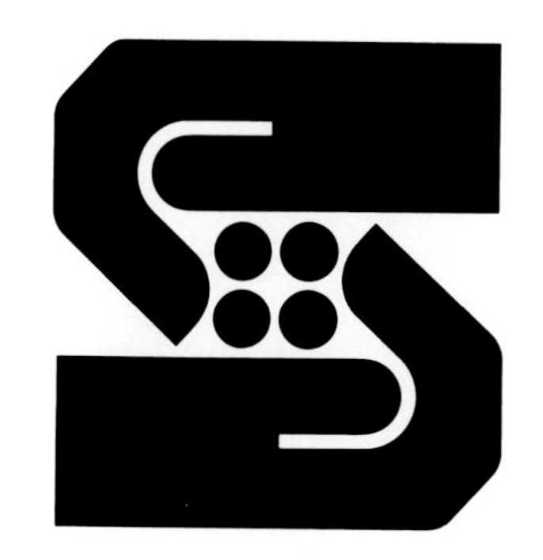
474

475

476

465 Tyler Pipe
subsidiary of Tyler Corporation
Tyler, Texas

466 Dodge Cork Co.
Lancaster, Pennsylvania

467 HMH Publishing Co.
Chicago

468 Metropolitan Life Insurance Co.
New York City

469 Weyerhaeuser Corporation
Tacoma, Washington

470 Temple Industries
Diboll, Texas

471 Capital National Corporation
Houston

472 Reeves Telecom Corporation
New York City

473 Hoffman-Taff, Inc.
Springfield, Mo.

474 Surety Savings & Loan Association
Burbank, California

475 International Paper Co.
New York City

476 General Oceanography
Cambridge, Massachusetts

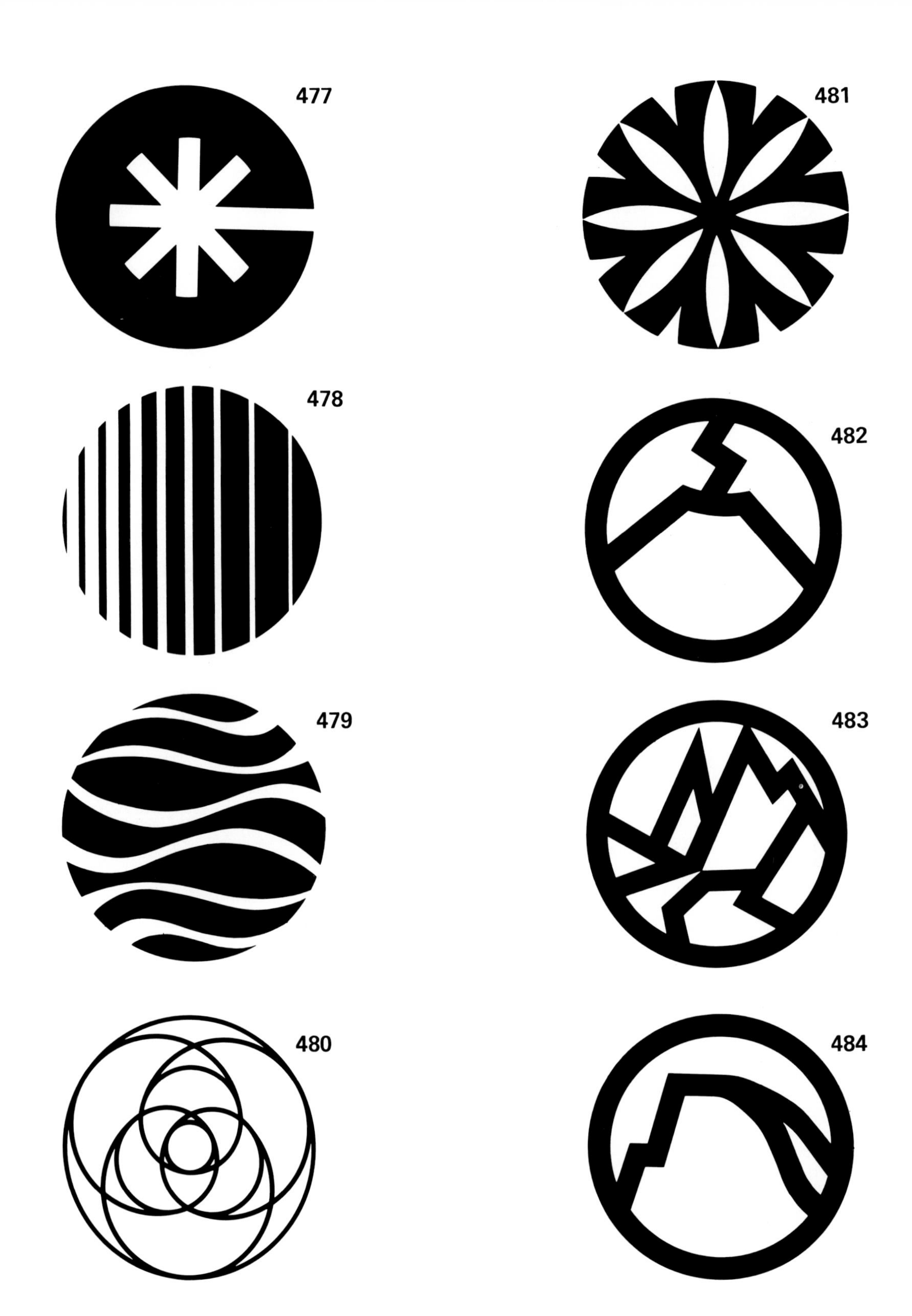
477
481
478
482
479
483
480
484

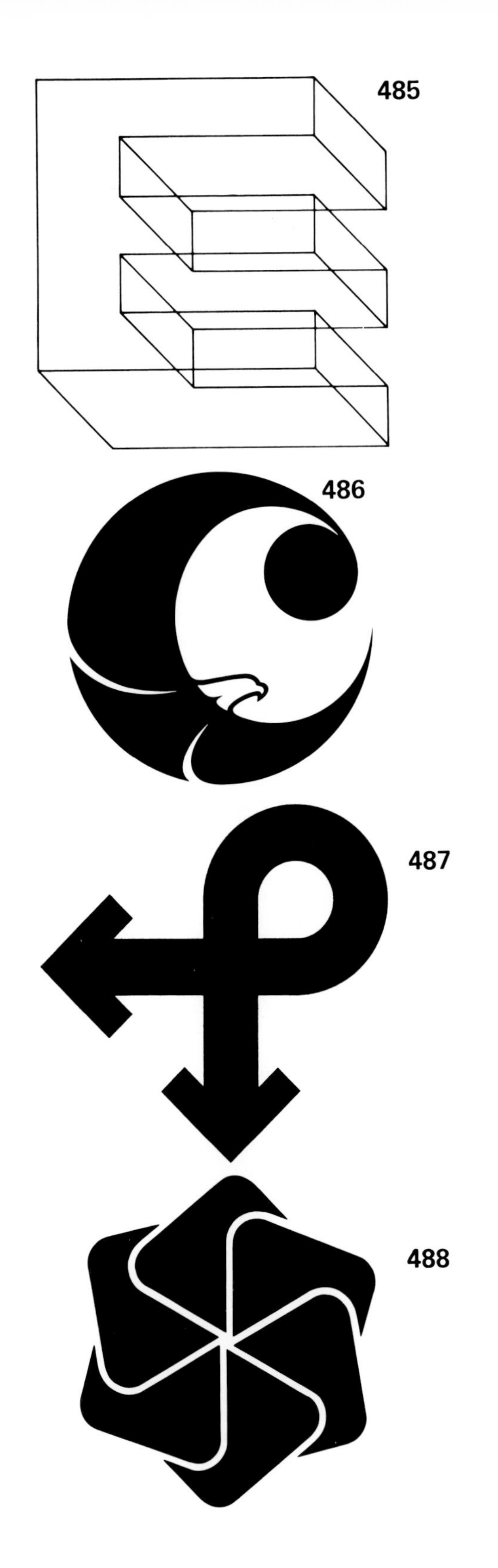

477 Coherent Radiation Laboratories
Palo Alto, California

478 Environmental Measurements, Inc.
San Francisco

479 Marine World
Redwood City, California

480 Aerojet Liquid Rocket Company
Sacramento, California

481 Salem Plaza
Salem, Oregon

482 Lassen Volcanic National Park
Menlo Park, California

483 Mount McKinley National Park
Menlo Park, California

484 Yosemite Park and Curry Co.
Yosemite National Park, Calif.

485 Educreative Systems, Inc.
New York City

486 Citizens Federal Savings & Loan Assn.
Pittsburgh

487 Penn's Southwest Association
Pittsburgh

488 Carteret Savings & Loan Association
Newark, New Jersey

489

490

491

492

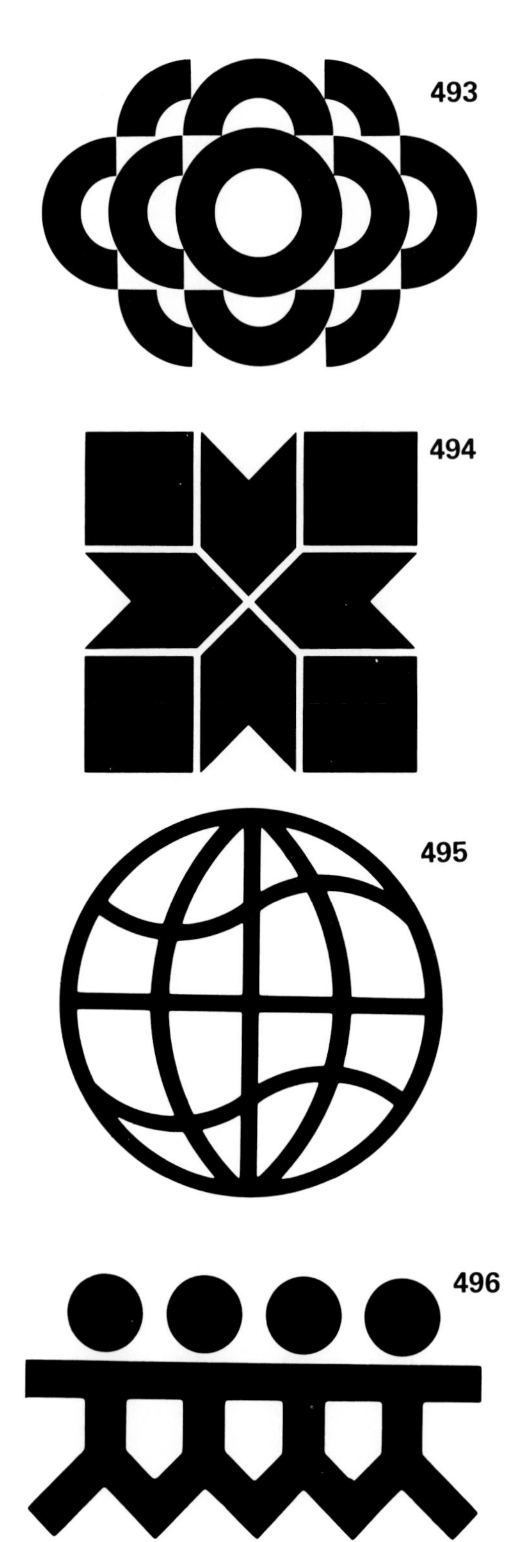

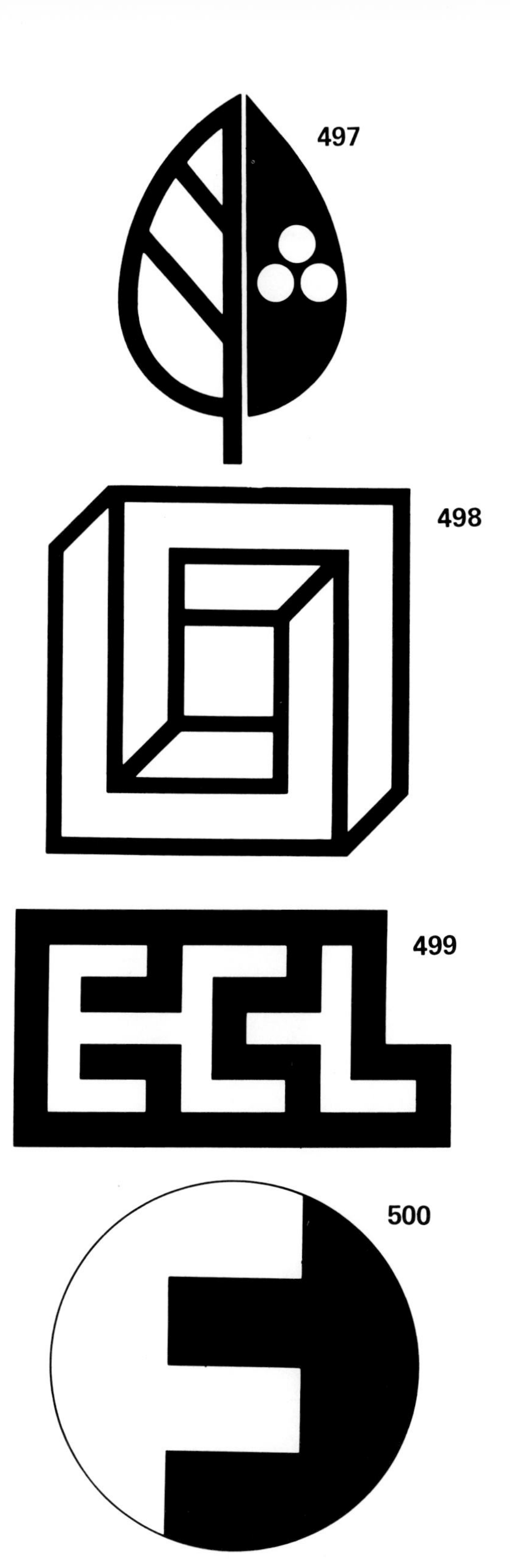

489 Security Corporation
Santa Ana, California

490 Hawaii Production Center
Honolulu

491 Cousins Properties, Inc.
Atlanta

492 Quillayote Camp
Olympic Peninsula, Washington

493 Nuclear Pacific, Inc.

494 National Forest Products Association
Washington, D. C.

495 Pepsi Cola International
Purchase, N.Y.

496 Pressman Corp. (toy manufacturers)
New York City

497 (insecticide product mark)
Upjohn Company
Kalamazoo, Michigan

498 Perfect Film & Chemical
New York City

499 ECL Industries
New York City

500 Franklin Typographers
New York City

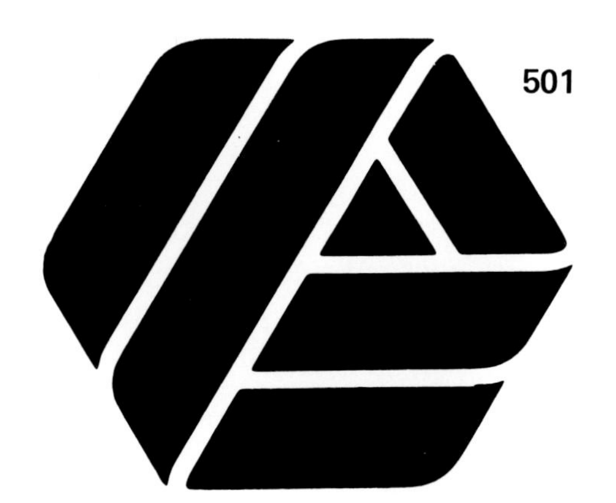

501

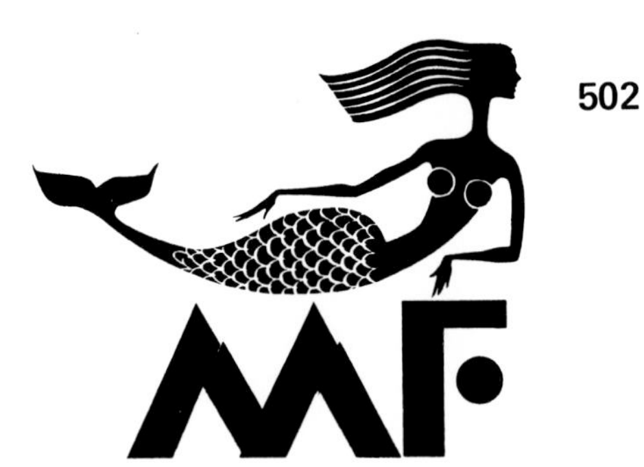

502

503

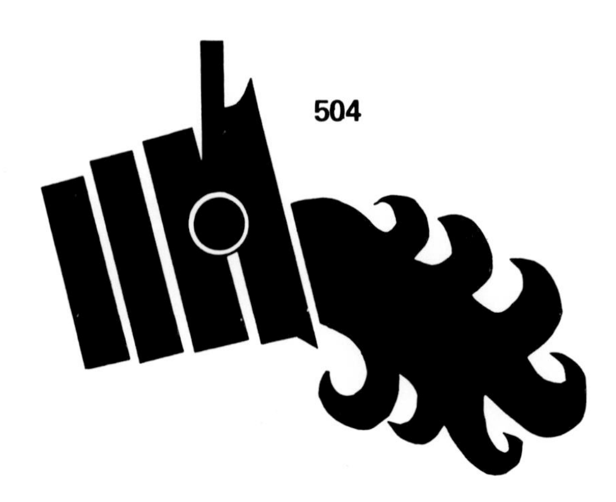

504

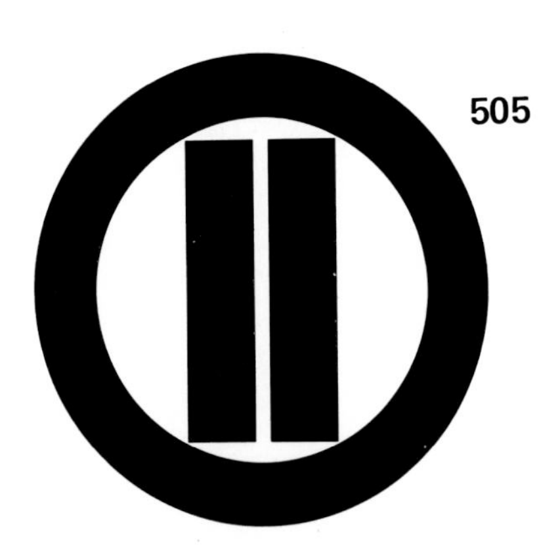

505

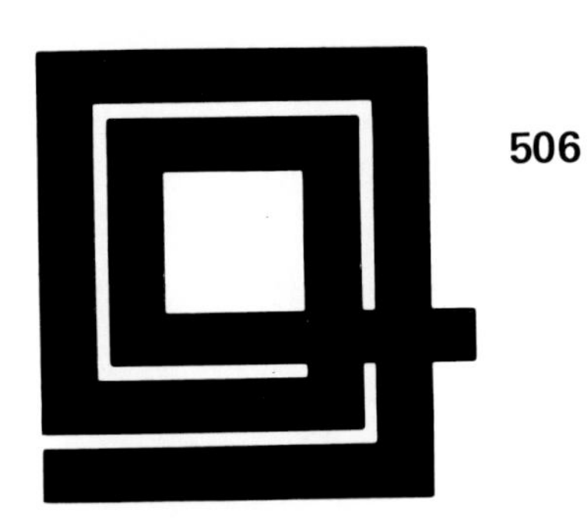

506

507

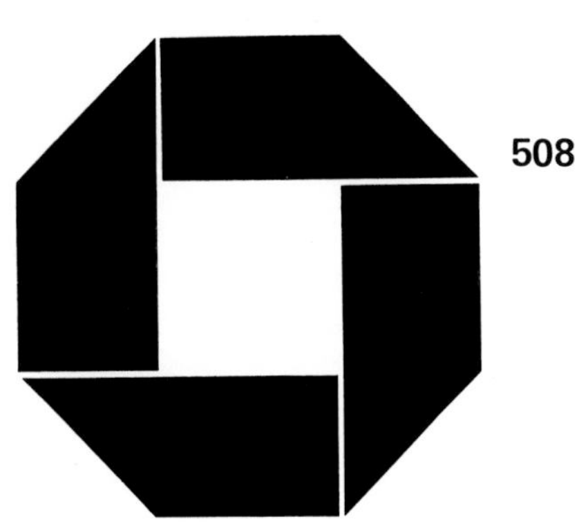

508

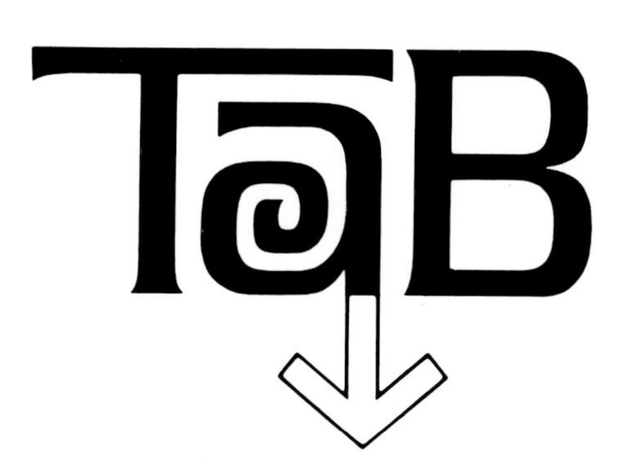

509

510

511

512

501 Bangor Punta Corporation
Greenwich, Connecticut

502 Milwaukee Faucets, Inc.
Milwaukee

503 Westinghouse Broadcasting Company
New York City

504 Kentucky Electric Steel Company
Ashland, Kentucky

505 WPIX Television
New York City

506 Olivetti Underwood Corporation
New York City

507 Wagner Industries, Inc.
Cicero, Illinois

508 The Chase Manhattan Bank
New York City

509 Tab
Coca-Cola Company
Atlanta

510 Armour-Dial, Inc.
Chicago

511 Kimberly-Clark Corp.
Neenah, Wisconsin

512 Comlab, Inc.
Chicago

513

514

515

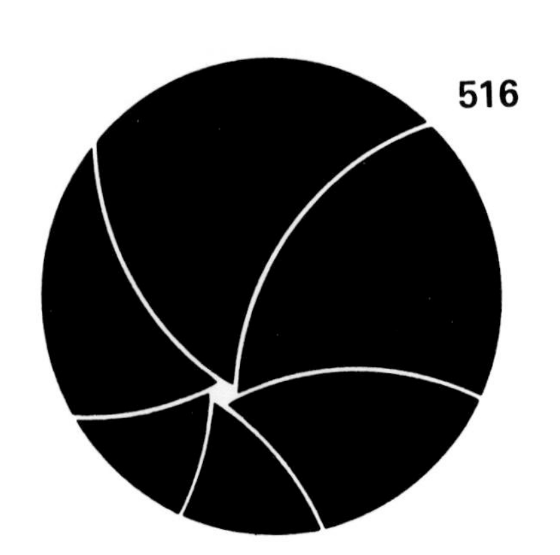

516

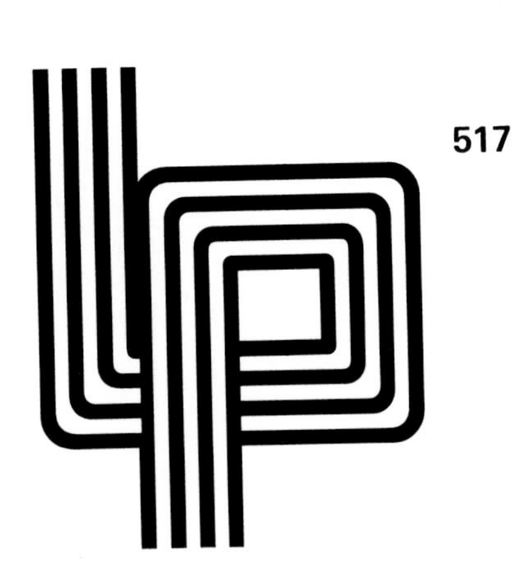

517

518

519

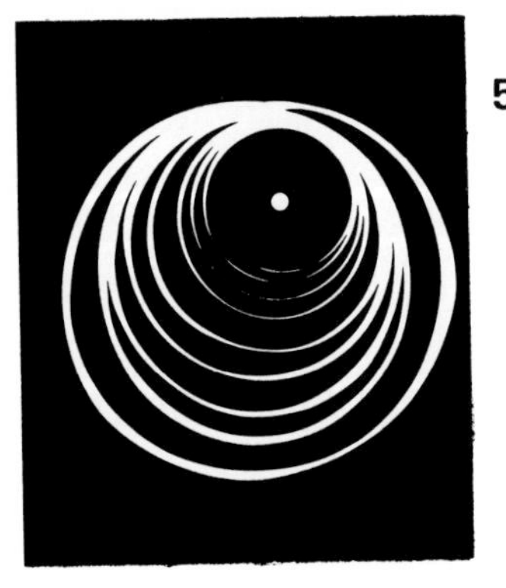

520

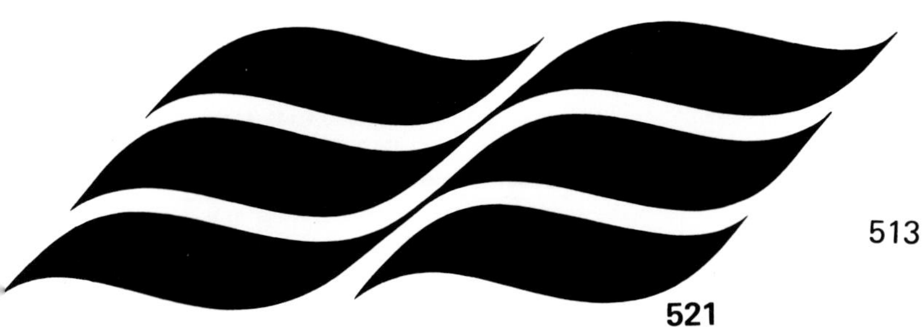

522

unit1

Amtrak

523

513 The Academy of Art College
San Francisco

514 Sonoco Products Co.
Hartsville, South Carolina

515 First National Bank
Baltimore

516 Omnibus Film Productions
Akron, Ohio

517 Burks Pumps
Decatur, Illinois

518 R.J. Reynolds Industries
Winston-Salem

519 Colt Industries
New York City

520 Precision Plating Co.
Chicago

521 Grossman Publishers
New York City

522 Unit 1
Denver

523 National Railroad Passenger Corp.
Washington, D.C.

524 Ex-Cell-O Corporation
Detriot

525
526
527
528
529
530
531
532

533

534

535

536

525 Spectra-Physics
Mountain View, California

526 Boise Cascade Corporation
Boise, Idaho

527 Sutro & Co., Inc.
San Francisco

528 U.S. Air Force Documentary
Art Program
Washington, D.C.

529 California Casualty Insurance Group
San Mateo, California

530 Westel Company
San Mateo, California

531 Squaw Valley Land and Livestock Co.
Tahoe City, California

532 Hagemeister-Lert, Inc.
San Francisco,

533 Tahoe Keys
Tahoe Valley, California

534 Crystal Shores
Crystal Bay, Nevada

535 The Red Radish (restaurant)
Olympic Valley, California

536 Committee of Arts and Lectures
University of California
Santa Cruz, California

537

538

539

540

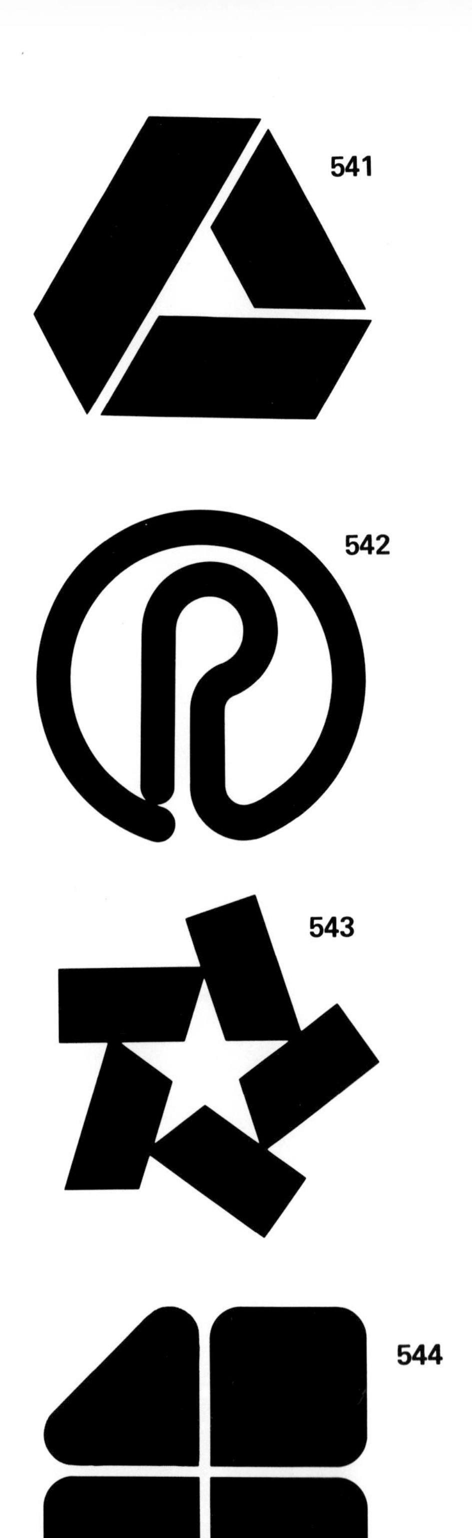

541

542

543

544

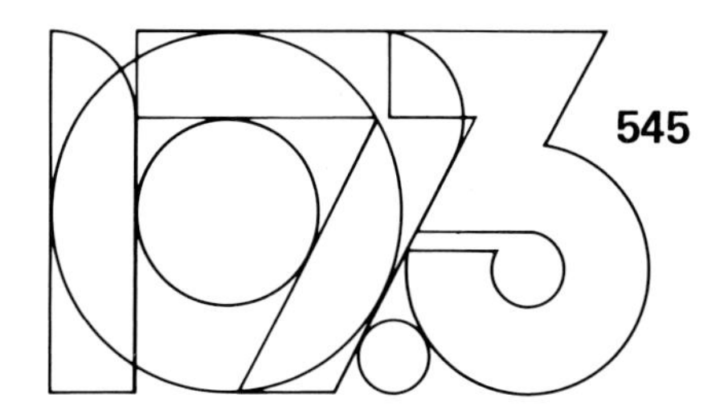
545

546

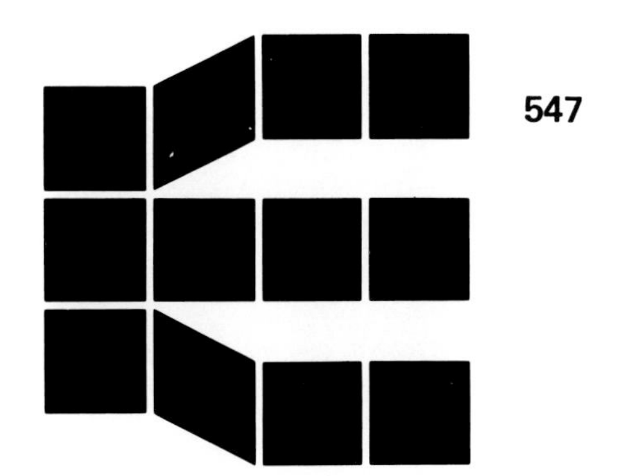
547

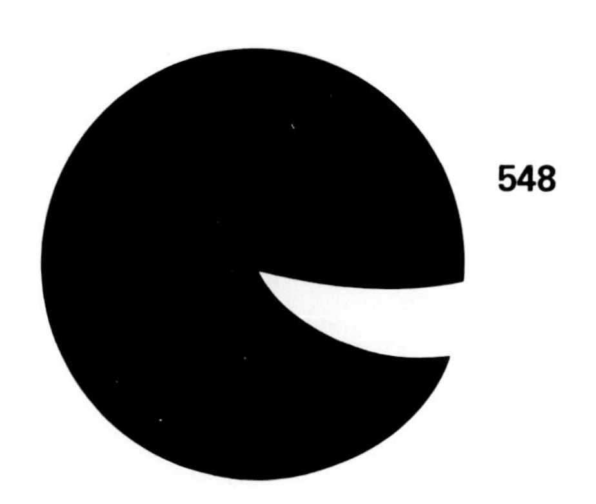
548

537 Montague-Spragens Printers
Berkeley, California

538 Nytron, Inc.
Palo Alto, California

539 Barr Chemical Products, Inc.
Berkeley, California

540 Pace Fund
Stanford University
Stanford, California

541 Consumer Alliance
Palo Alto, California

542 Patchcord Productions, Inc.
Beverly Hills, California

543 WMAL TV
Washington, D. C.

544 WCIV Television
Mount Pleasant, S.C.

545 WMAL FM
Washington, D.C.

546 The San Francisco Experience
Electrovision Productions, Inc.
San Francisco

547 Electrovision Productions, Inc.
San Francisco

548 Cornnuts, Inc.
Oakland, California

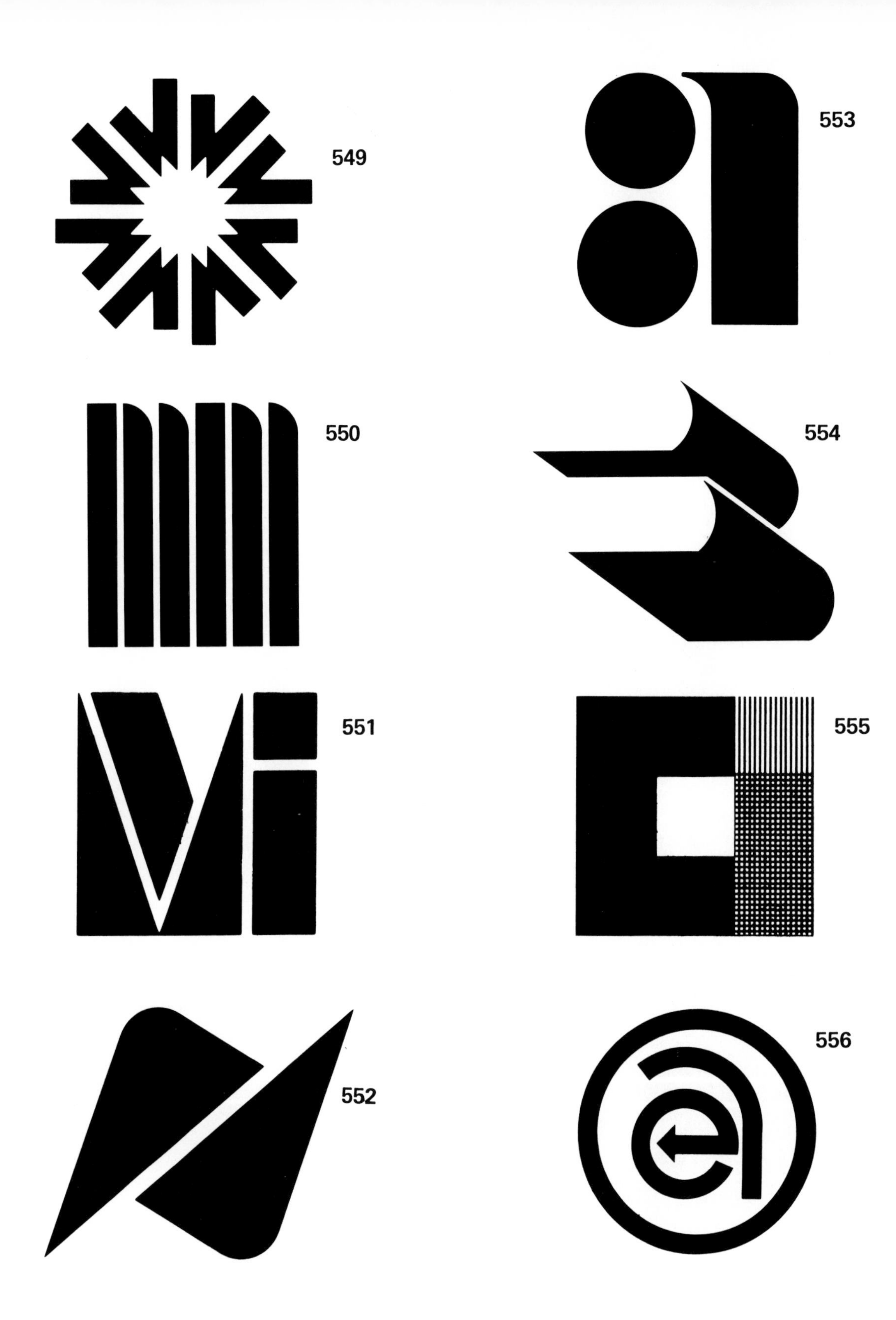
549
553
550
554
551
555
552
556

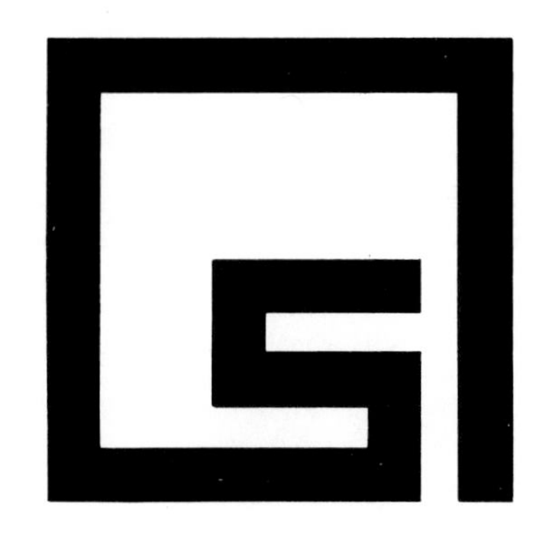

557

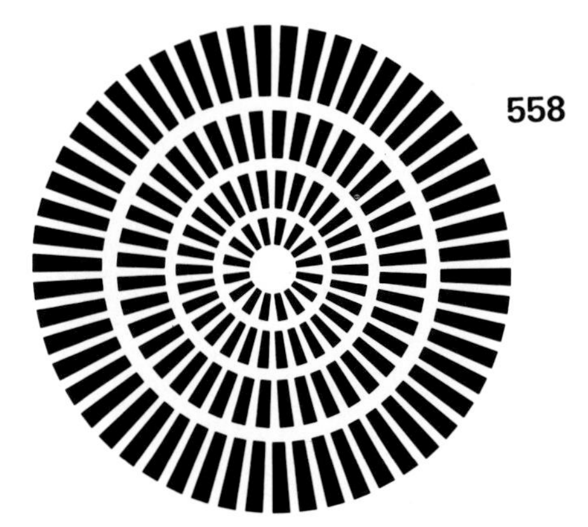

558

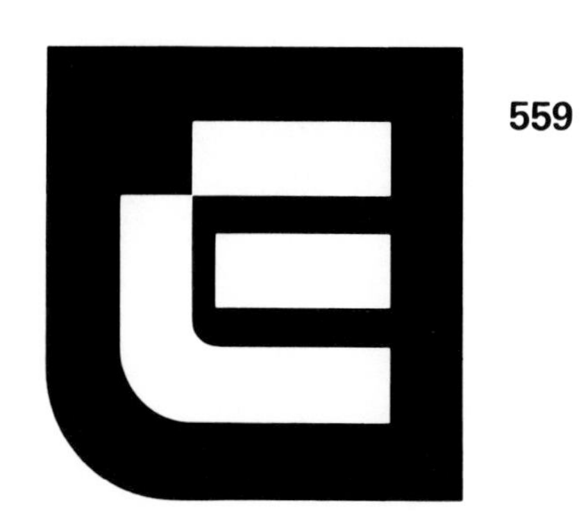

559

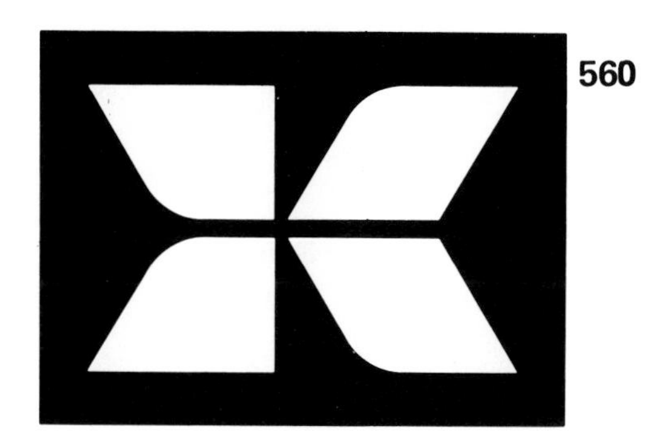

560

549 Duquesne Light
Pittsburgh

550 Majors & Majors Realtors
Dallas

551 Monogram Industries, Inc.
Los Angeles

552 Nalco Chemical Co.
Chicago

553 The Ansul Company
Marinette, Wisconsin

554 Bellarmine College
Louisville

555 Contract Interiors, Inc.
Chicago

556 Aerotron, Inc.
Raleigh

557 Signetics Corporation
Sunnyvale, California

558 First National Bank
Miami

559 Equitable Trust Bank
Baltimore

560 Koracorp Industries
San Francisco

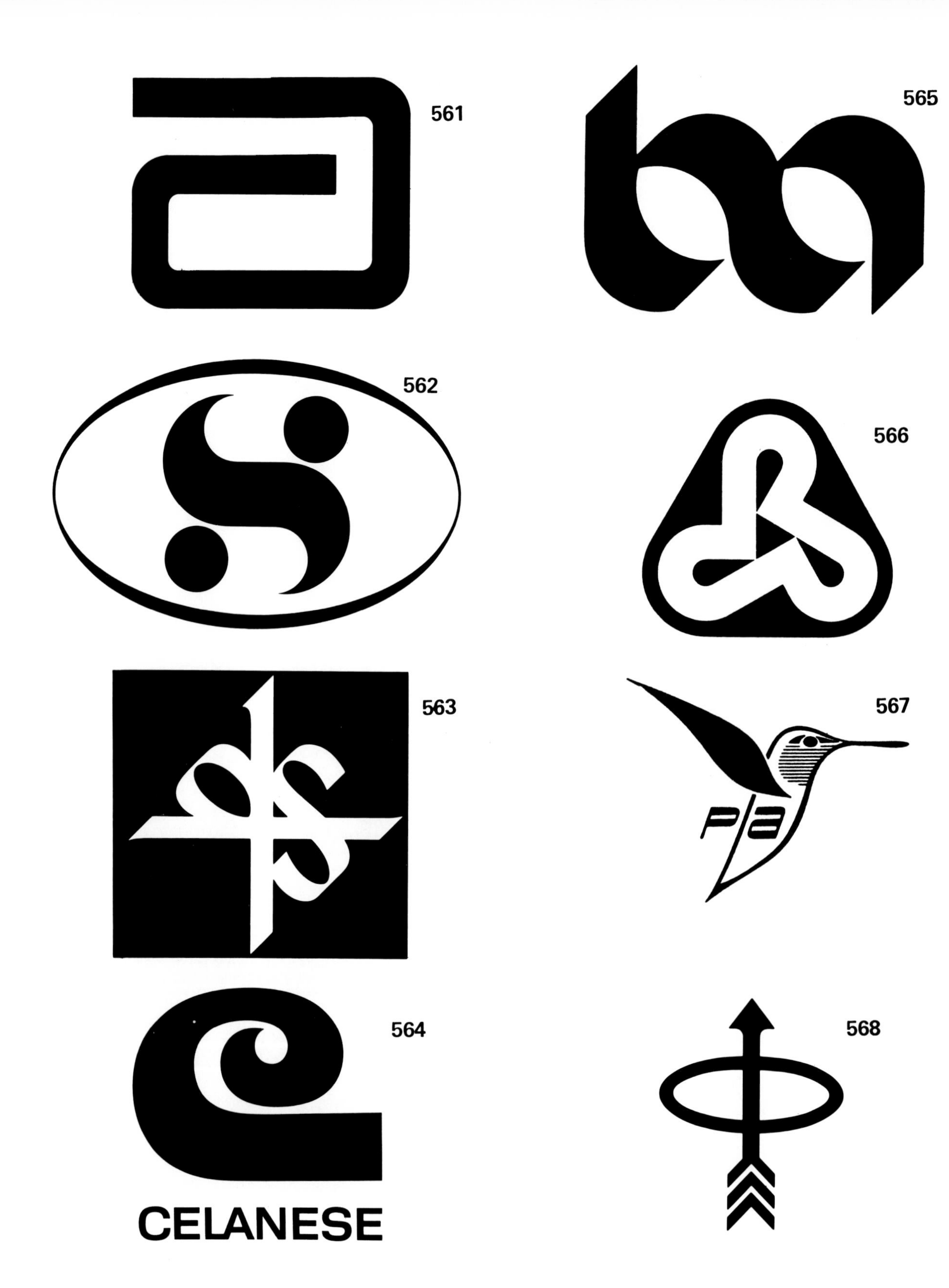
561
562
563
564
CELANESE
565
566
567
pa
568

569

570

571

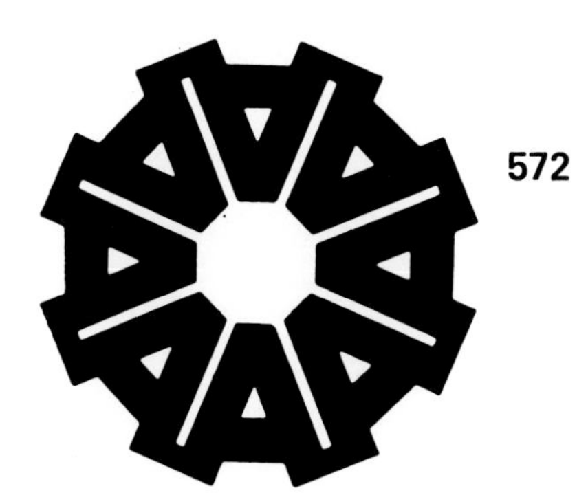
572

561 Abbott Laboratories
North Chicago, Ill.

562 Scott Paper Company
Philadelphia

563 Dayton Typographic Service
Dayton

564 Celanese Corporation
New York City

565 Bank Marketing Association
Chicago

566 Royal Industries
Pasadena

567 Pittsburgh Airways, Inc.
Pittsburgh

568 Parker Pen Co.
Janesville, Wisconsin

569 Direct Mail Advertising Assn.
New York City

570 Atlas Van Lines
Evansville, Indiana

571 Waters Associates
Framingham, Massachusetts

572 American National Bank & Trust
Chattanooga

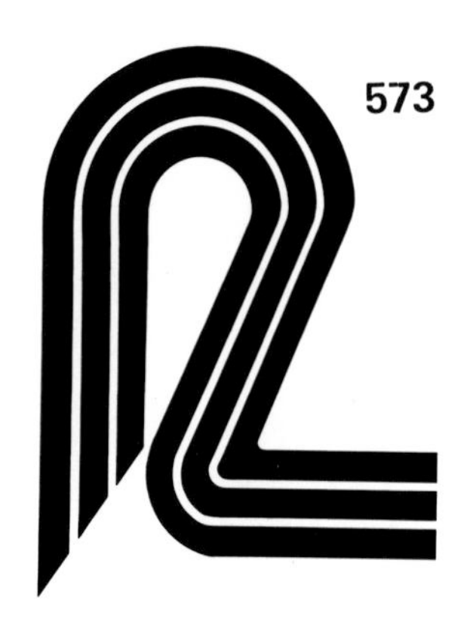

573

574

575

576

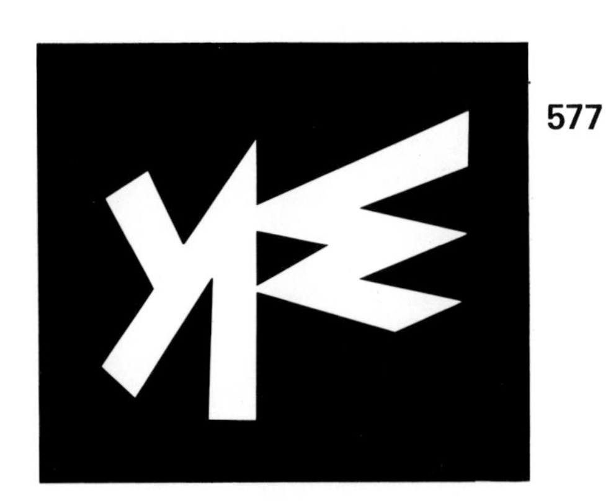

577

578

EWi

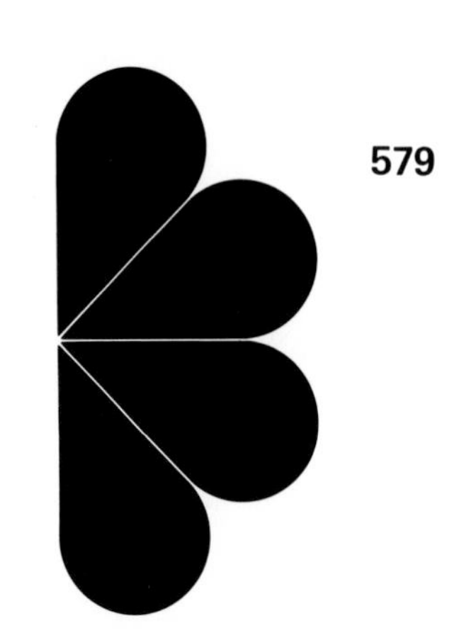

579

580

581

MeadJohnson

LABORATORIES

582

Kirsch

583

Republicsteel

584

Abex

573 Rose Engineering Company
Los Angeles

574 L.J. Globus Advertising, Inc.
Los Angeles

575 Propinquity
Los Angeles

576 Rohm and Haas Company
Philadelphia

577 Keller Williams Furniture Mfg. Co.
Oklahoma City

578 Edinger-Wyckoff, Inc.
Stroudsburg, Pennsylvania

579 Kovler Gallery
Chicago

580 Higgins Hegner Genovese, Inc.
Chicago

581 Mead Johnson Laboratories
Evansville, Indiana

582 The Kirsch Company
Sturgis, Michigan

583 Republic Steel Corporation
Cleveland

584 Abex Corporation
New York City

585

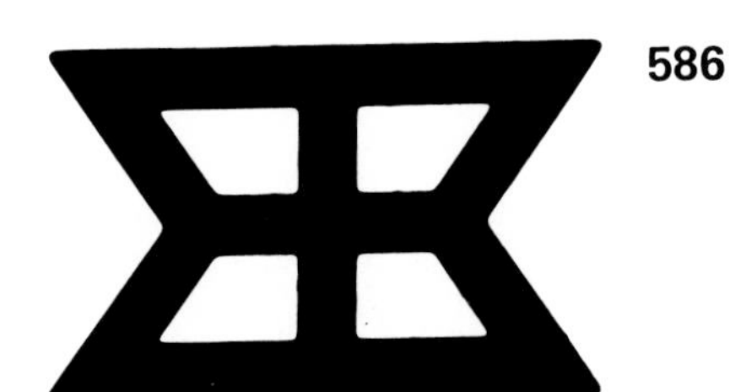
586

587

588

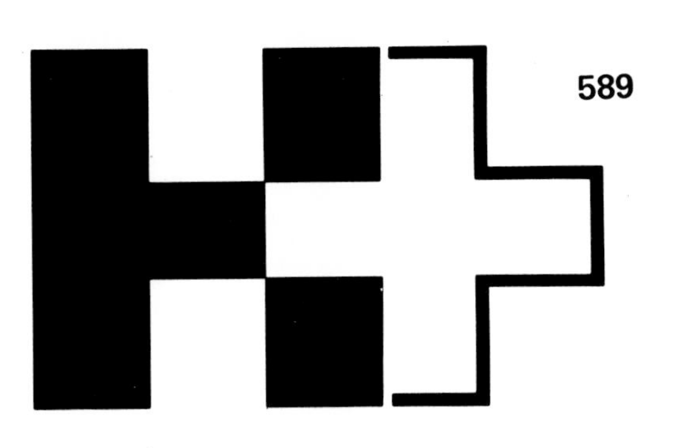
589

590

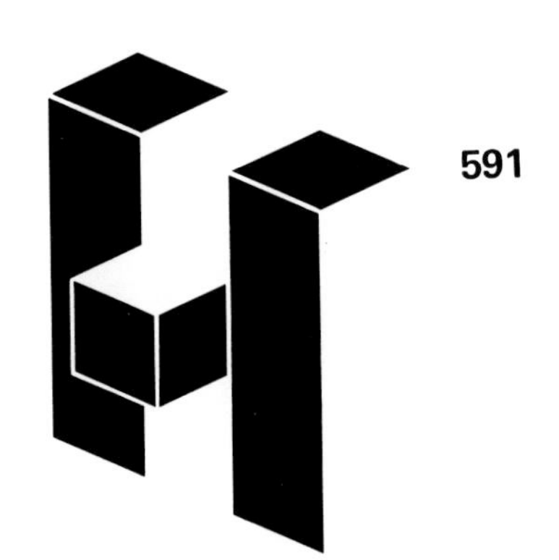
591

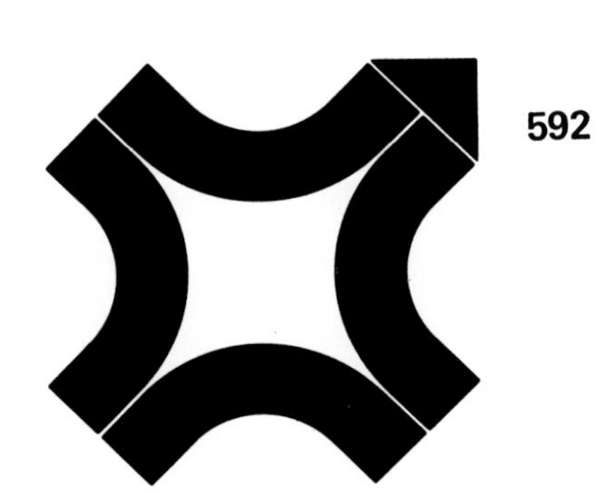
592

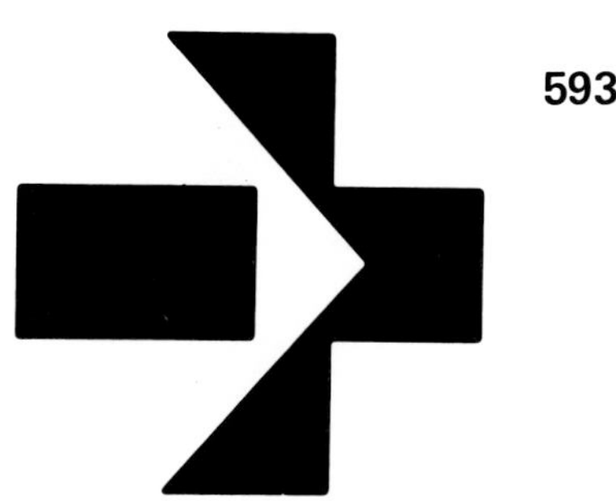

594

595

596

585 Bank Printing Co., Inc.
Los Angeles

586 Travenol Laboratories, Inc.
Morton Grove, Illinois

587 International Geomarine Corp.
Los Angeles

588 Aerospace Corporation
Los Angeles

589 Hospicare, Inc.
Los Angeles

590 Ohio Trailways
Oxford, Ohio

591 National Corp. for Housing
Partnerships
Washington, D. C.

592 Northeast Subway Extension
Philadelphia

593 Gould, Inc.
Chicago

594 National Energy Systems Corp.
San Francisco

595 Nashua Corp.
Nashua, New Hampshire

596 Metals Research Instrument Corp.

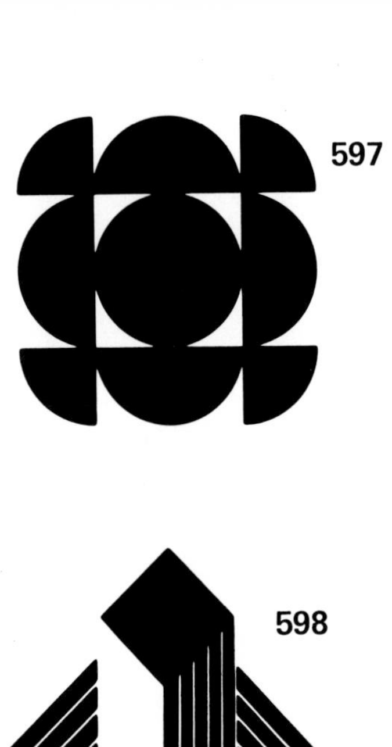
597

598

599

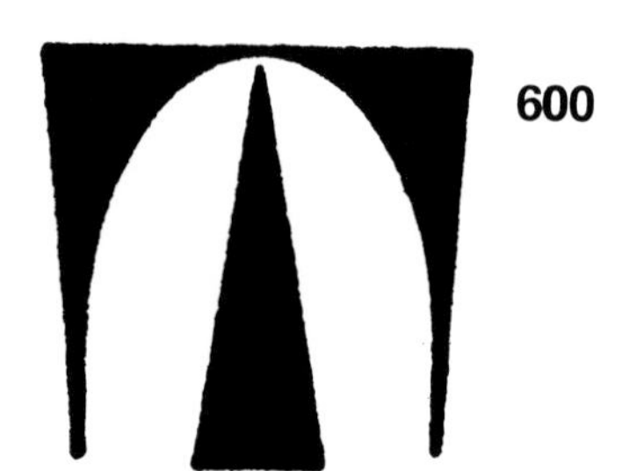
600

601

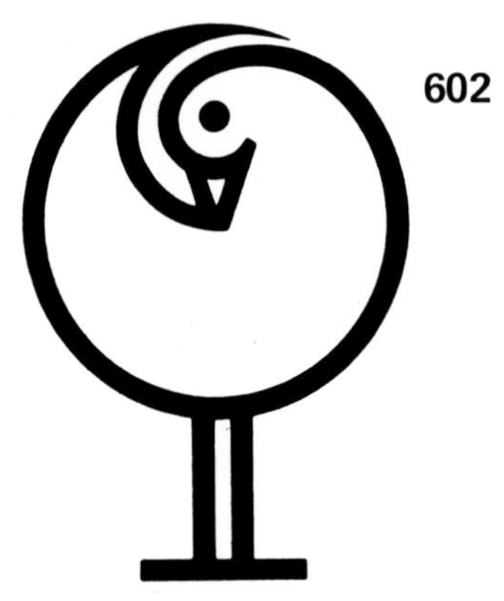
602

603

604

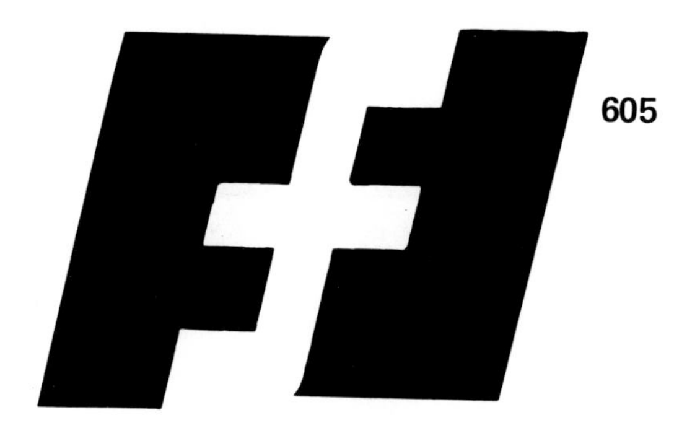

605

606

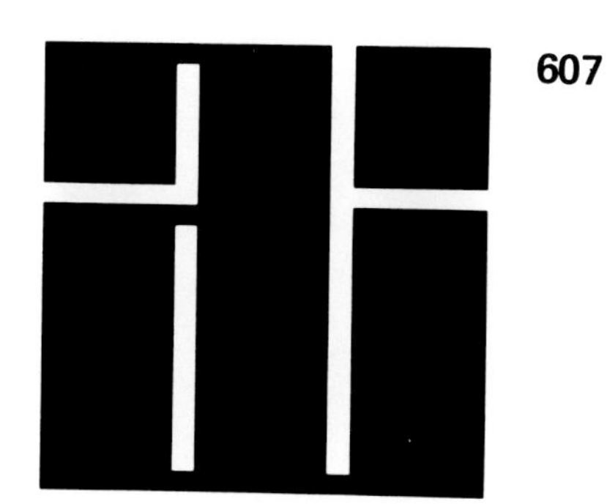

607

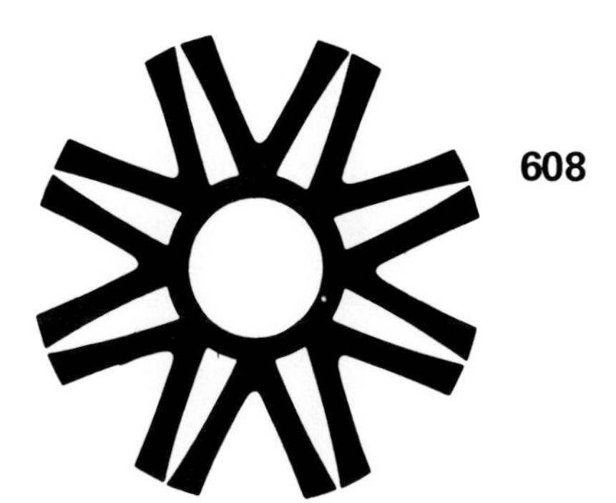

608

597 Dayton Hudson Corp.
Minneapolis

598 U.S. Leasing Realty Advisers, Inc.
San Francisco

599 GAC Corporation

600 Timber Structures, Inc.
Portland, Oregon

601 Diversey Corporation
Chicago

602 Bird Precision Jewels
Waltham, Massachusetts

603 Erica Wilson, Inc.
New York City

604 Evers Savings Association
Cincinnati

605 Foremost Lithograph
Providence, Rhode Island

606 Color Concentrate Corp.
Woonsocket, Rhode Island

607 Arkwright-Interlaken, Inc.
Fiskeville, Rhode Island

608 Virginia National Bank
Norfolk, Virginia

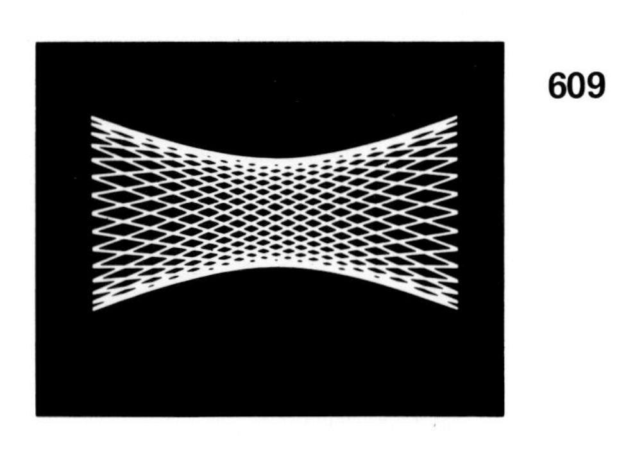

609

610

611

612

613

614

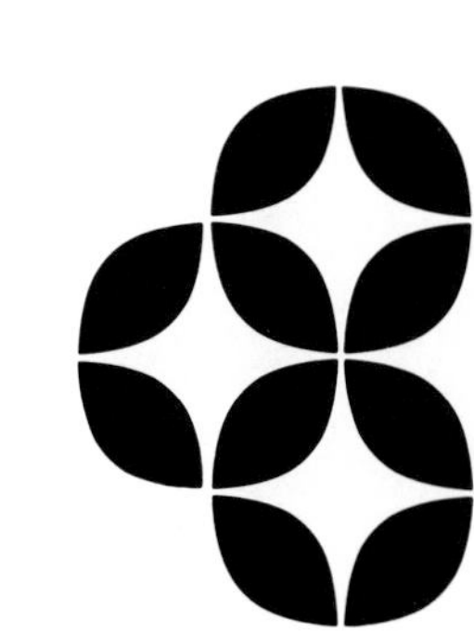

615

616

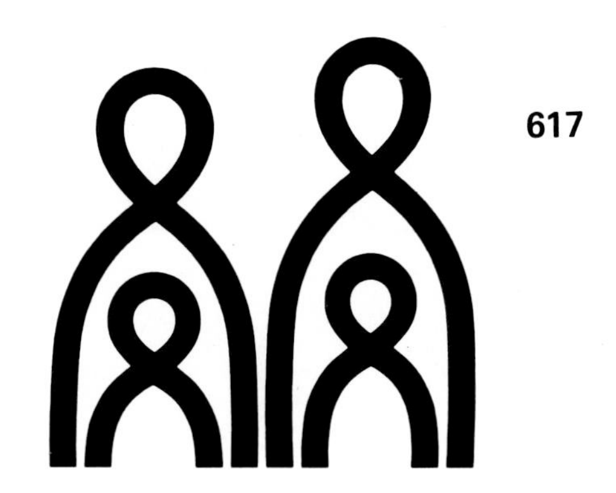

617

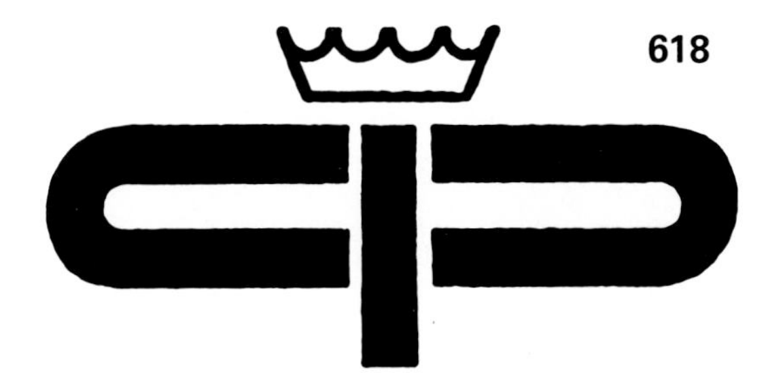

618

619

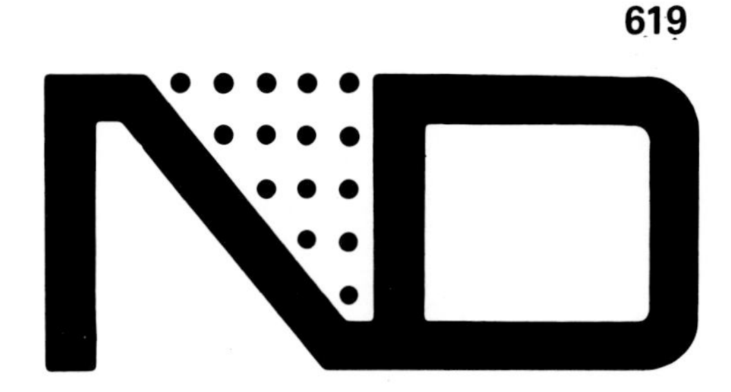

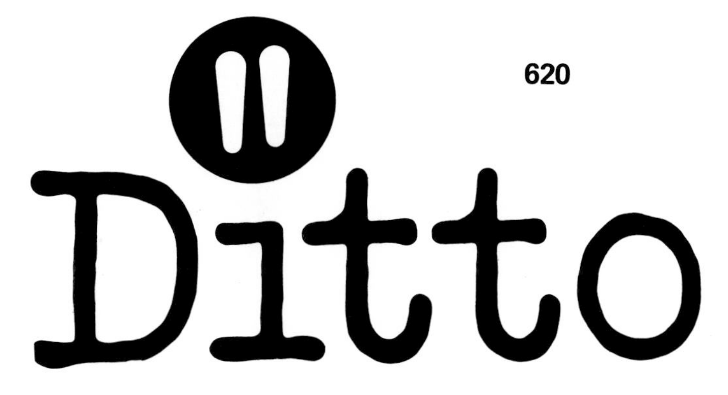

620

609 Bauer & Black
Chicago

610 LaSalle Steel

611 Bank of Maine
Augusta

612 Weschsler Coffee Corp.
New York City

613 Jeffries Banknote Co.
Los Angeles

614 Bank of the Commonwealth
Detroit

615 Steel Service Center Institute
Cleveland

616 Logan Clay Products
Logan, Ohio

617 The Pathfinder Fund
Boston

618 Crown Paper
Yonkers, New York

619 Nuclear Data Inc.
Palatine, Illinois

620 Ditto Inc.
Lincolnwood, Illinois

621

622

623

Goodall

624

625

626

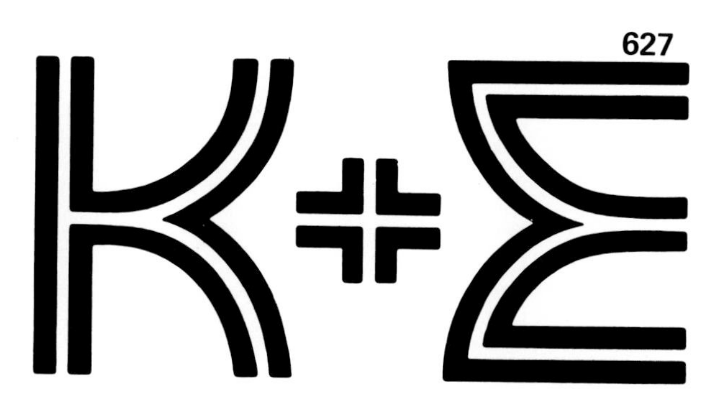

627

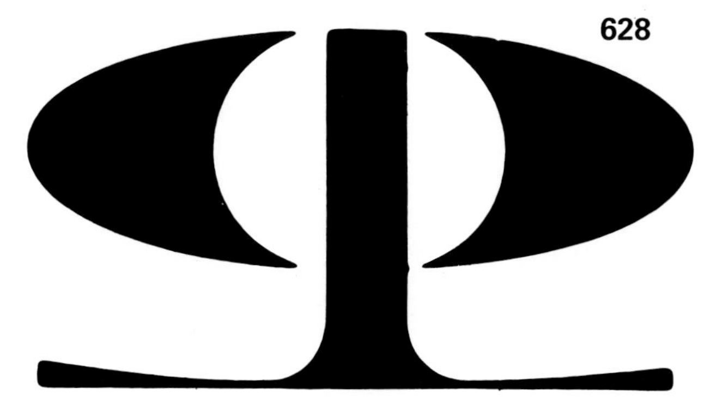

628

621 Helipot Division
Beckman Instruments
Fullerton, California

622 Marine Sciences
Los Angeles

623 Utica Duxbax Corp.
Utica, New York

624 Goodall Rubber Co.

625 United Refining Co.
Warren, Pennsylvania

626 North American Van Lines
Ft. Wayne, Indiana

627 Keuffel & Esser Co.
Morristown, New Jersey

628 Children's Press
Chicago

629

630

631

632

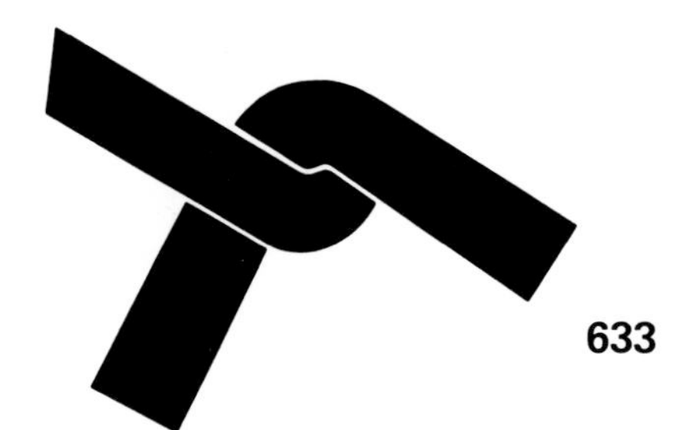

633

634

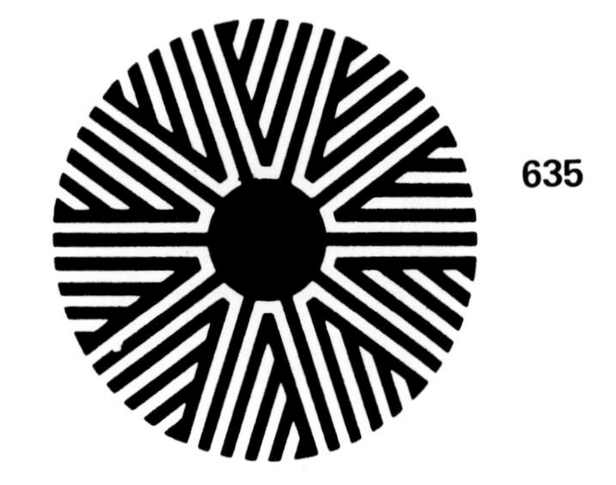

635

636

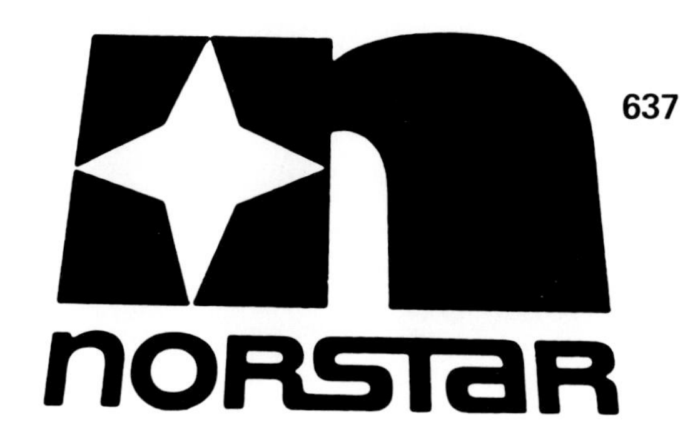

637

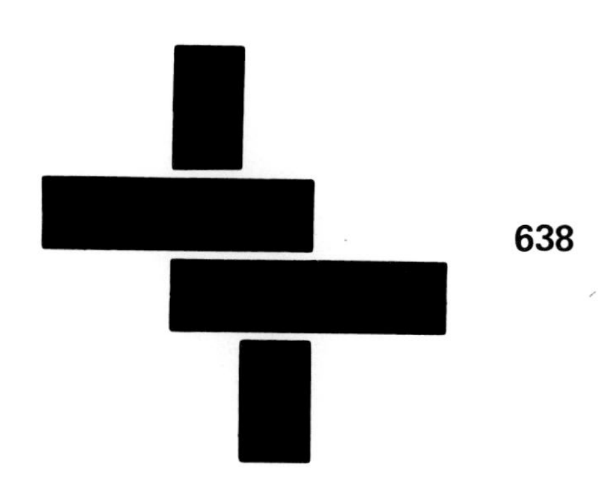

638

639

640

629 National Bank of Commerce
San Antonio

630 The Wool Bureau, Inc.
New York City

631 National Central Bank
Lancaster, Pennsylvania

632 Alpine State Bank
Rockford, Illinois

633 Ford Wire Products
Indianapolis, Indiana

634 Gate City Steel
Omaha, Nebraska

635 Universal Development Corp.
Chicago

636 KSTP Television
St. Paul, Minnesota

637 Norstar Sales Inc.
Minneapolis, Minnesota

638 Seven Lakes
Tampa, Florida

639 The Nilsen Group
Philadelphia

640 T.C. Miller Realty Co.
Akron, Ohio

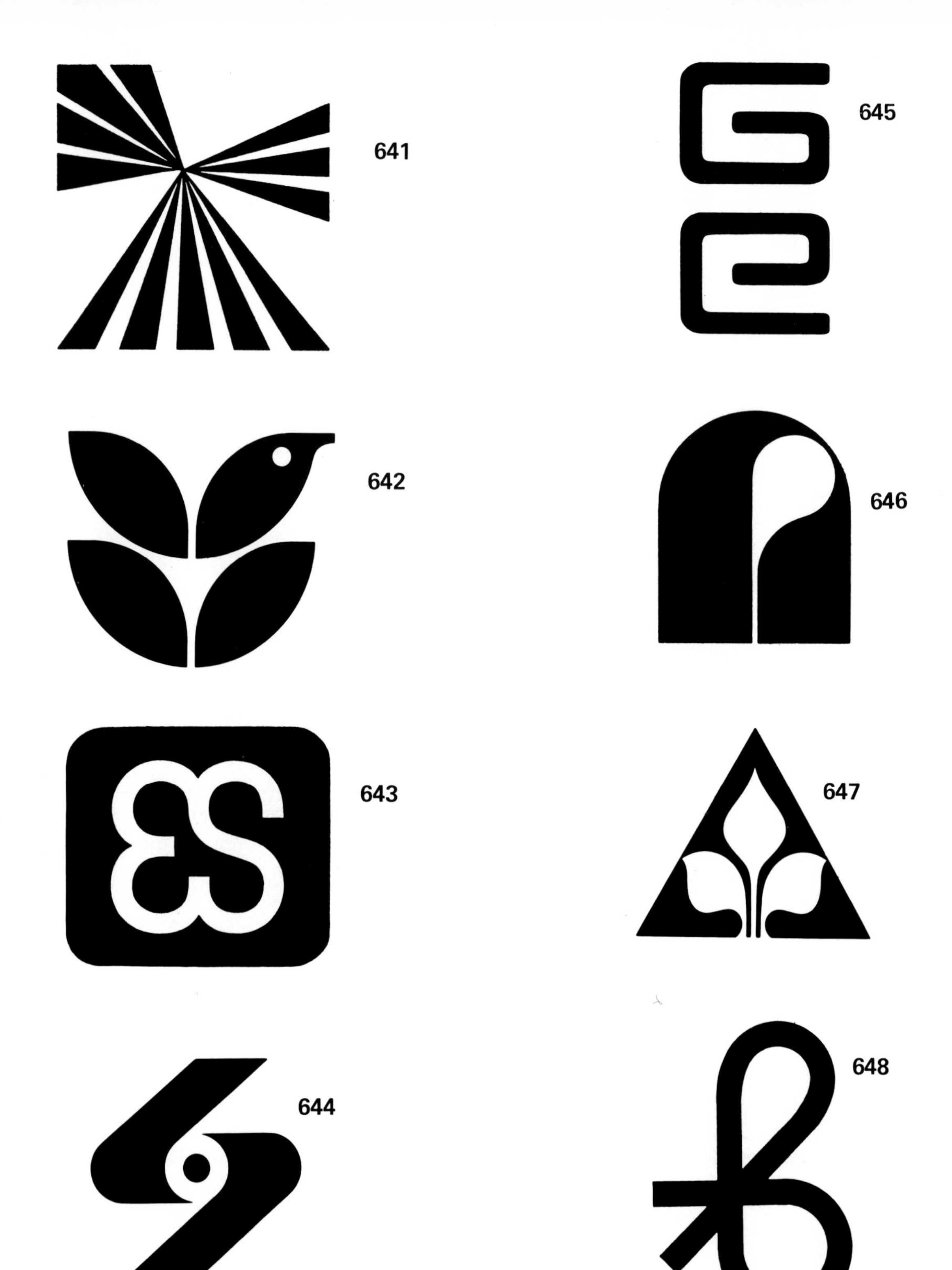
641
645
642
646
643
647
644
648

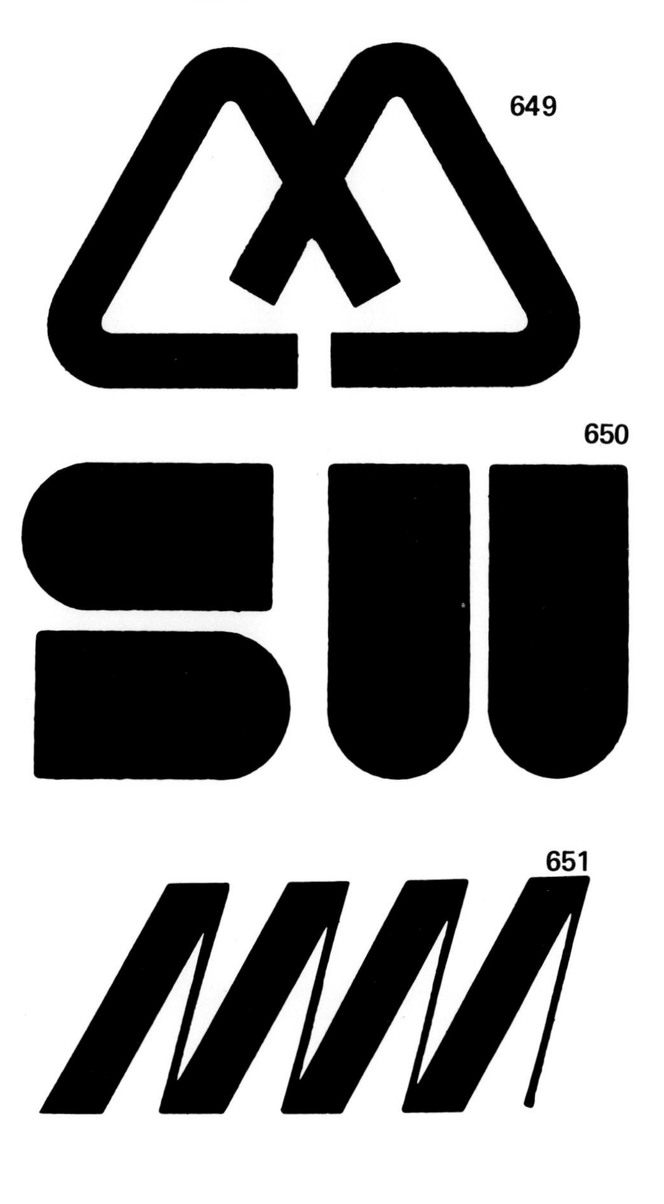

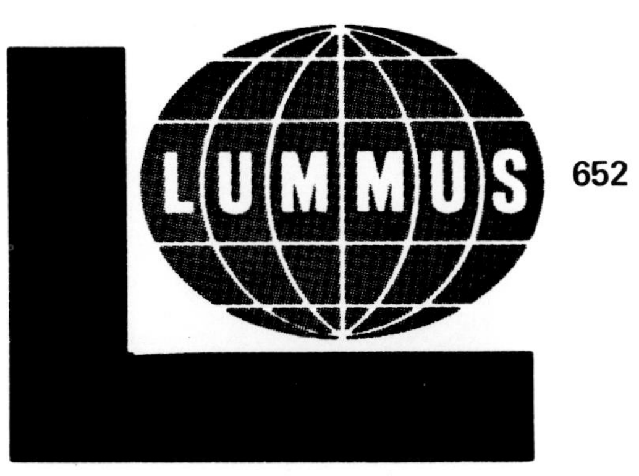

641 United Management Services, Inc.
Houston

642 Cheyenne Mountain Ranch
Colorado Springs, Colorado

643 Eastern Stainless Steel Co.
Baltimore, Maryland

644 Screen Gems
New York City

645 Glass Containers Corporation
Fullerton, California

646 Pacific Fashion Institute
San Francisco

647 Union Planters National Bank
Memphis, Tennessee

648 Berven Carpets Corp.
Fresno, California

649 Merrill Manufacturing Corp.
Merrill, Wisconsin

650 Shelby Williams Industries, Inc.
Chicago

651 Midland Mortgage Co.
Oklahoma City, Oklahoma

652 The Lummus Co.
Bloomfield, New Jersey

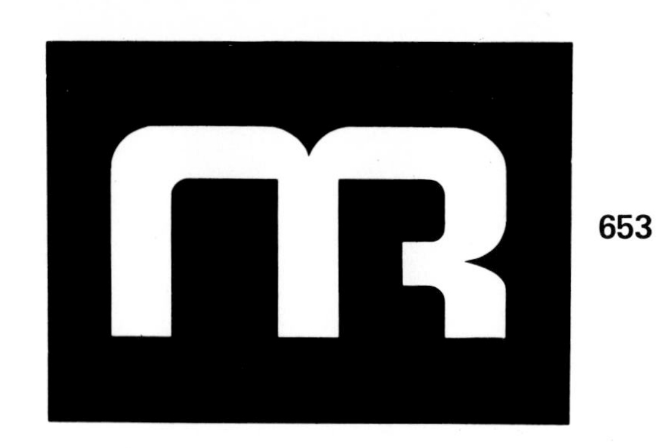
653

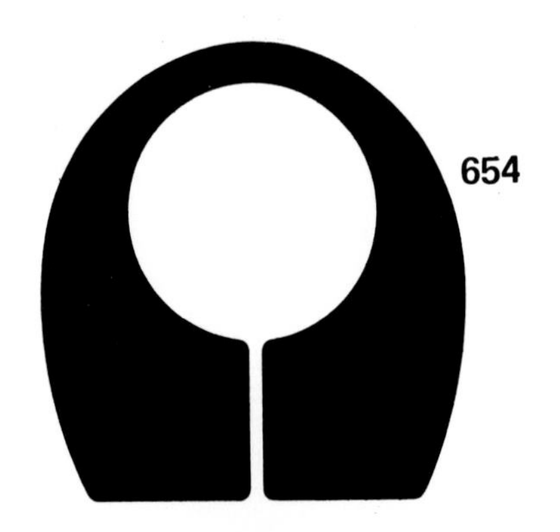
654

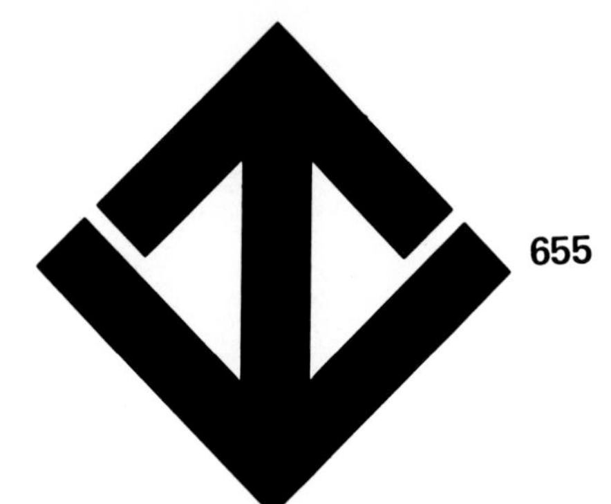
655

656

657

658

659

660

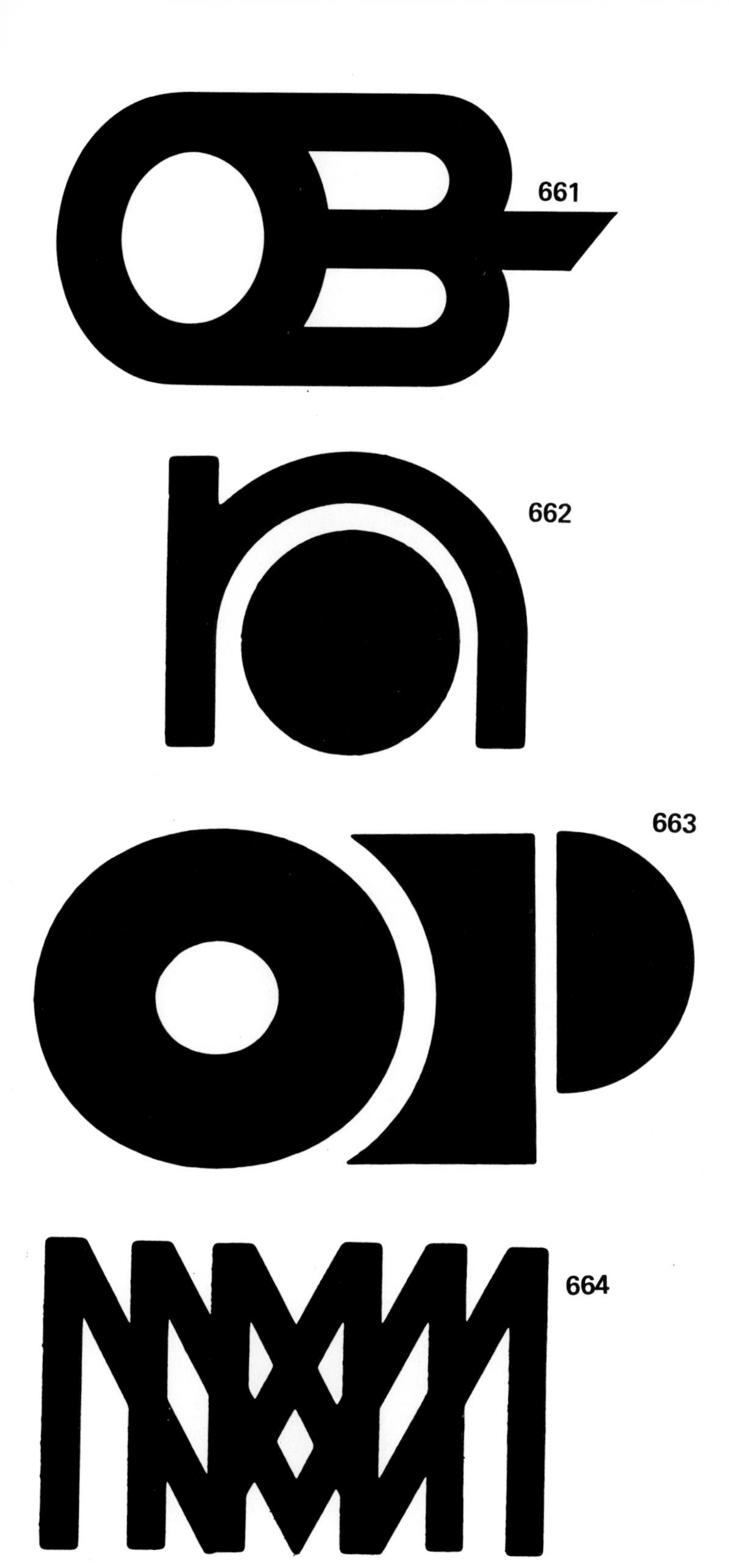

653 Midland-Ross Corporation
Cleveland

654 Acushnet Company
New Bedford, Massachusetts

655 Western New York Savings Bank
Buffalo, New York

656 Consolidated International Corp.
Chicago

657 Diversified Products Co.
Opelika, Alabama

658 Sid Gelpe & Associates
Landscape Designers
Tarzana, California

659 Texas Gas Transmission Co.
Owensboro, Kentucky

660 Mutron
Brockton, Massachusetts

661 The Ohio Brass Co.
Mansfield, Ohio

662 A.J. Nystrom & Co.
Chicago

663 Oxford Papers
New York City

664 Multiples, Inc.
New York City

665

666

667

668

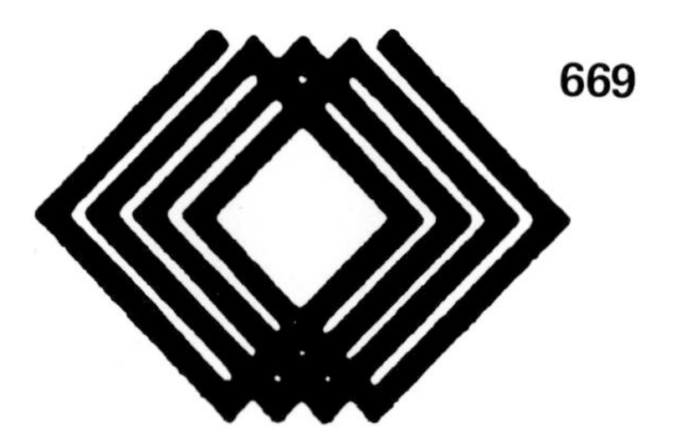
669

670

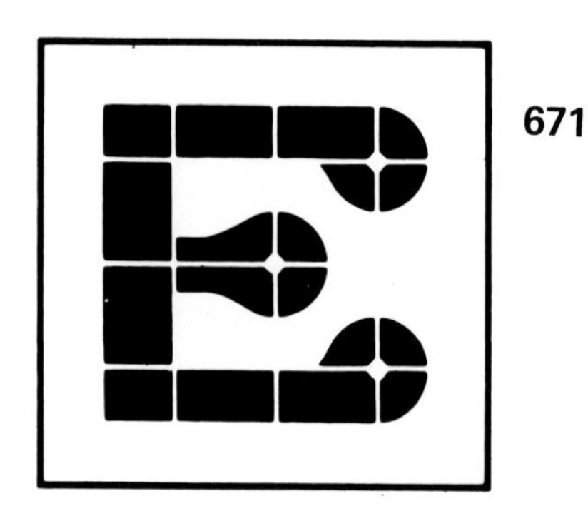
671

672

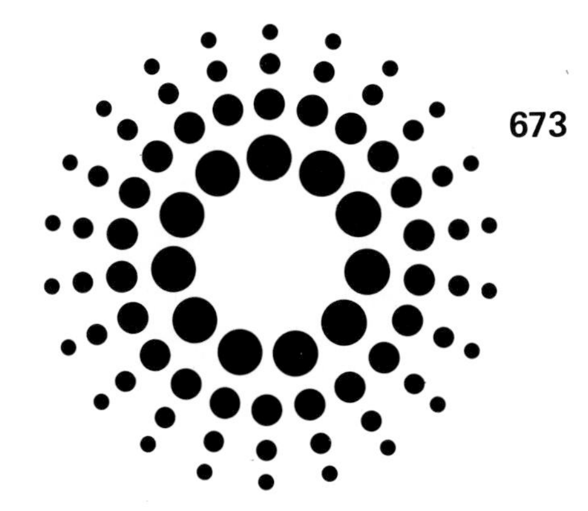

673

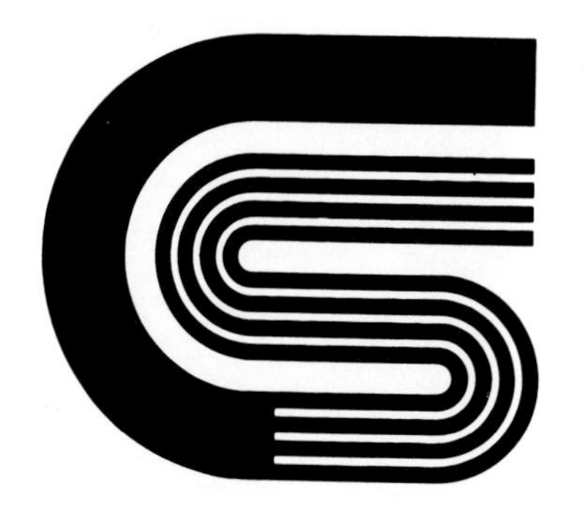

674

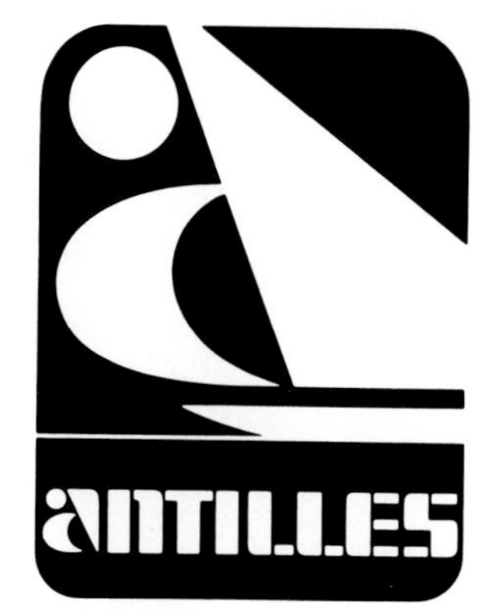

675

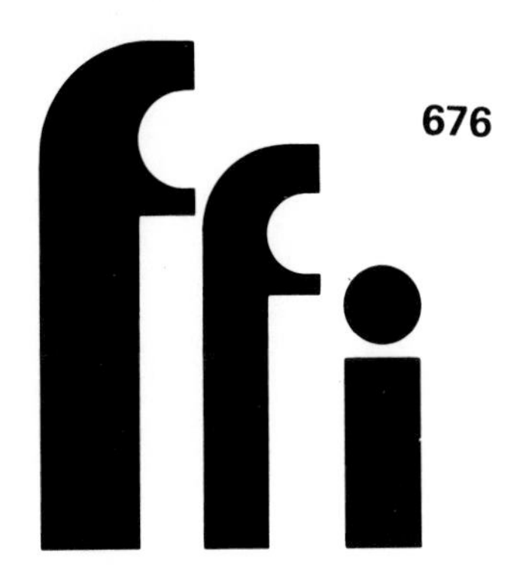

676

665 Vision Craft Ltd.
Fayetteville, New York

666 The Bunker-Ramo Corp.

667 D.G. Mountz Associates, Inc.
San Jose, California

668 Matheson Scientific
Chicago

669 Standard & Poors/InterCapital, Inc.
New York City

670 Arlen Realty & Development Corp.
New York City

671 Excellon Industries
Torrance, California

672 Hitchiner Mfg. Co., Inc.
Milford, New Hampshire

673 Everbrite Electric Signs, Inc.
South Milwaukee, Wisconsin

674 Continental Steel Corp.
Kokomo, Indiana

675 Antilles Yachting Service
St. Thomas, U.S. Virgin Islands

676 Family Funding, Inc.
Cambridge, Massachusetts

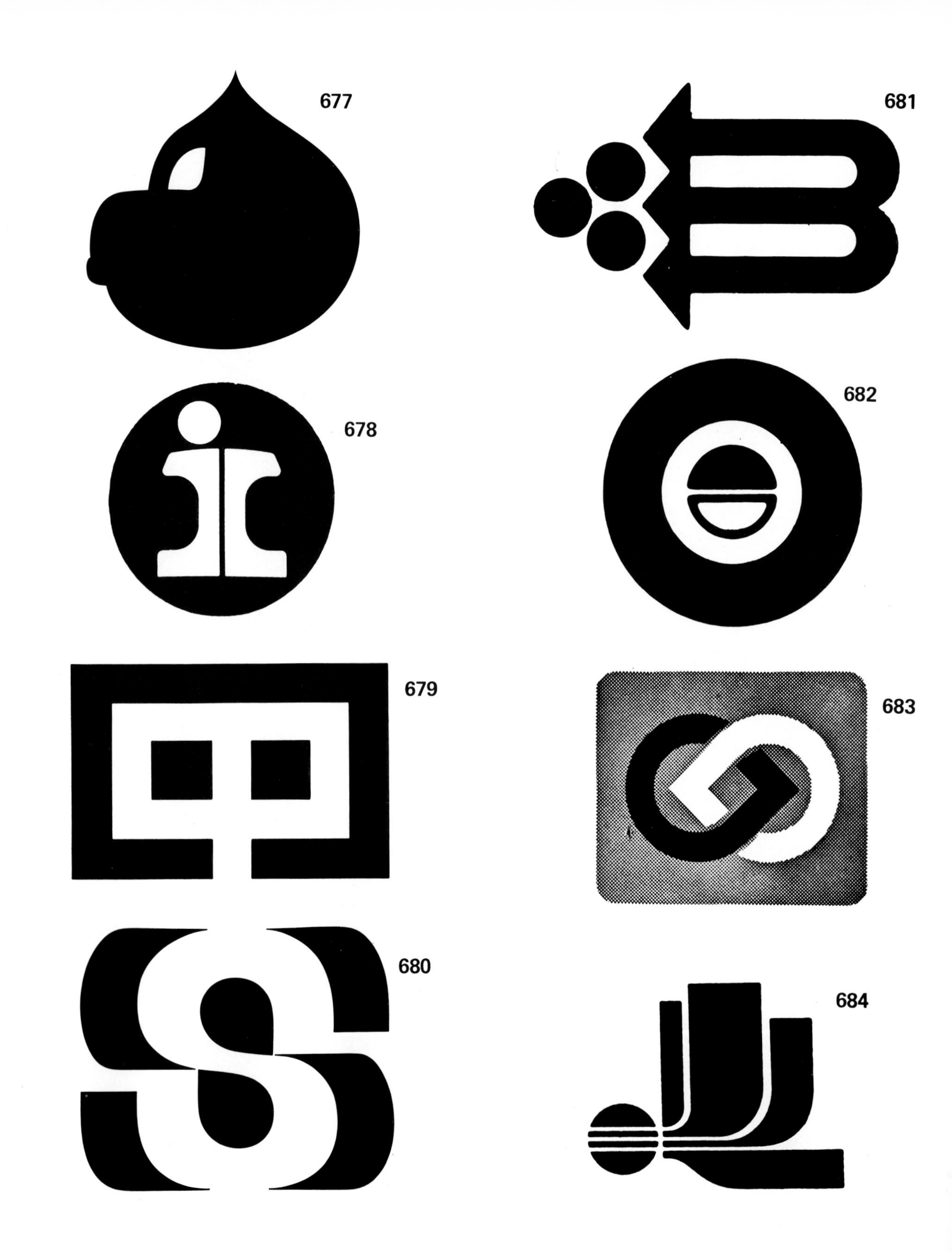
677
678
679
680
681
682
683
684

685

686

687

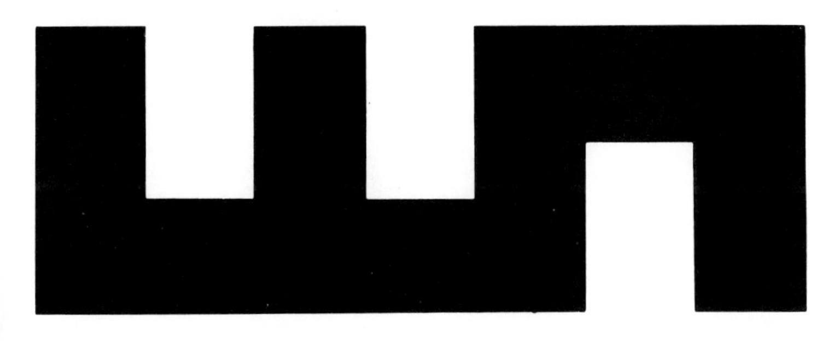

688

677 Hollywood Car Wash
Hollywood, California

678 Illinois Central Railroad
Chicago

679 Creative Packaging
Indianapolis

680 Southland Corporation
Dallas

681 Berg Hayslette Dupar, Inc.

682 Federal-Mogul
Detroit

683 The Bankers Life
Des Moines, Iowa

684 Realty Systems, Inc.
Denver, Colorado

685 Shultzy's
Boston

686 Delaware River Port Authority
Camden, New Jersey

687 Weltz Ad Service, Inc.
New York City

688 Ward Nassee Art Gallery
Boston

689

690

691

692

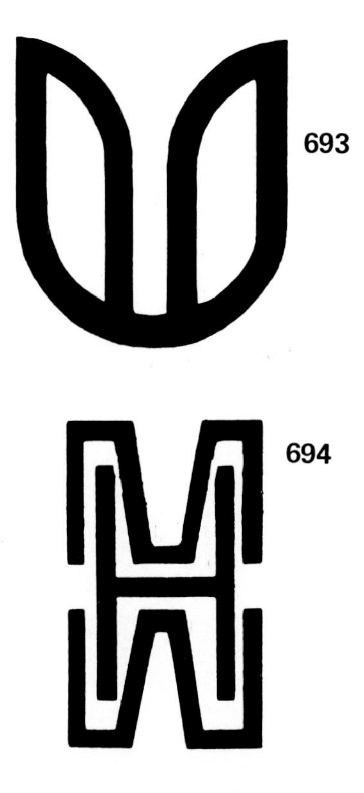
693

694

695

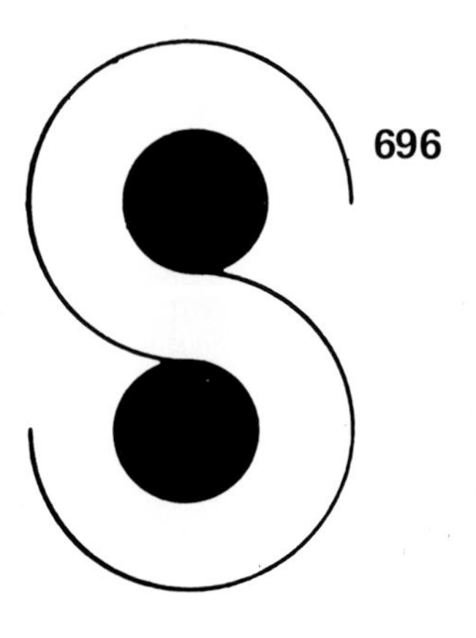
696

697

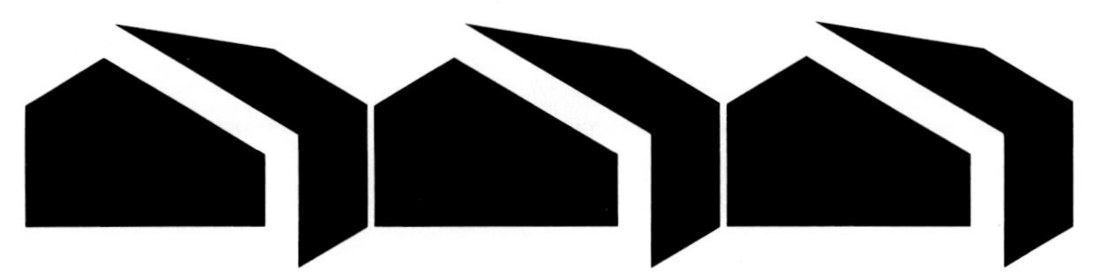

698

699

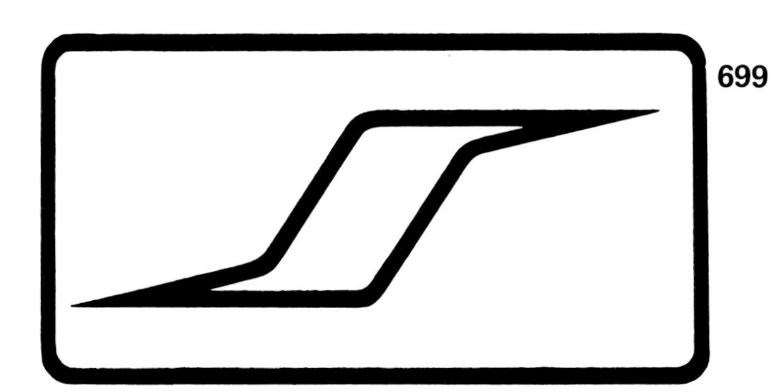

700

689 Directions or Dilemmas
Aspen, Colorado

690 American Film Institute
Washington, D.C.

691 Gottesman Central National Corp.
New York City

692 Knapp Bros. Shoe Manufacturers
Brockton, Massachusetts

693 Renauld International Ltd.
Fitchburg, Massachusetts

694 M.H.&W.
Englewood Cliffs, New Jersey

695 Jalart House
Port Chester, New Jersey

696 Suburban Printers

697 Modular Building
Benicia, California

698 Colonie Center
Albany, New York

699 Scintrex, Inc.
Tonawanda, New York

700 J.I. Case Co.
Racine, Wisconsin

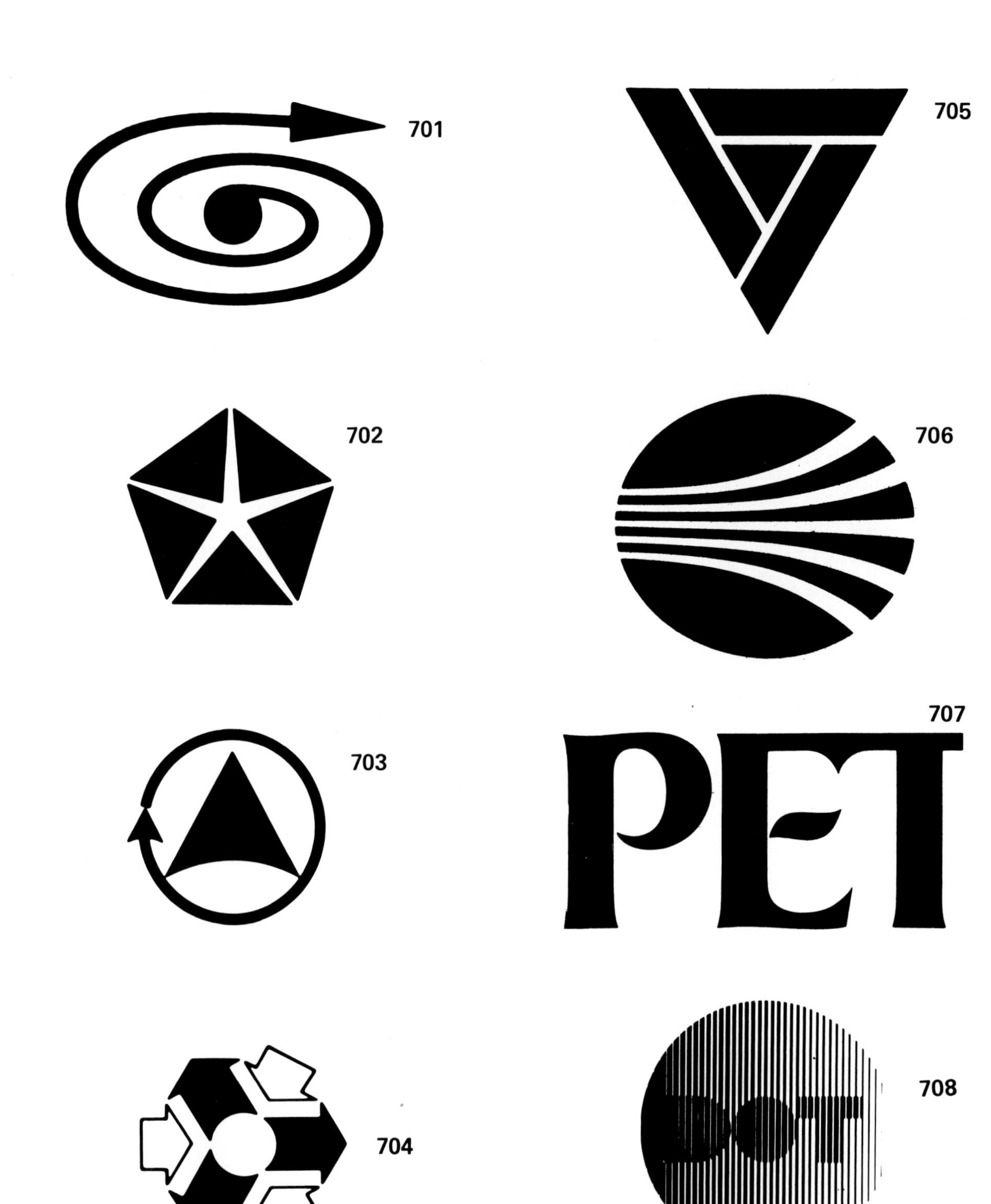
701
705
702
706
707
PET
703
704
708

709

710

711

712

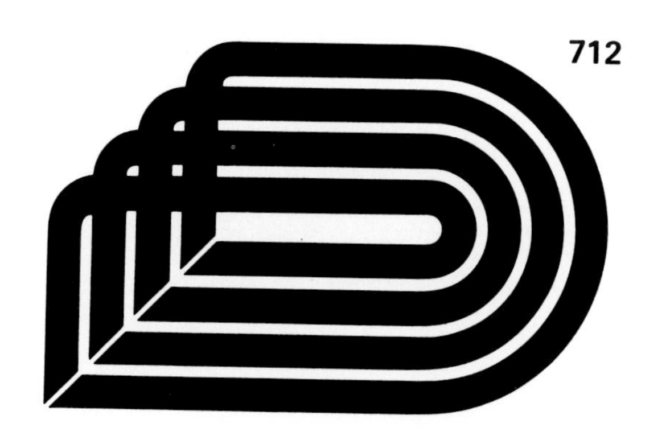

701 Genesco
New York City

702 Chrysler Corporation
Detroit

703 Anderson Corporation
Worcester, Massachusetts

704 McKesson & Robbins Drug Co.
New York City

705 Pittsburgh National Bank
Pittsburgh

706 Continental Airlines
Los Angeles

707 Pet, Inc.
St. Louis

708 Dot Records
Los Angeles

709 Gates Aviation Corp.
Denver

710 Joseph Love & Co.
New York City

711 American Building Maintenance Industries
San Francisco

712 DiGiorgio Development Corp.
San Francisco

713
714
715
MASTER
716
717
718
719
720

721

722

723

western union

724

713 Bank of America
San Francisco

714 Washington Mutual Savings Bank
Seattle, Washington

715 Master Lock Co.
Milwaukee, Wisconsin

716 Aluminum Corp. of America
Pittsburgh

717 School of Visual Arts
New York City

718 Southwest Forest Industries
Phoenix, Arizona

719 Scintillonics
Fort Collins, Colorado

720 Atlantic National Bank
Norfolk, Virginia

721 Cone Mills Marketing Co.
New York City

722 Kallir, Phillips, Ross, Inc.

723 Western Union
New York City

724 Anixter Bros., Inc.
Skokie, Illinois

725

726

727

728

729

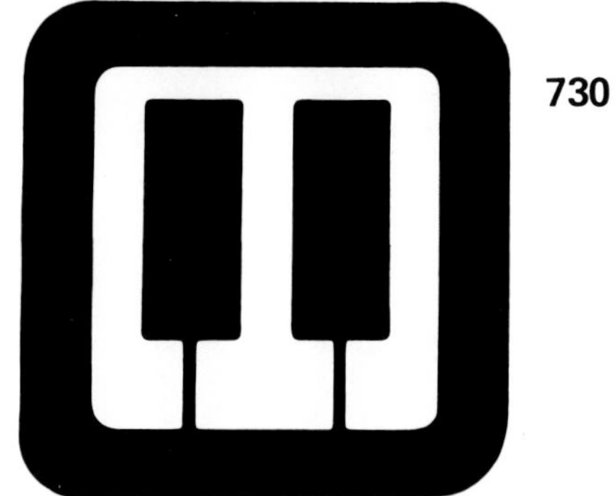

730

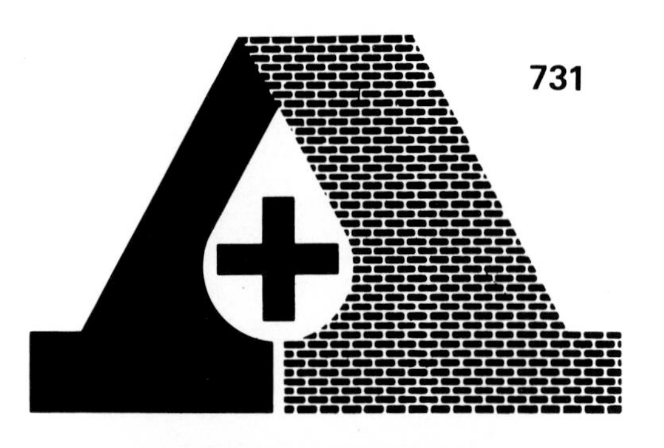

731

732

733

734

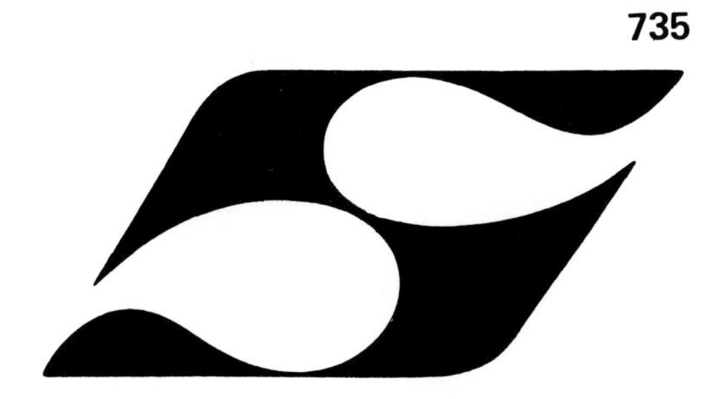
735

736

725 Brazos Graphics
Bryan, Texas

726 Spring '71 Bookfair
New York City

727 Trust Company Bank
Atlanta, Georgia

728 Windecker Research, Inc.
Midland, Texas

729 Art's Photo
Los Angeles

730 Magnus Organ Corporation
Linden, New Jersey

731 "Additive A"
Kimberly Clark
Neenah, Wisconsin

732 Crown Zellerbach
San Francisco

733 McDowell Wellman Engineering Co.
Cleveland

734 Atlas Chemical Industries, Inc.

735 The Setwell Corp.
Traverse City, Michigan

736 Sargent-Welch Scientific Co.
Skokie, Illinois

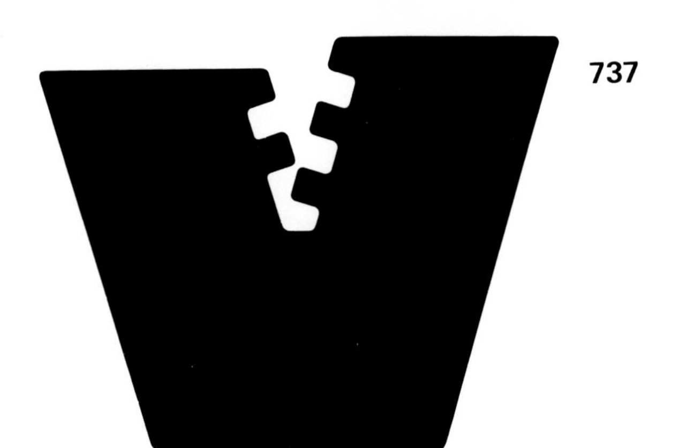
737

738

739

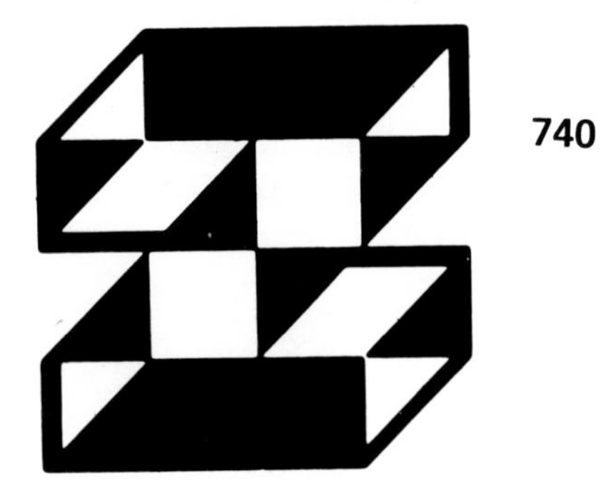
740

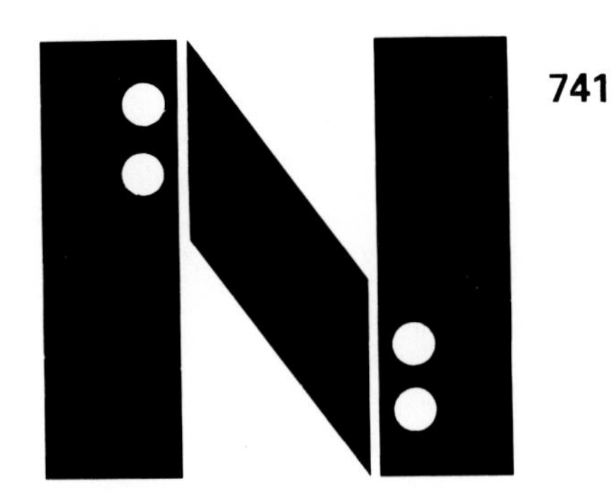
741

742

743

744

745

746

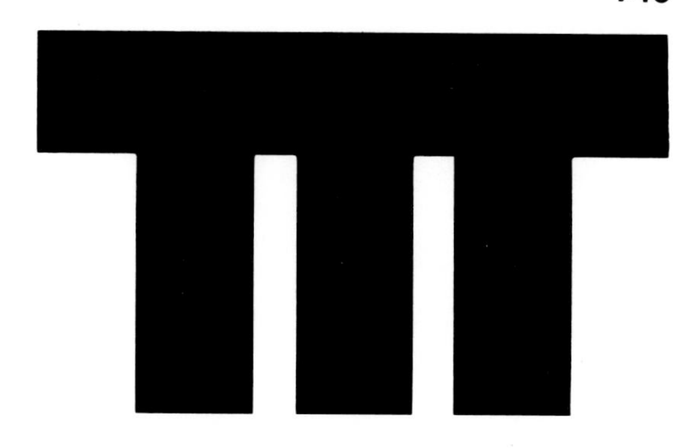

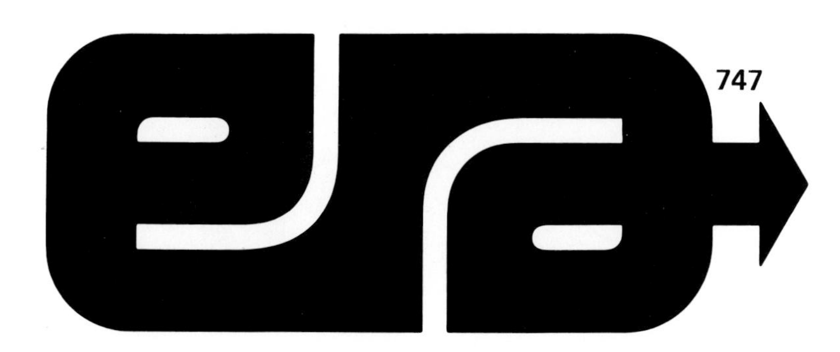

747

748

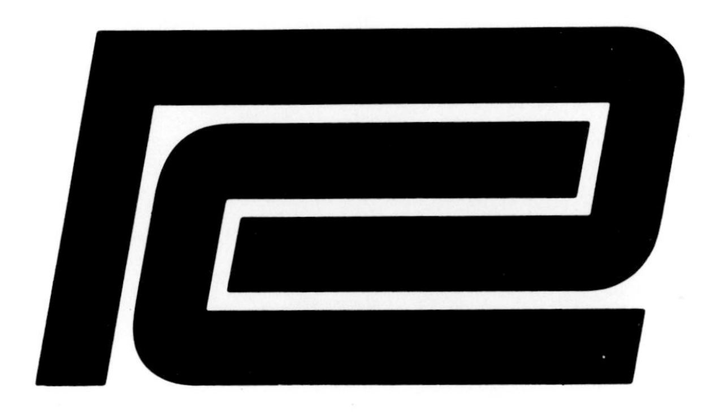

737 Vargas Zippers
Los Angeles

738 Cargill
Minneapolis

739 Motion Picture Film Services, Inc.
Pittsburgh

740 International Design Center
Minneapolis

741 Neiman Construction Co.
Los Angeles

742 Cal Mode Contract Furniture Mfrs.
Culver City, California

743 Capital National Bank
Houston

744 San Francisco International
Market Center
San Francisco

745 Sport Magazine
Bartell-Media Corp.
New York City

746 Triplett Corporation
Bluffton, Ohio

747 Economic Research Associates, Inc.
Los Angeles

748 Penn Central Transportation Co.
Philadelphia

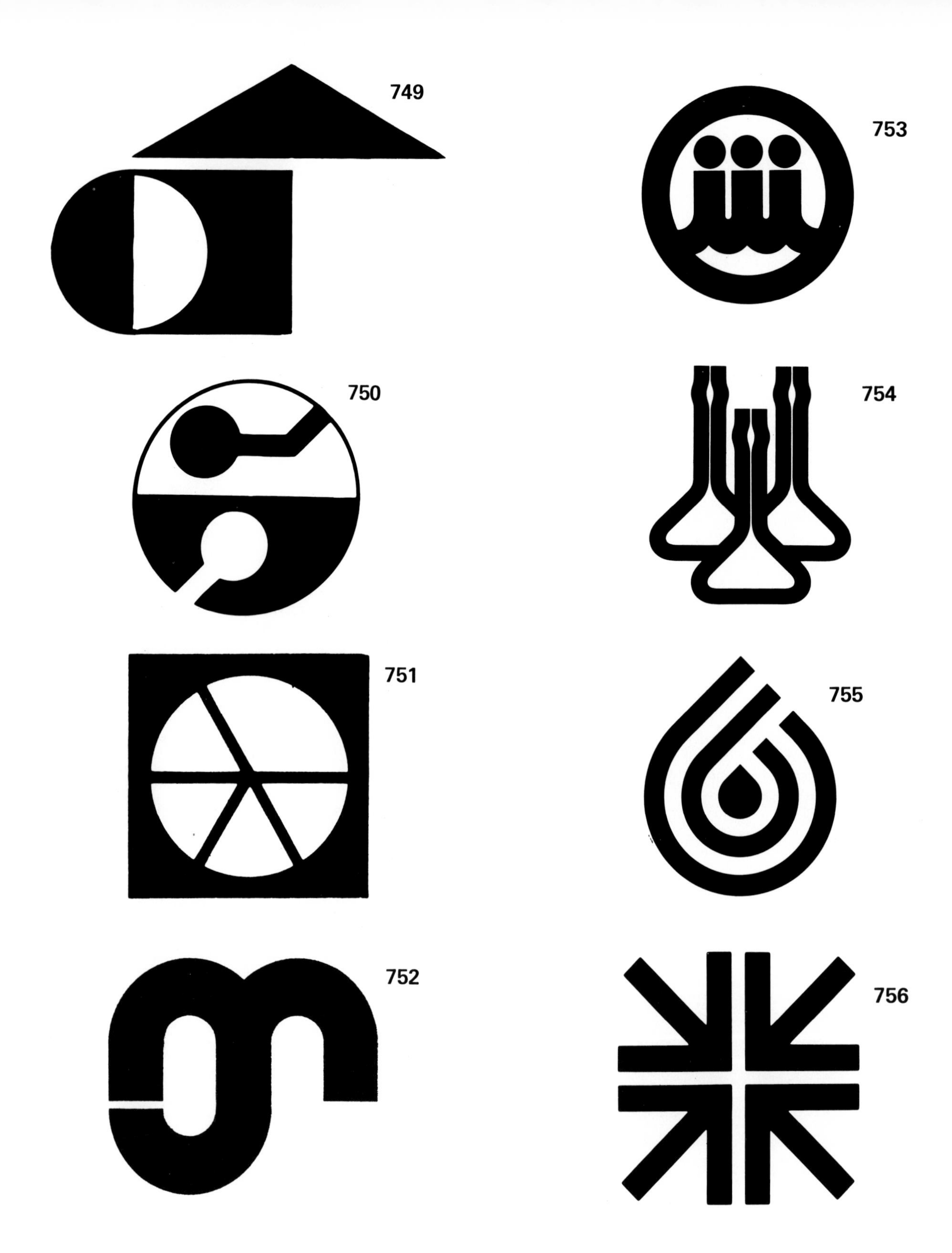
749
753
750
754
751
755
752
756

757

758

759

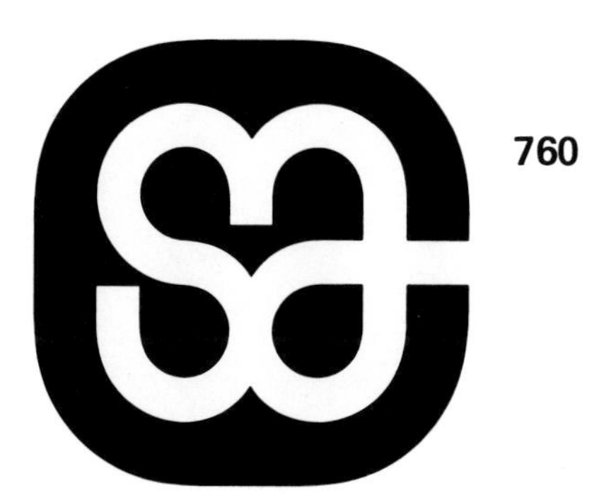

760

749 Cemcar Co.
Hackensack, New Jersey

750 Lumatrol Co.
Midland Park, New Jersey

751 Mary Friley, Inc.
Financial Consultants
New York City

752 Jack H. Morgan, Architect
Dallas

753 Illumination Industries, Inc.
Sunnyvale, California

754 Bio Science Laboratory
Van Nuys, California

755 Barkow Petroleum
Richmond, California

756 Recognition Devices
Great Neck, New York

757 National Hospital Corp.
Los Angeles

758 Magellan Ltd.
Los Angeles

759 Operation Match
New York City

760 Santa Anita Consolidated, Inc.
Los Angeles

761
765
762
766
763
767
764
768

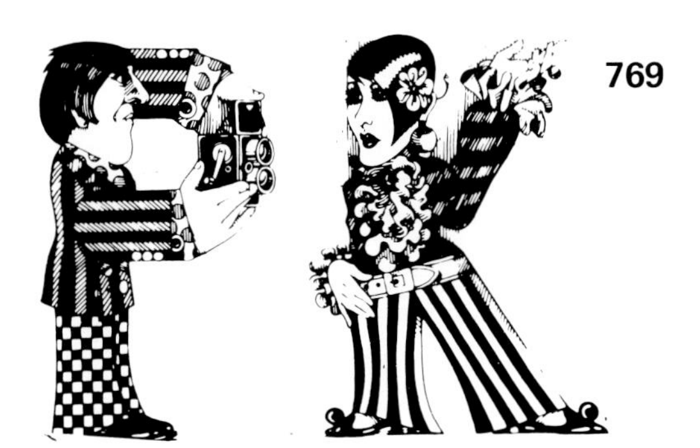

769

770

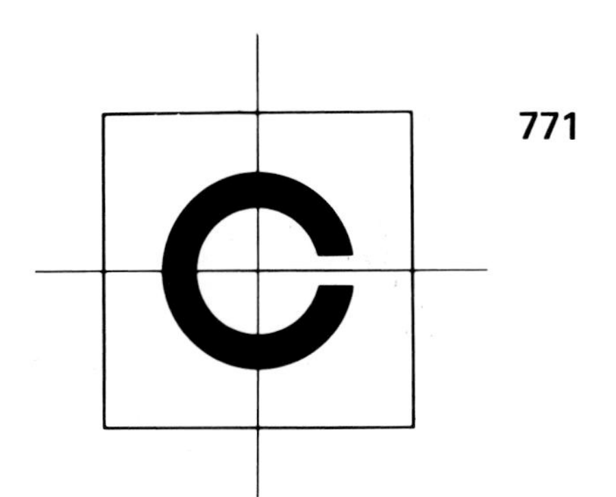

771

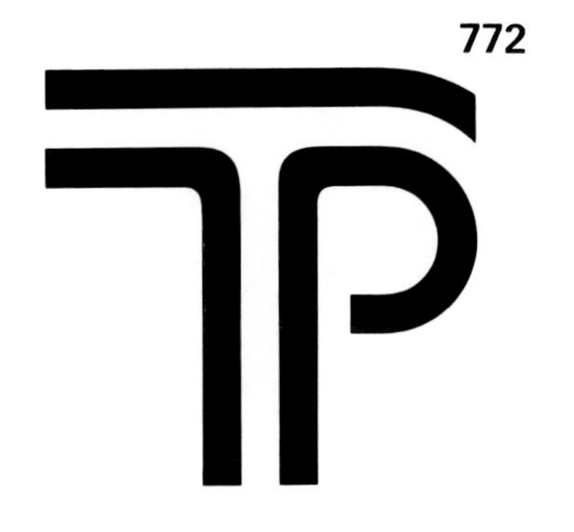

772

761 Massachusetts Financial Services, Inc.
Boston

762 U.S. Air Force Systems Command
Washington, D.C.

763 The Vitriform Corp.
Orange, California

764 Financial Congeneric, Inc.
Los Angeles

765 Interactive Data Services
New York City

766 Torin Corporation
Torrington, Connecticut

767 Massachusetts Bay Transportation Authority
Boston

768 Indian Head, Inc.
New York City

769 Peter Kenner Photography
New York City

770 Liquid Paper Corp.
Dallas

771 Calumet Mfg. Co.
Chicago

772 Tioga Pipe Supply Co., Inc.
Philadelphia

773

774

775

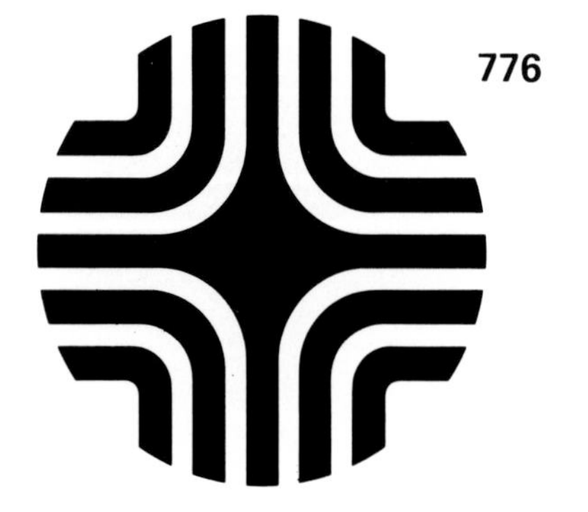

776

777

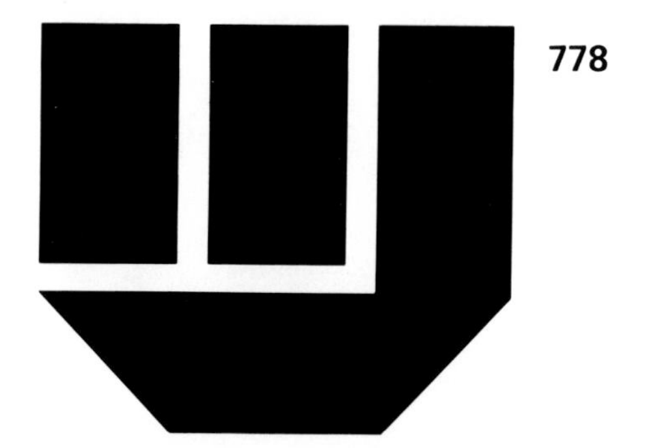

778

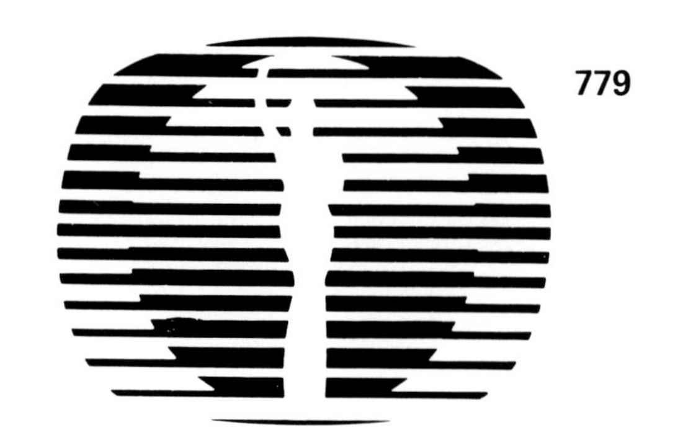

779

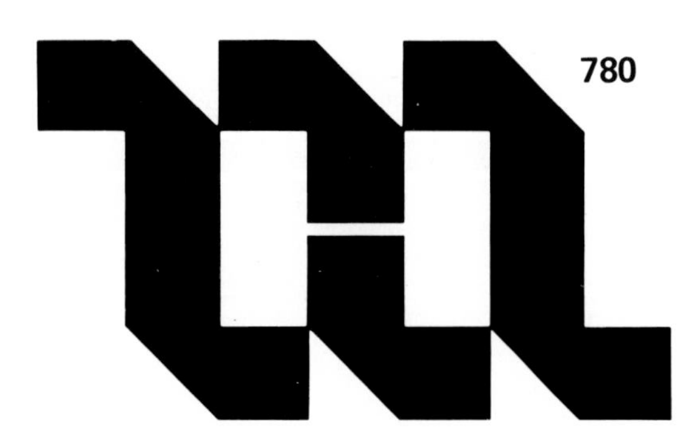

780

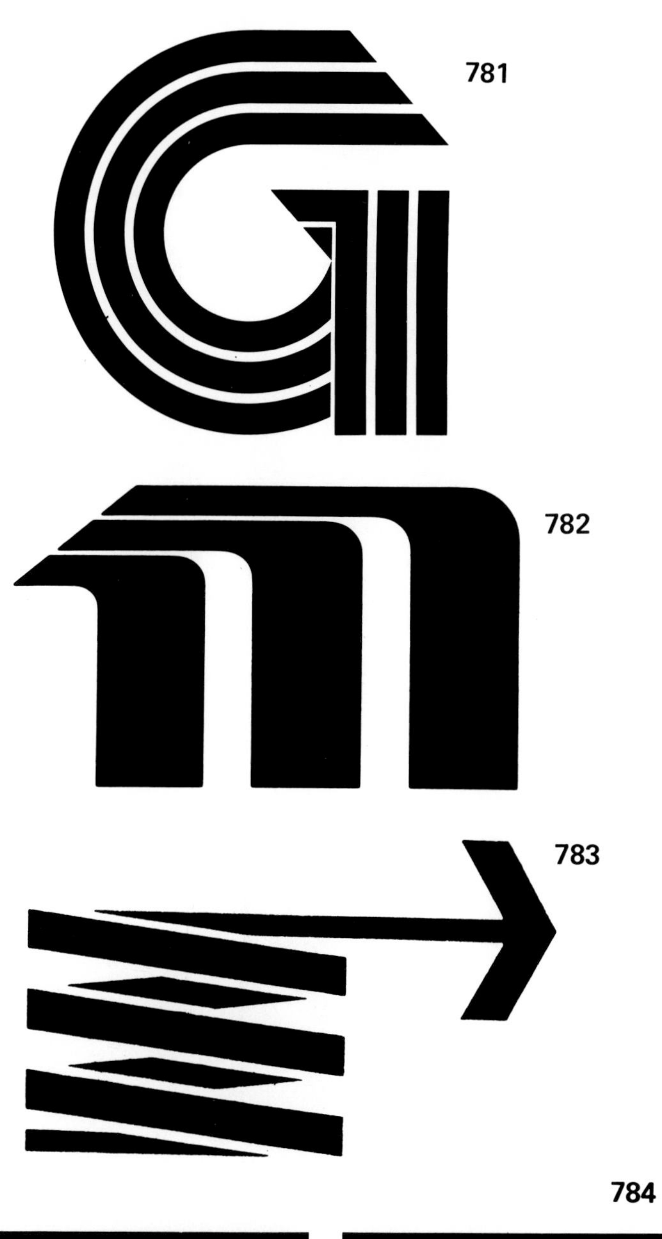

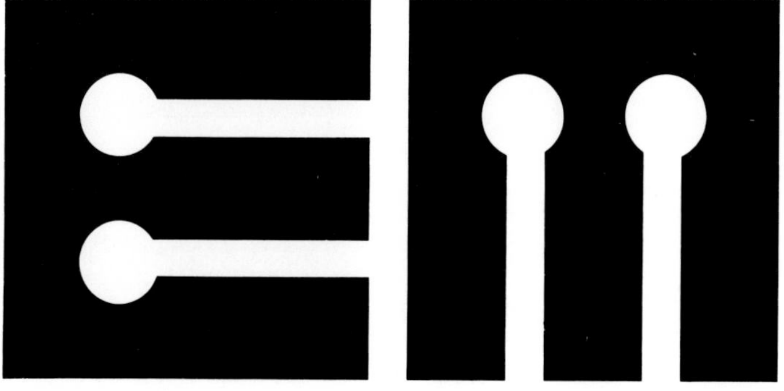

773 Amcap Fund, Inc.
Los Angeles

774 Land Management, Inc.
Porterville, California

775 Dixon Corporation
Briston, Rhode Island

776 Sunbeam Lighting
Los Angeles

777 Tower Manufacturing Co.
(tacks and nails)
Madison, Indiana

778 National Bank of Washington
Washington, D.C.

779 Columbia Pictures Cassettes
New York City

780 Mount Holyoke College
South Hadley, Massachusetts

781 Getz Corporation
San Francisco

782 Masonite Corporation
Chicago

783 Mid-Continent Helicopter Assoc., Inc.
Omaha, Nebraska

784 Electronic Memories, Inc.
Hawthorne, California

785

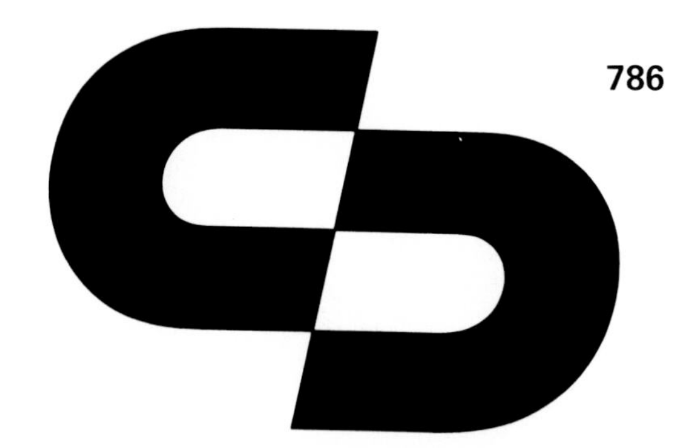

786

787

788

789

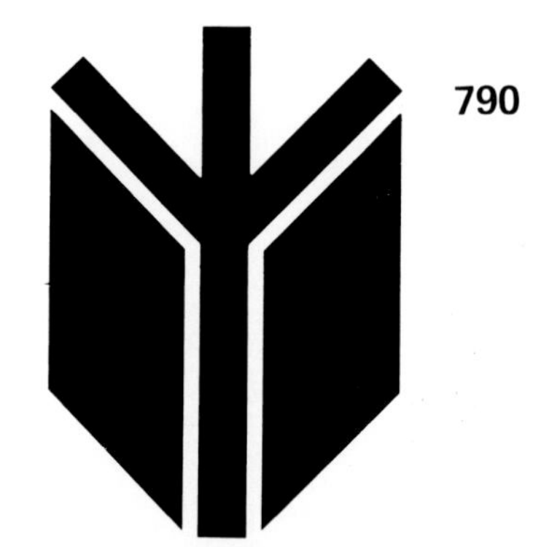

790

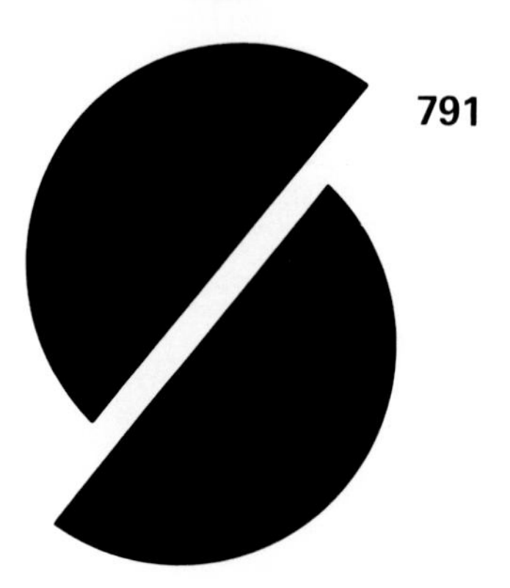

791

792

793

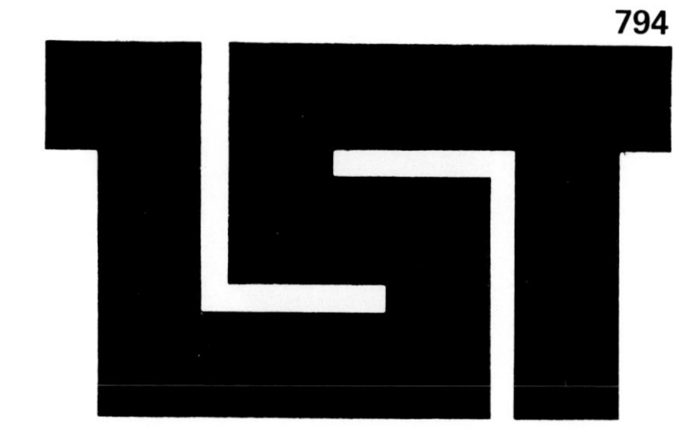

794

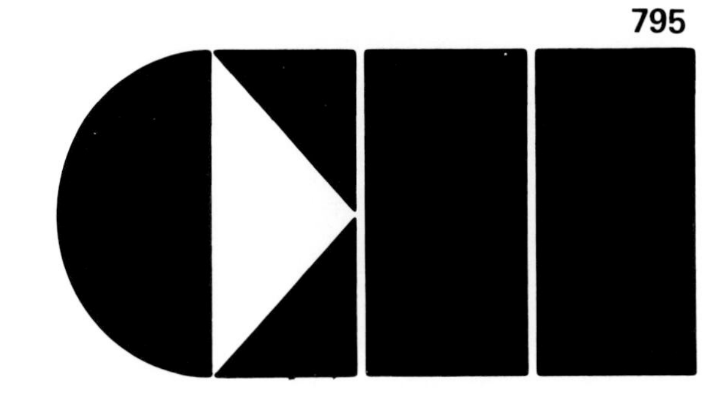

795

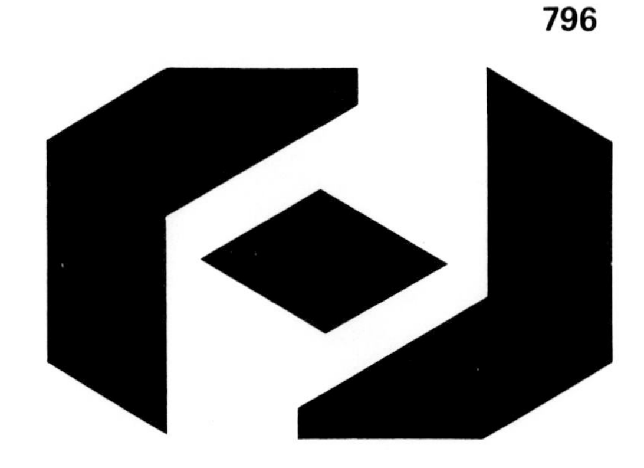

796

785 The Bellwood Company
Orange, California

786 Converse, Davis & Assoc.
Pasadena, California

787 Burlington Industries
New York City

788 U.S. National Park Service
Harpers Ferry Center
Harpers Ferry, West Virginia

789 National Health Enterprises
Milwaukee

790 Johns Hopkins Press
Baltimore

791 The Signal Companies
Los Angeles

792 Soiltest, Inc.
Evanston, Illinois

793 Saxon Industries, Inc.
New York City

794 First National Bank of Maryland
Baltimore

795 Cone-Heiden
Seattle, Washington

796 The Raymond Corporation
Greene, New York

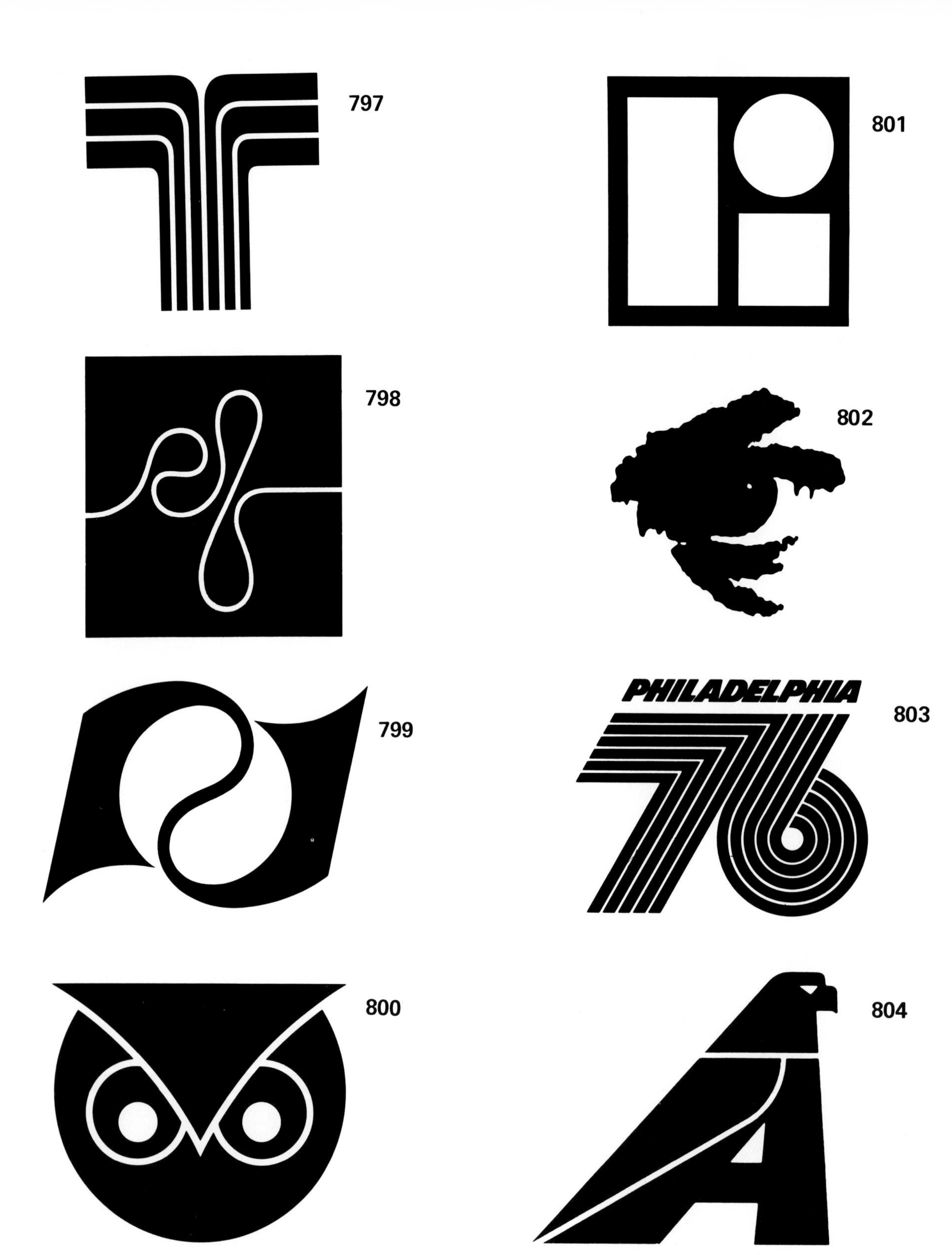
797
798
799
800
801
802
PHILADELPHIA
803
804

805

806

807

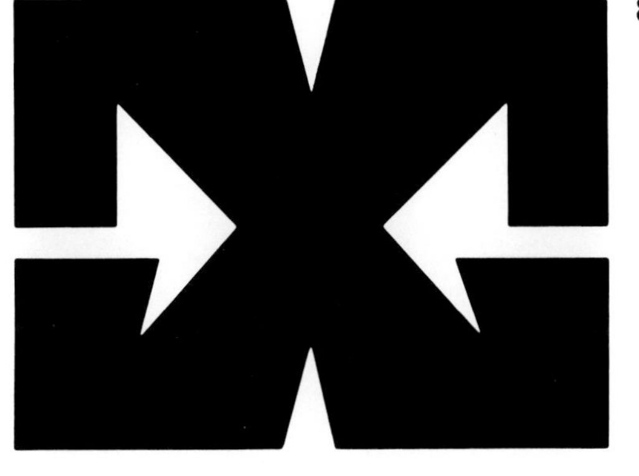

808

797 Transamerica Corporation
Los Angeles

798 Encounter Films
New York City

799 Major League Baseball
Office of the Commissioner
New York City

800 Fowler & More & Co.
Englewood, Colorado

801 Litton Industries
Beverly Hills, California

802 Curt Cole Burkhart
Chicago

803 Philadelphia Bicentennial Committee
Philadelphia

804 American Stencil Mfg. Co.
Denver

805 Hunt-Wesson Foods, Inc.
Fullerton, California

806 Bank of the Southwest
Houston

807 Omark Industries
Portland, Oregon

808 General Graphics
San Francisco

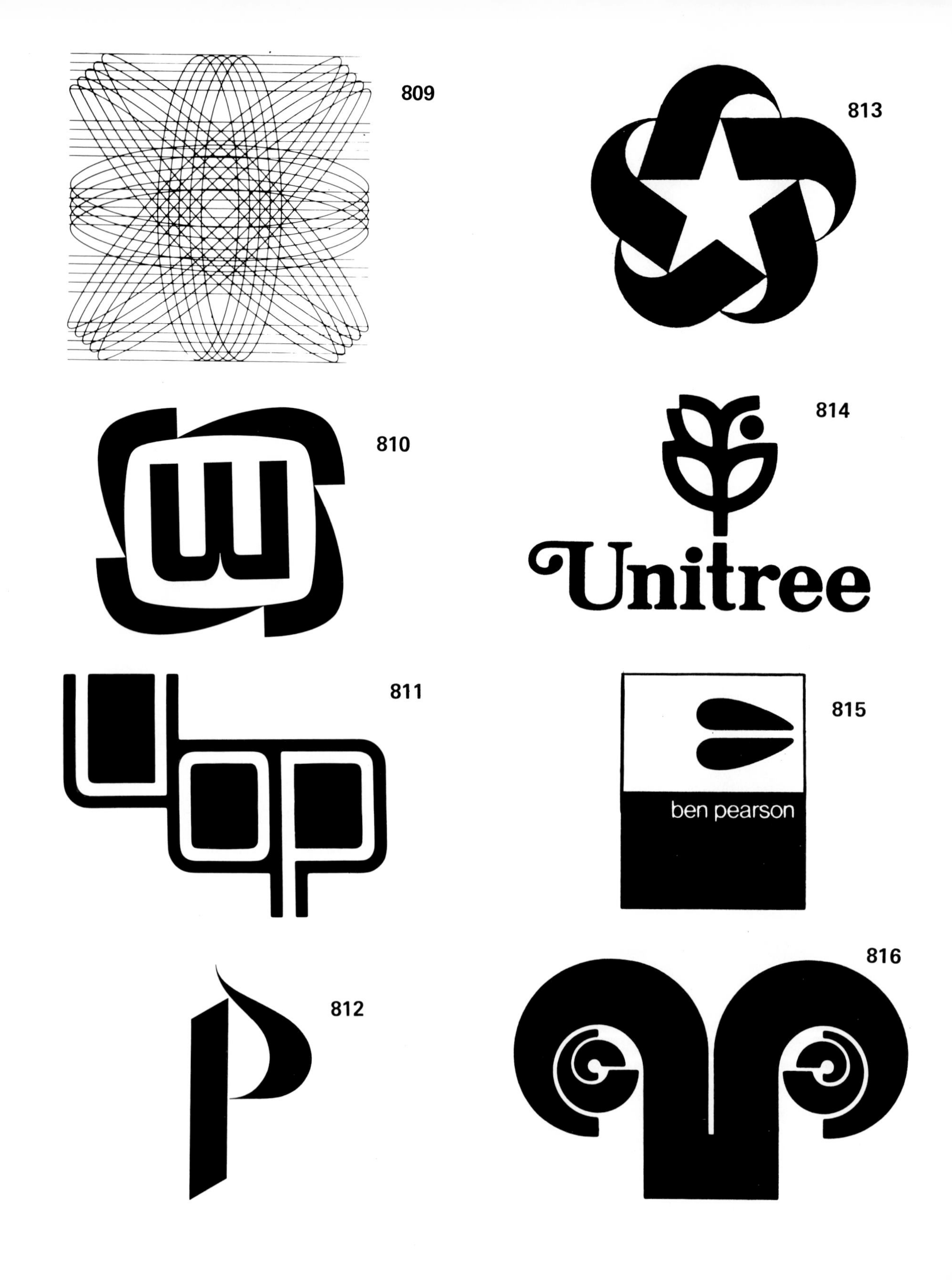
809
813
810
814
Unitree
811
815
ben pearson
812
816

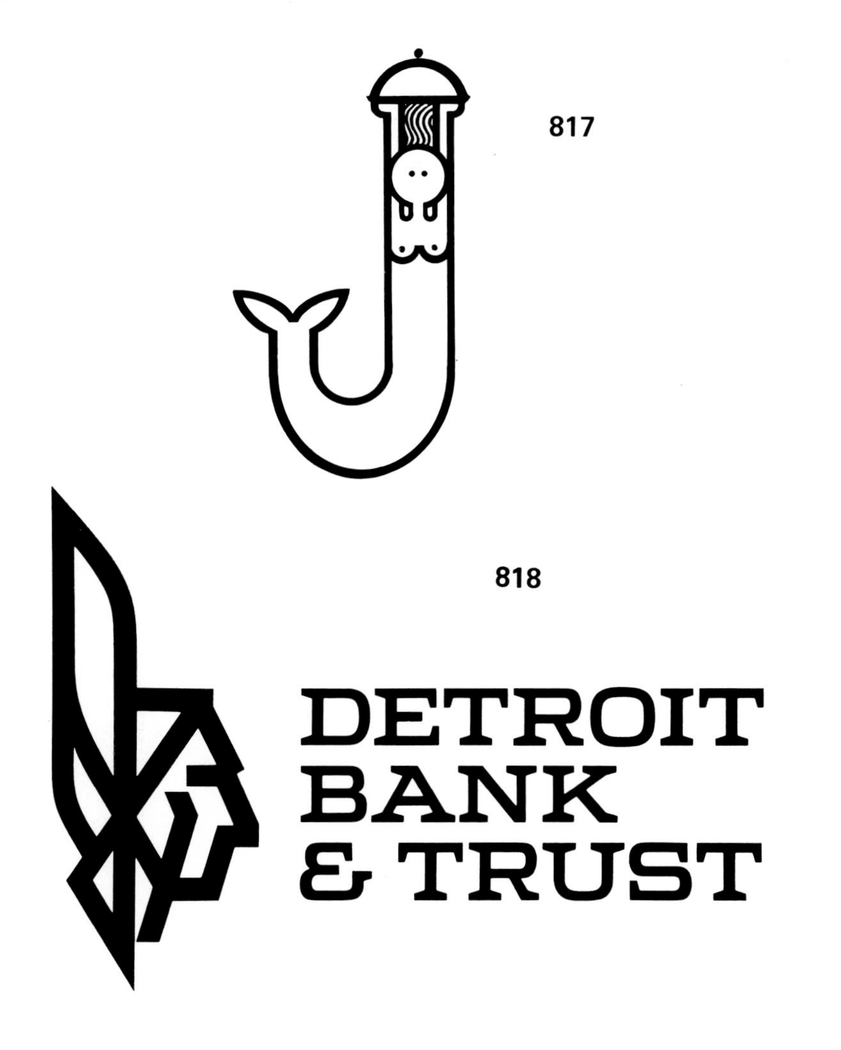

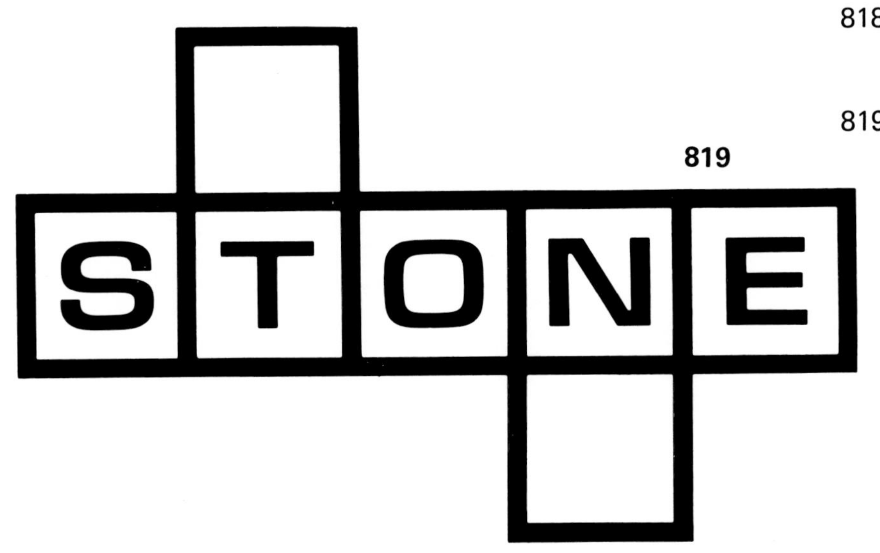

809 Manhattan School of Music
New York City

810 Waring Products Division
New Hartford, Connecticut

811 Universal Oil Products
Des Plaines, Illinois

812 Pierce Pre-Cooked Foods
Moorefield, West Virginia

813 Clarendon Trust Co.
Arlington, Virginia

814 Unitree
Cheektowaga, New York

815 Ben Pearson Archery
Pine Bluff, Arkansas

816 Sea Ranch
San Francisco

817 Jack's at the Beach
Seafood Restaurant
Santa Monica, California

818 Detroit Bank & Trust
Detroit

819 Stone Container Corp.
Chicago

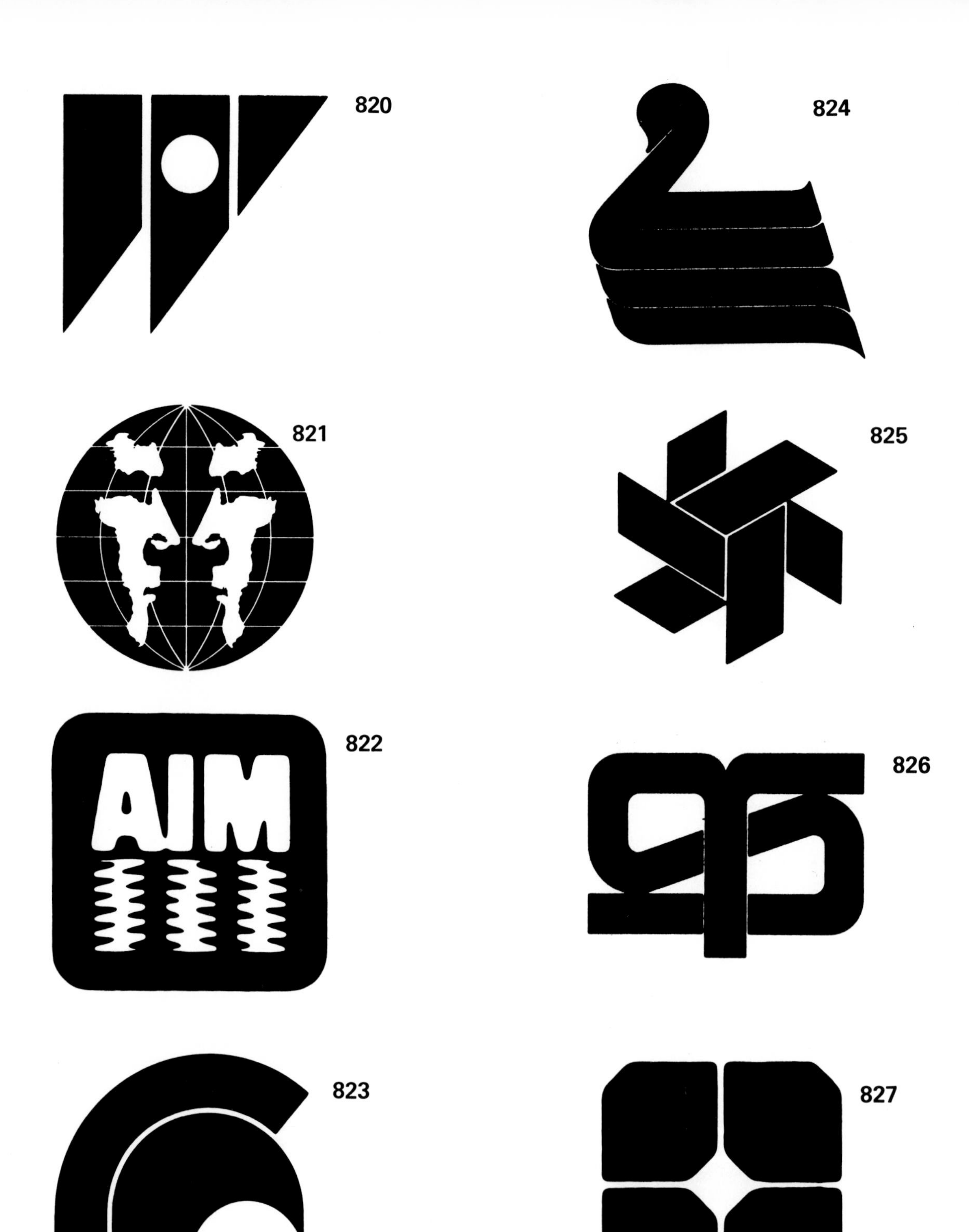
820
824
821
825
822
AIM
826
823
827

828

829

830

831

820 Worcester Center
Worcester, Massachusetts

821 Face to Face
The Adams Group
Silver Spring, Maryland

822 American Innerspring Mfrs.
Memphis, Tennessee

823 Trojan Yacht
Lancaster, Pennsylvania

824 Park Bellevue Apartments

825 Northstar at Tahoe
Ski Resort

826 Taxshield
San Francisco

827 Old Stone Bank
Providence, Rhode Island

828 Minter Homes Corporation
Huntington, West Virginia

829 United Missouri Bancshares, Inc.
Kansas City

830 Federal Envelope Division of
Champion Papers
New York City

831 LaMonte-Shimberg Corp.
Tampa, Florida

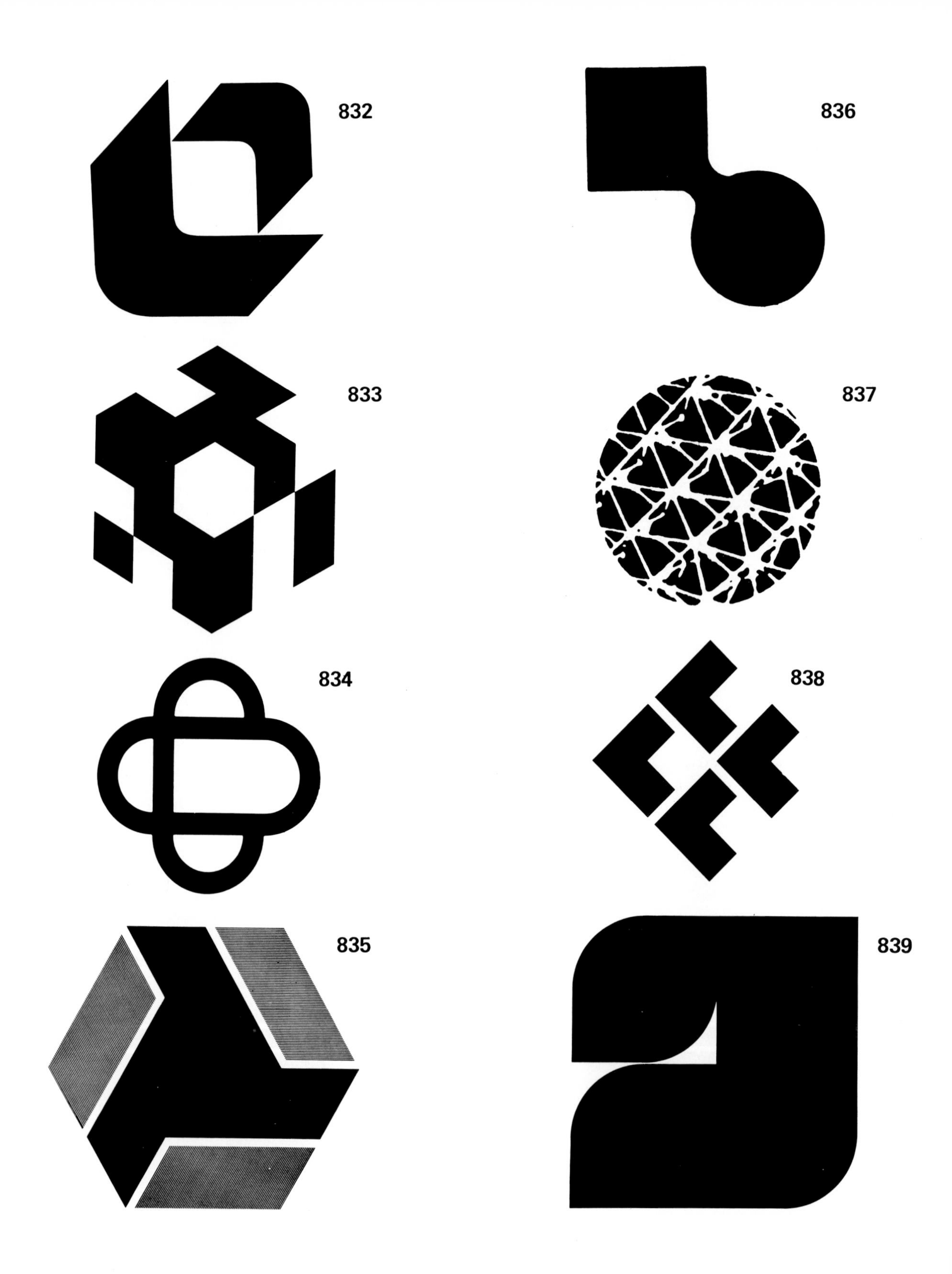
832
833
834
835
836
837
838
839

841

842

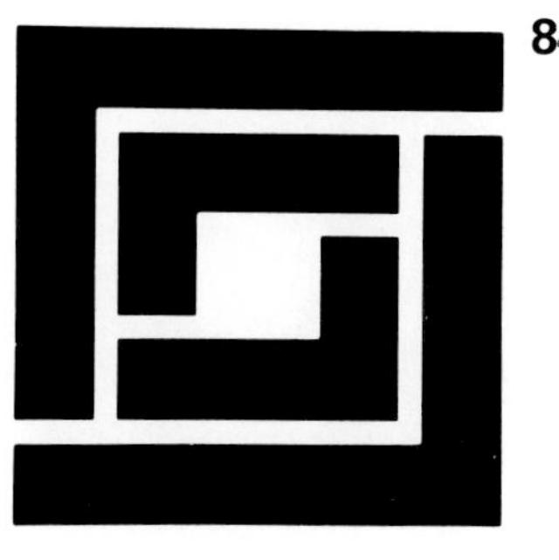

843

832 City Investing Co.
New York City

833 InfoServ Corp.
Peoria, Illinois

834 Damon Corporation
Needham, Heights, Massachusetts

835 Meinhard-Commercial Corporation
New York City

836 Color Control Co.
Ft. Lee, New Jersey

837 Urban Systems, Inc.
Cambridge, Massachusetts

838 Institute of Management Sciences
Schaumburg, Illinois

839 Marvin Atkins & Associates
North Hollywood, California

840 Merrimack Valley Textile Museum
North Andover, Massachusetts

841 Western Savings & Loan Association
Phoenix, Arizona

842 Coordinating Council for Higher Education
Sacremento, California

843 Forel
New York City

844
845
846
847
848
849
850
851

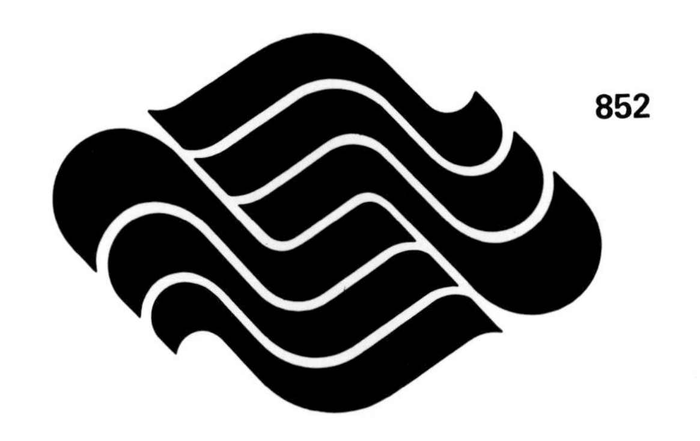

852

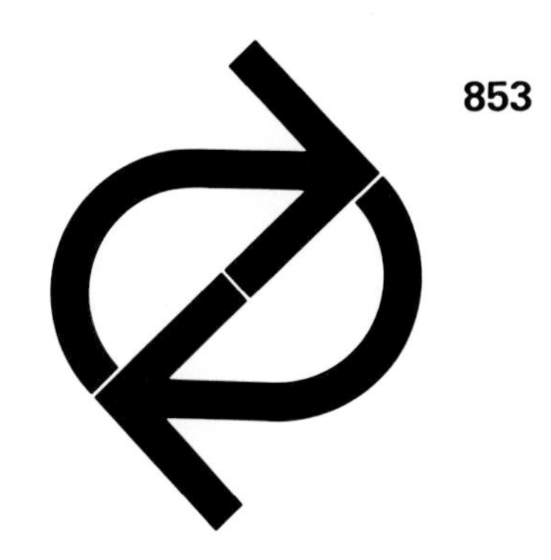

853

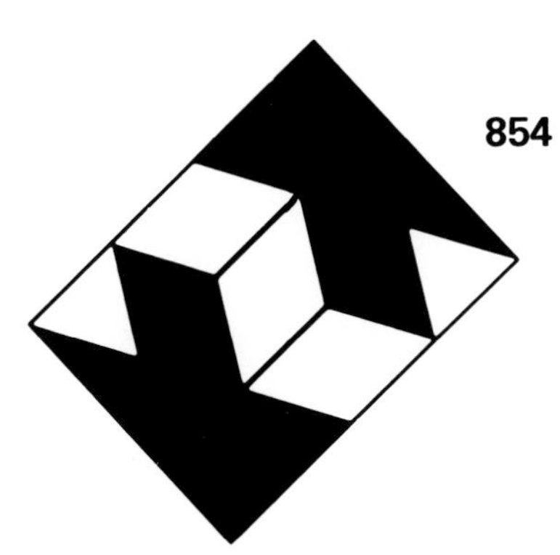

854

855

844 Associated Credit Bureaus
Houston

845 Diamond Crystal Salt Co.
St. Clair, Michigan

846 Pacific Lighting Corp.
Los Angeles

847 Allergan Pharmaceuticals
Santa Ana, California

848 Rhode Island Arts Festival
Providence, Rhode Island

849 Dalco Chemical Corp.
Minneapolis

850 Carl E. Erickson
Chicago

851 Southland Corporation
Dairies Division
Dallas

852 Laguna Niguel Corp.
Laguna Niguel, California

853 Short Line, Inc.
Providence, Rhode Island

854 National Association of the
Partners of the Americas
Washington, D.C.

855 Safety Management Magazine
A.M. Best Company
Morristown, New Jersey

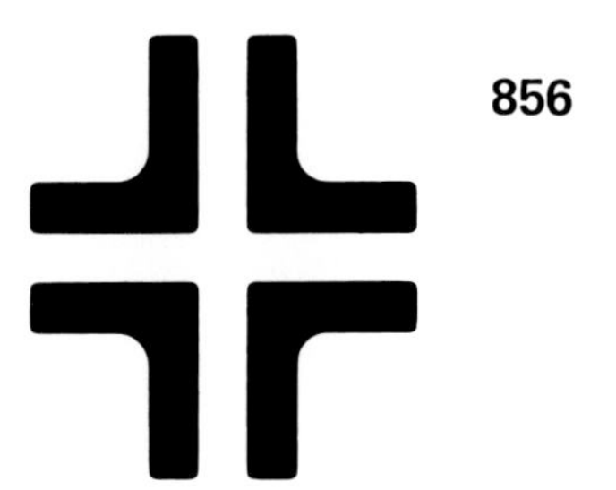

856

857

858

859

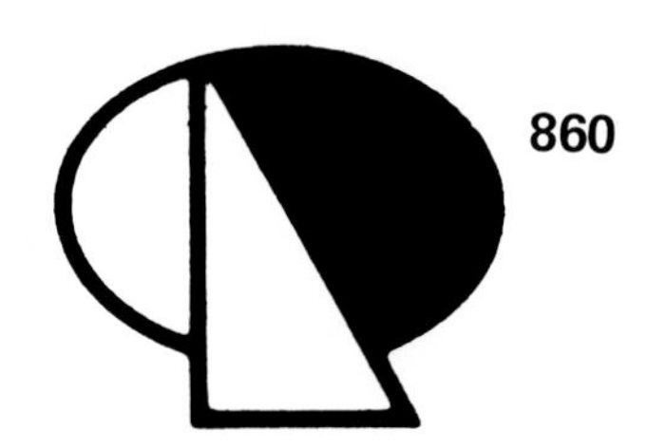

860

861

862

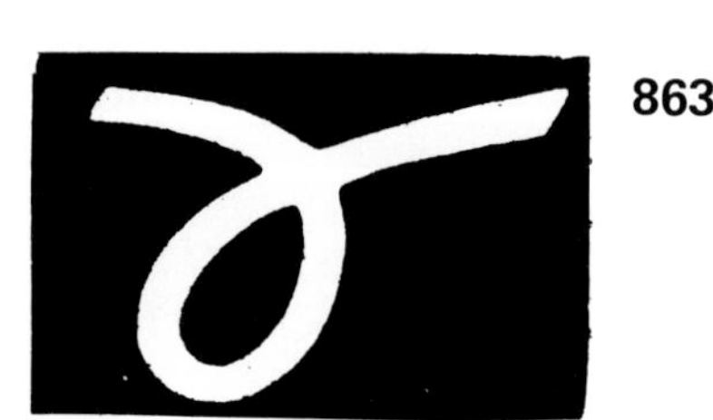

863

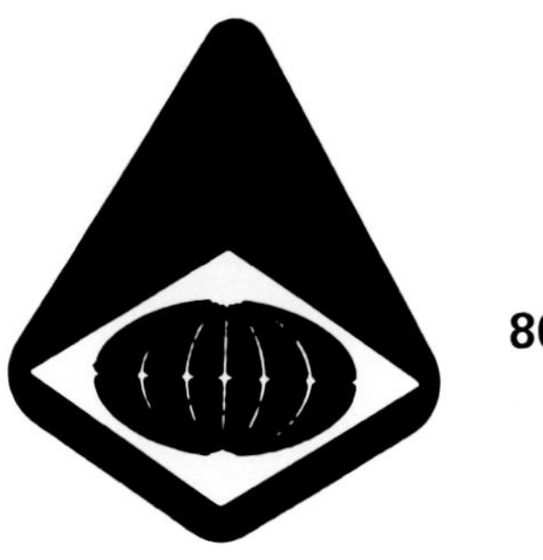

864

865

866

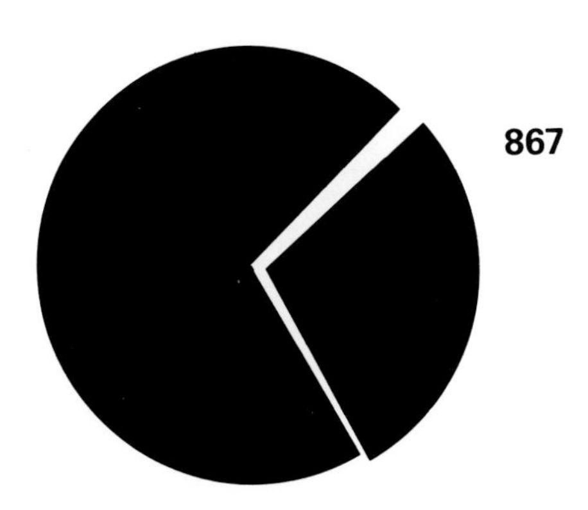

867

856 Louisville Area Chamber of Commerce
Louisville, Kentucky

857 Merrill, Lynch, Pierce, Fenner & Smith
New York City

858 Charles Jourdan Salon
New York City

859 Groos National Bank
San Antonio

860 Purdue Airlines, Inc.
West Lafayette, Indiana

861 Southern California Edison Co.
Los Angeles

862 Homestead Federal Savings & Loan
Dayton, Ohio

863 Princeton Gamma-Tech

864 Sybron Corporation
Rochester, New York

865 Beech Mountain
Banner Elk, North Carolina

866 Worthington Foods
Worthington, Ohio

867 Cordage of Cincinnati
Cincinnati

868

869

870

872

873

874

871

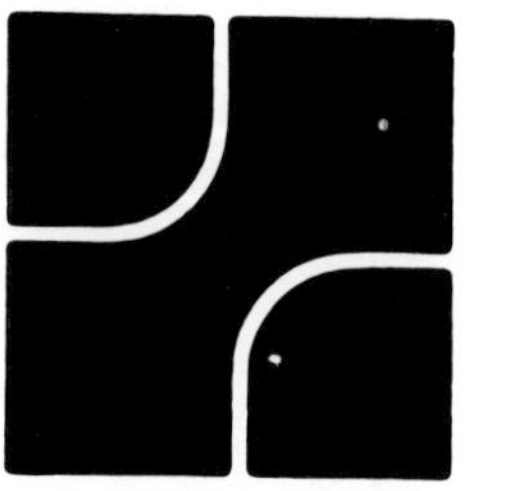

875

876

SIMPSON LEE PAPER COMPANY

877

878

879

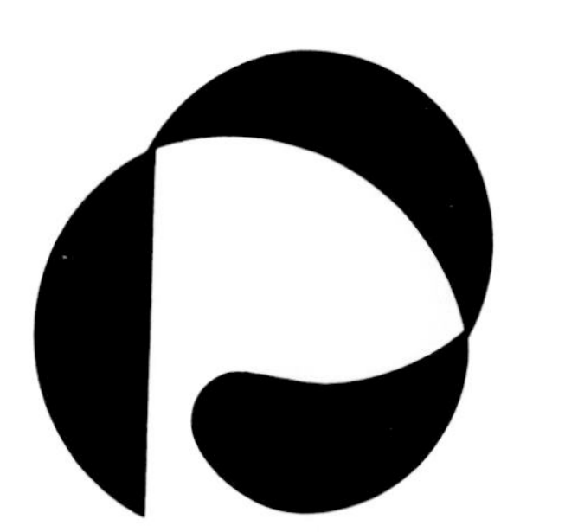

868 Dallas Baptist College
Dallas

869 Bergstrom Paper Co.
Neenah, Wisconsin

870 Spear & Staff
Babson Park, Massachusetts

871 Marcona Corporation
San Francisco

872 Playhouse Pictures
Hollywood, California

873 Jay Peak (ski village)
Jay, Vermont

874 Hartford National Bank & Trust Co.
Hartford, Connecticut

875 Johnson Reprint Corporation
New York City

876 Simpson Lee Paper Co.
San Francisco

877 First Exchange National Bank
Roanoke, Virginia

878 Deepsea Ventures, Inc.
Gloucester Point, Virginia

879 Piedmont Trust Bank
Martinsville, Virginia

880
881
882
883
884
885
886
887

FAIRMONT 888

889

890

891

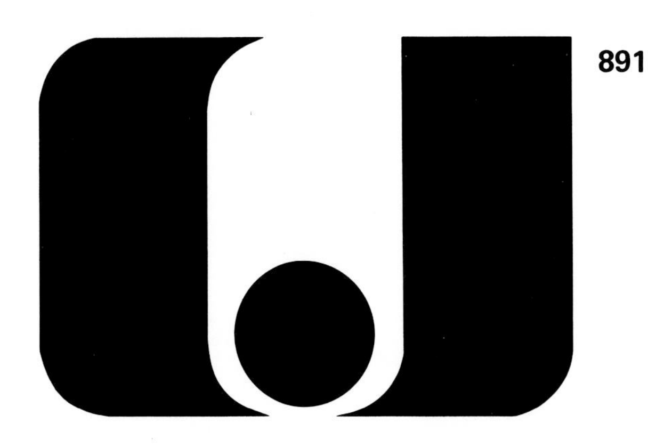

880 Optical Products Division of
Aleon Laboratories, Inc.

881 Bryon Weston Co.
Dalton, Massachusetts

882 Foulds Macaroni
Libertyville, Illinois

883 Gregory Fosella Associates
Boston

884 Crown Controls Corp.
New Bremen, Ohio

885 Infotron, Inc.
Burlington, Massachusetts

886 Bank Building Corporation
St. Louis

887 Klein Associates
Salem, New Hampshire

888 Fairmont Foods Co.
Omaha, Nebraska

889 Apex Business Systems, Inc.
Flushing, New York

890 Cryogenic Technology, Inc.
Waltham, Massachusetts

891 Cranford-Johnson & Associates
Little Rock, Arkansas

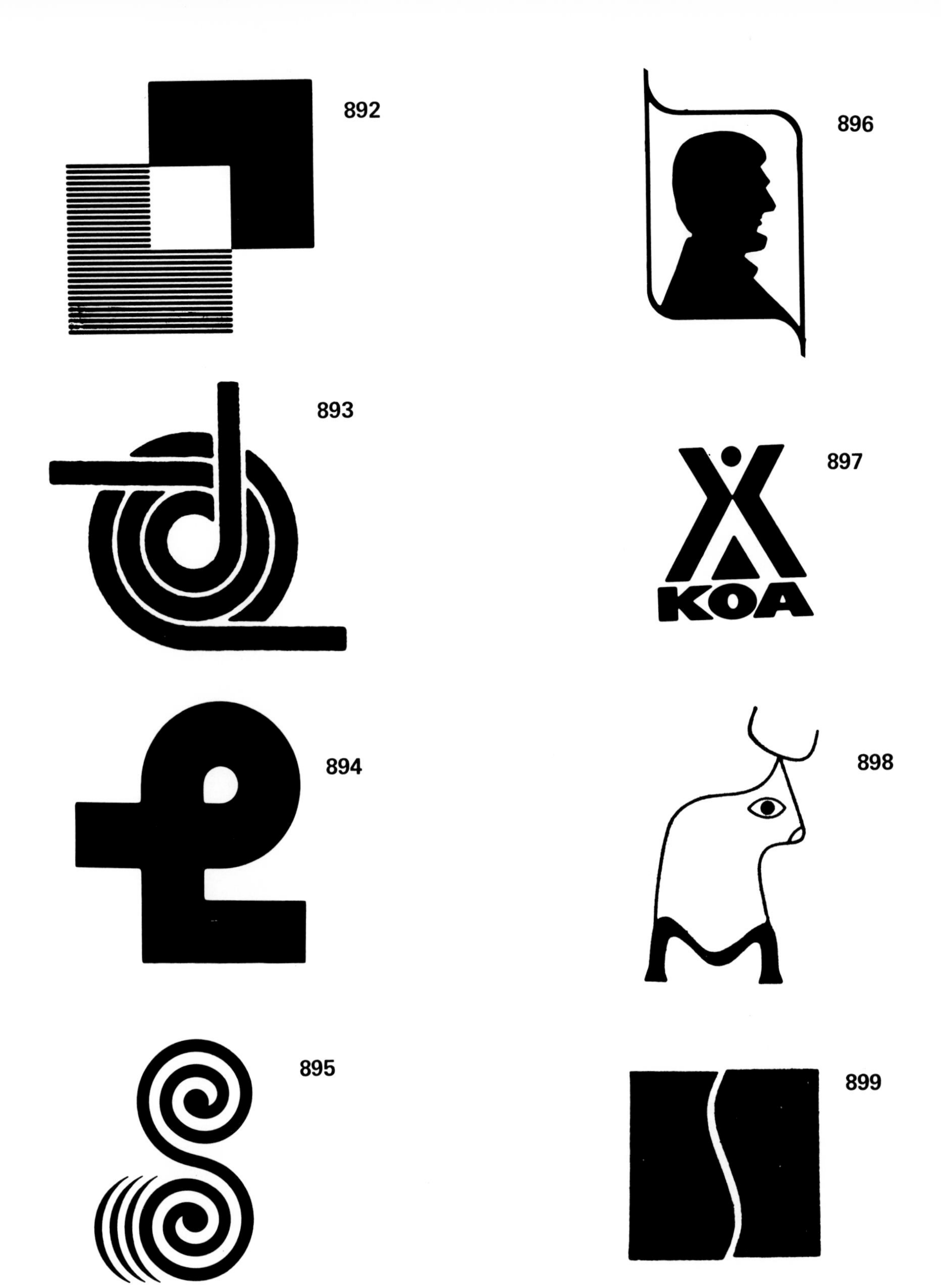
892
893
894
895
896
897
KOA
898
899

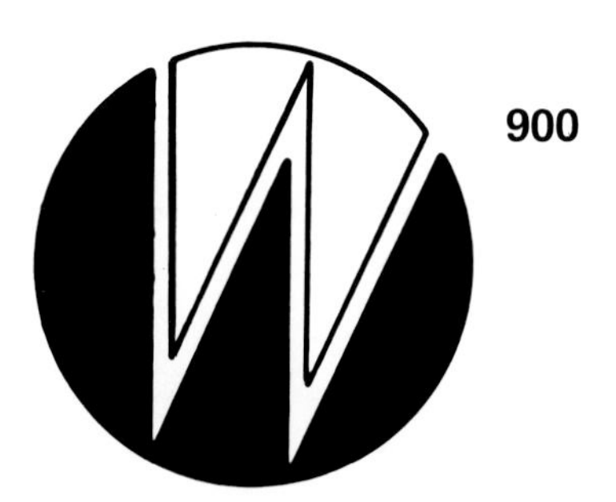

900

901

902

903

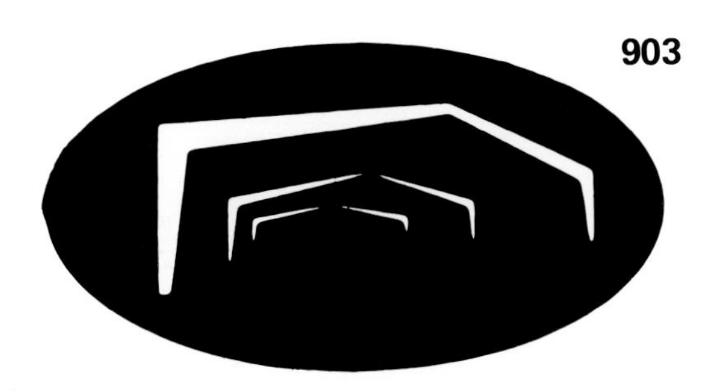

892 Provident Mutual Life Insurance Co.
Philadelphia

893 Oceanic Properties
Honolulu

894 Learning Corporation of America
New York City

895 E.F. Schmidt Co. Lithographers
Milwaukee

896 Lincoln Trail Bank
Fairview, Illinois

897 Kampgrounds of America
Billings, Montana

898 Museum Books, Inc.
New York City

899 Silver's
Highland Park, Michigan

900 Watson Mfg.
Jamestown, New York

901 Wood Electric Corporation
Danvers, Massachusetts

902 Imperial Bank
Beverly Hills, California

903 Butler Mfg. Co.
Kansas City

904

905

906

907

908

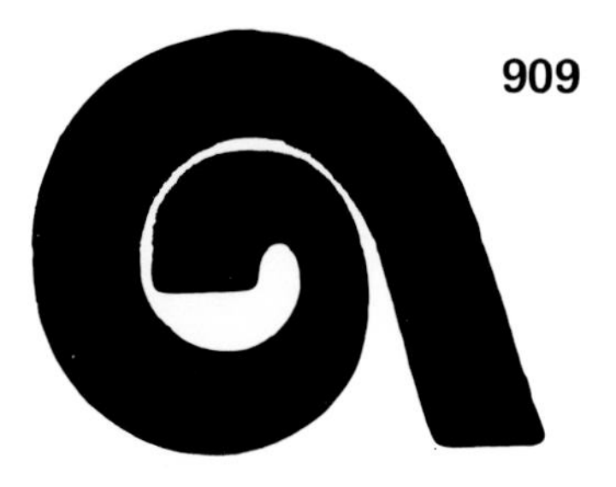
909

910

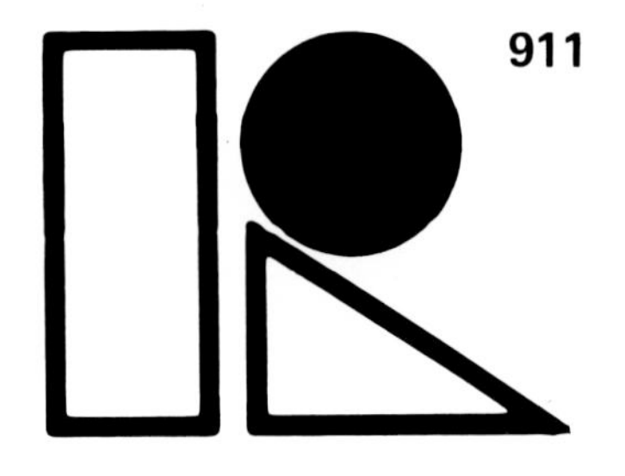
911

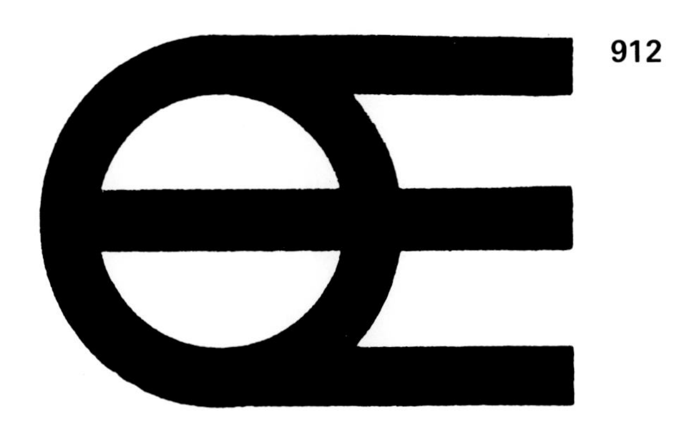
912

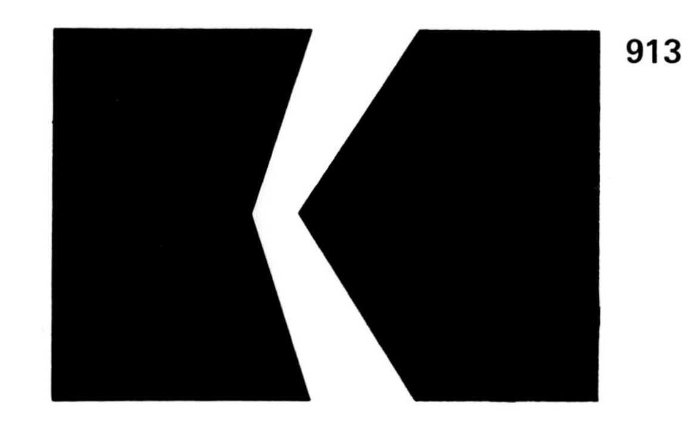
913

914

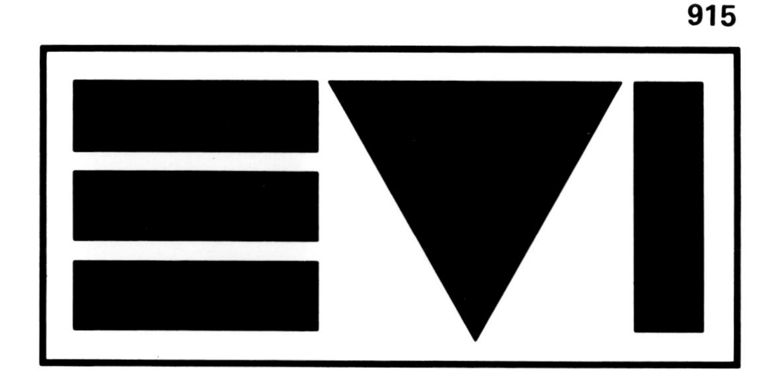
915

904 Hollister, Incorporated
Chicago

905 Beldon Roofing & Remodeling
San Antonio, Texas

906 Statler Tissue Corp.
Medford, Massachusetts

907 Ohio University Press
Athens, Ohio

908 Plan Hold
Los Angeles

909 Akro Corporation
Canton, Ohio

910 General Boushelle Inc.
Chicago

911 Richard P. Rita Personnel System
Hartford, Connecticut

912 Oregon Handling Equipment Co.
Portland, Oregon

913 Koch Products

914 Anchor Fence
Baltimore

915 Electronic Voice, Inc.
Los Angeles

916

917

918

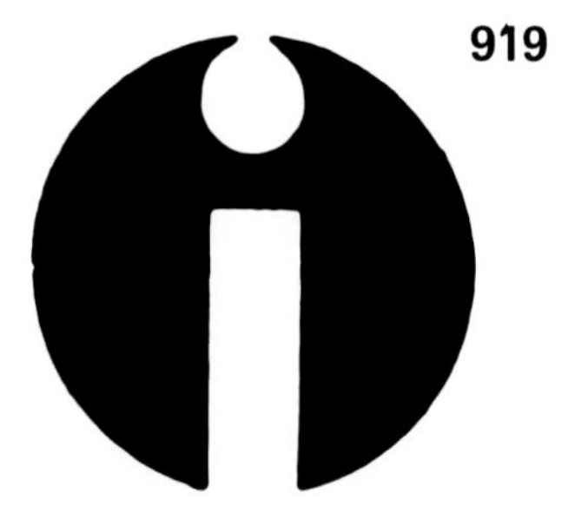

919

920

921

922

923

924

925

926

927

916 Evergreen State Builders, Inc.
Tacoma, Washington

917 Fernstrom Moving System
Rosemont, Illinois

918 Bank of Commerce
Tulsa, Oklahoma

919 Intergold Corp.
Albany, New York

920 Youngstown Steel
Youngstown, Ohio

921 Polaris Enterprises, Inc.
Chicago

922 Amprobe Instrument
Lynnbrook, New York

923 Microdot Inc.
Los Angeles

924 U.S. Plywood
New York City

925 Collins Radio Co.
Dallas

926 Balance Technology, Inc.
Ann Arbor, Michigan

927 Armco Steel Corp.
Middletown, Ohio

928

929

930

932

933

934

931

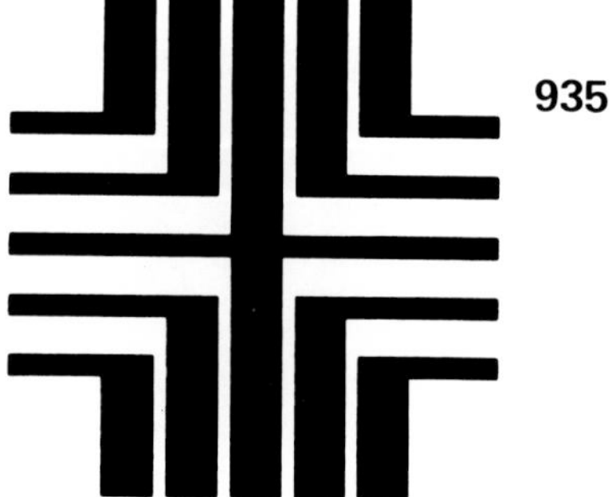

935

936

937

Entertainment
world

938

939

GENERAL CINEMA CORPORATION

928 The Louitt Corporation
Providence, Rhode Island

929 Ashland Area Chamber
of Commerce
Ashland, Kentucky

930 MIT Lincoln Laboratory
Lexington, Massachusetts

931 WGN Television
Chicago

932 Eastern Airlines
New York City

933 Westinghouse
Pittsburgh

934 Cranfill Gallery
Dallas

935 Pitney Bowes
Stamford, Connecticut

936 Connecticut General Life Ins. Co.
Hartford

937 Entertainment World Magazine

938 Eaton Corporation
Cleveland

939 General Cinema Corporation

940
944
941
945
FURNAS
942
946
943
947

948

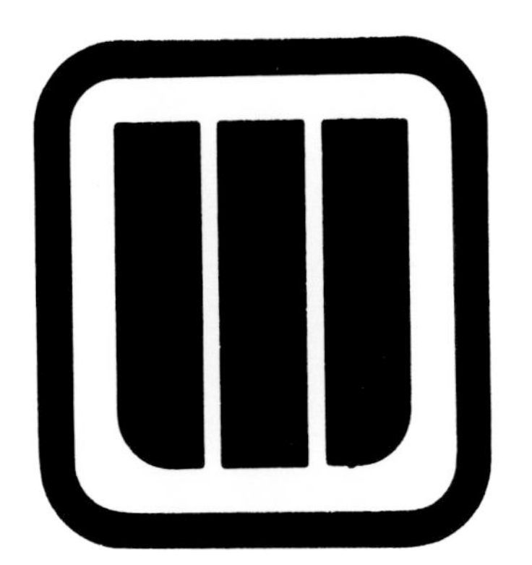

949

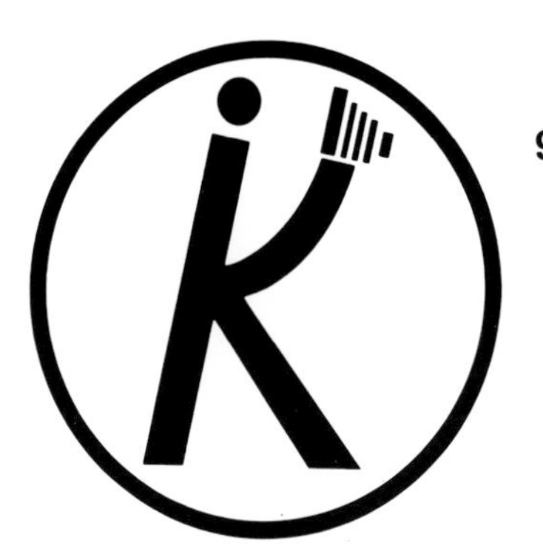

950

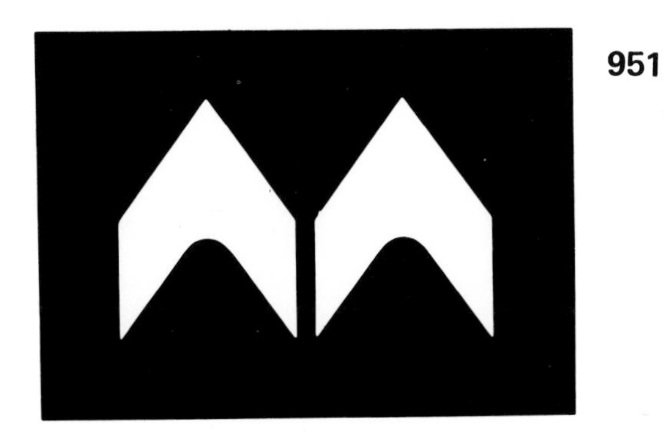

951

940 Berg Electric Corporation
Los Angeles

941 Pelican Productions
New York City

942 Uptrend
Trend Industries
Atlanta

943 Harbor Industries, Inc.
Grant Haven, Michigan

944 Hoerner Waldorf Corporation
St. Paul, Minnesota

945 Furnas Electric Corporation
Batavia, Illinois

946 Title Insurance Co. of Minnesota
Minneapolis

947 The Bank of Virginia

948 3M Company
St. Paul, Minnesota

949 Worthen Bank & Trust Co.
Little Rock, Arkansas

950 Ben Koolin Studio
New Burnswick, New Jersey

951 Modine Mfg. Co.
Racine, Wisconsin

952

953

954

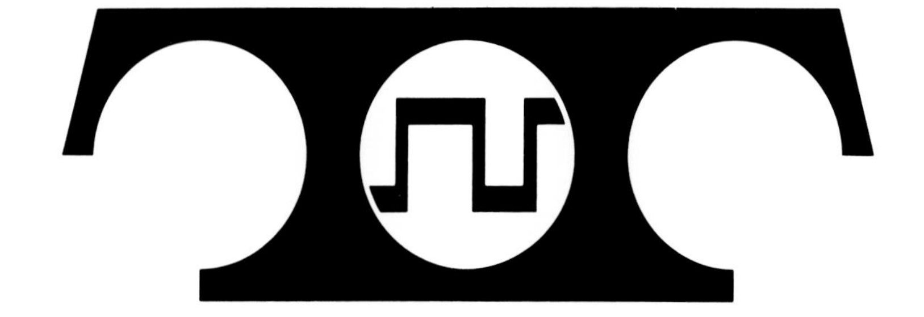

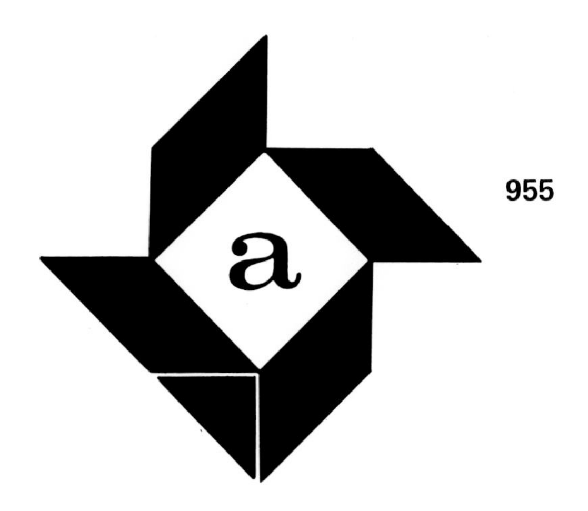

955

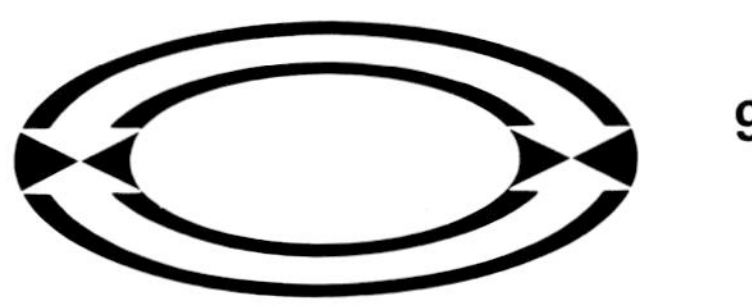

956

957

952 Equitable Life Insurance Co. of Iowa
Des Moines, Iowa

953 Washington Natural Gas Company
Seattle, Washington

954 Teletype Corporation

955 Allpak Container, Inc.
Seattle, Washington

956 D.H. Overmyer Co., Inc.
New York City

957 Schenck Trebel Corporation
Farmingdale, L.I., New York

958 World Carpets
Dalton, Georgia

958

WORLD CARPETS

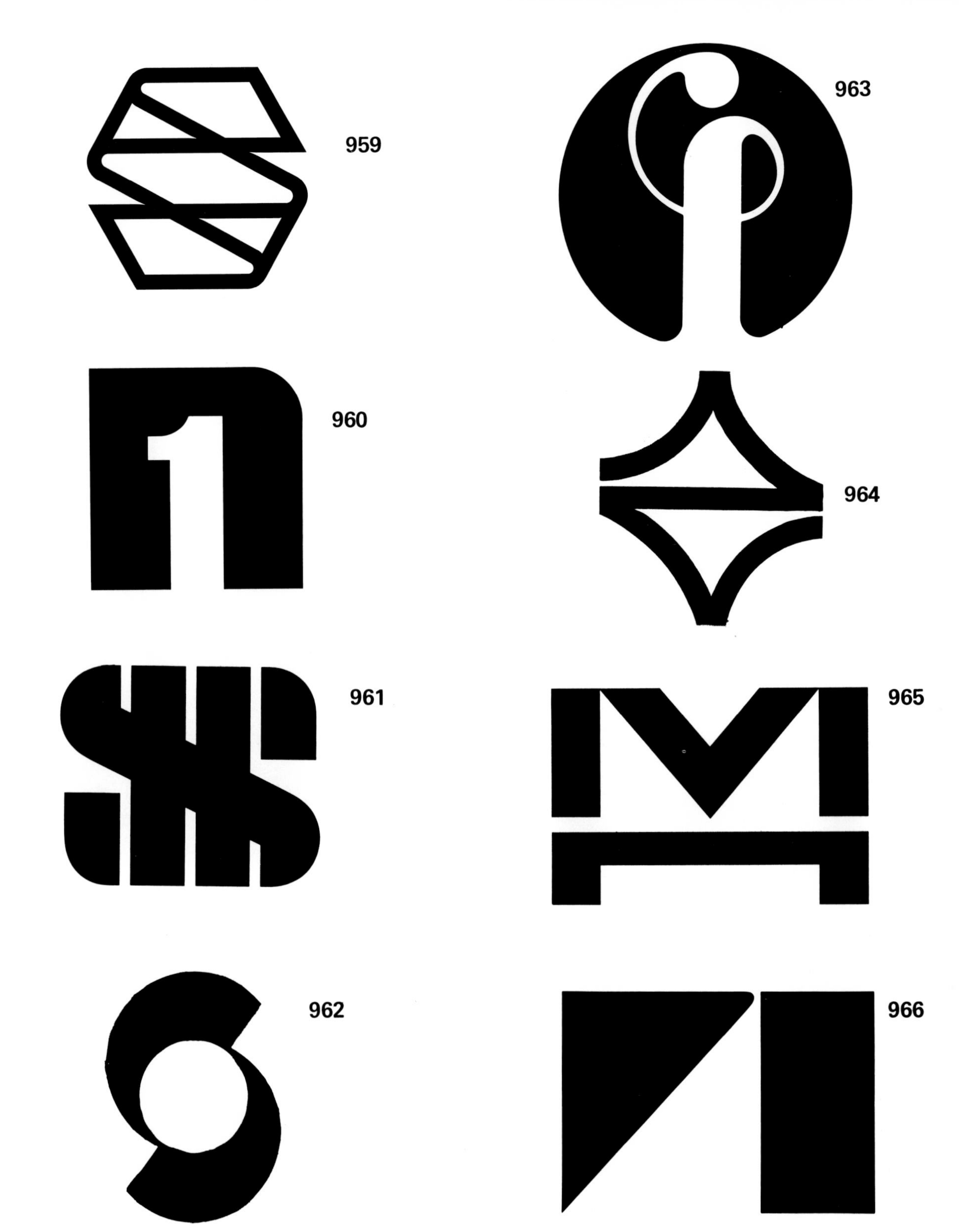
959
960
961
962
963
964
965
966

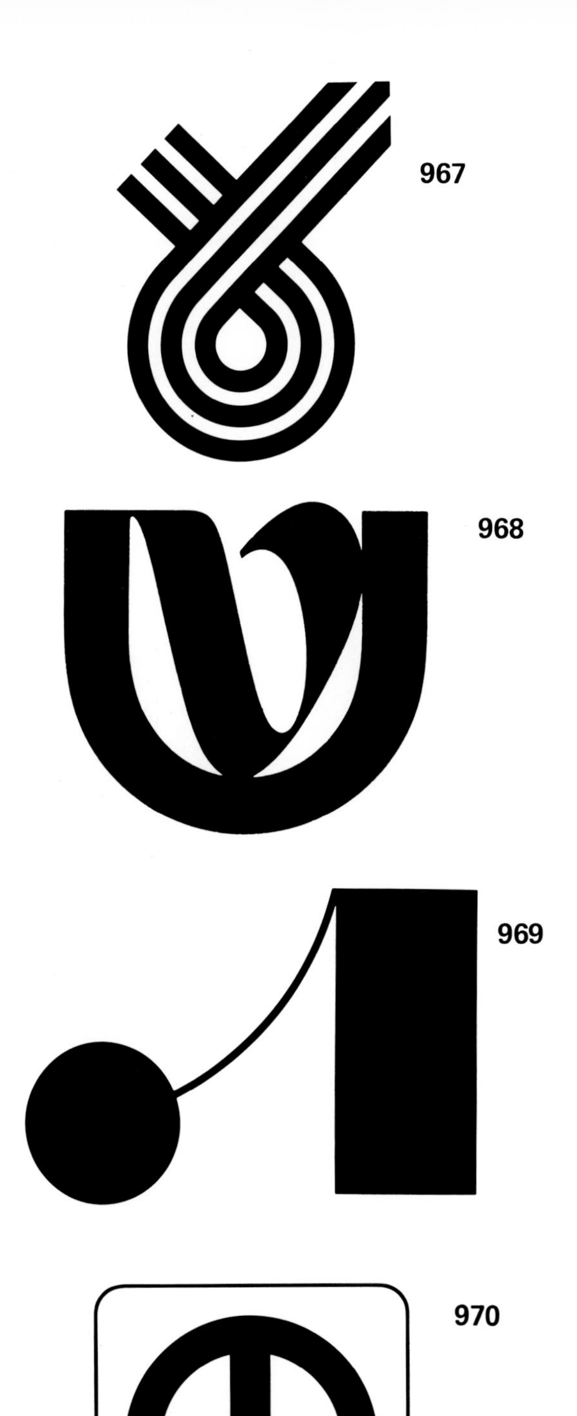

959 Sierracin Corporation
Sun Valley, California

960 National First Corporation
Santa Ana, California

961 Shearson Hammill & Co.

962 Sturm Machine Co., Inc.
Barboursville, West Virginia

963 Inmarco, Inc.
Los Angeles

964 B.C. Ziegler and Co.
West Bend, Wisconsin

965 Mohawk Paper Mills
Cohoes, New York

966 American Motors
Detroit

967 Republic Corporation
Los Angeles

968 United Virginia Bank

969 American Demolition
Denver

970 Diners Club
New York City

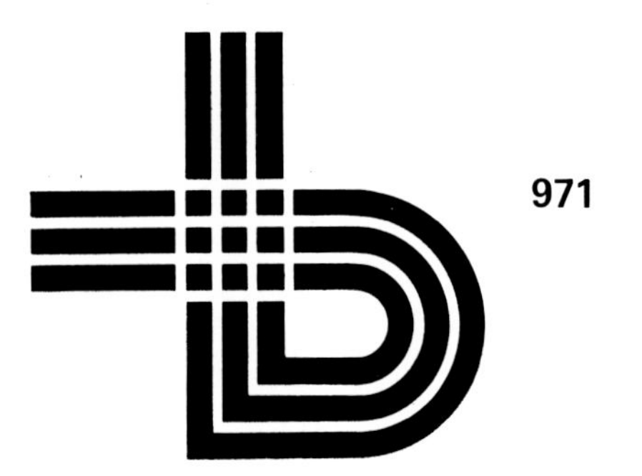

971

972

973

974

975

976

977

978

979

980

XEROX

981

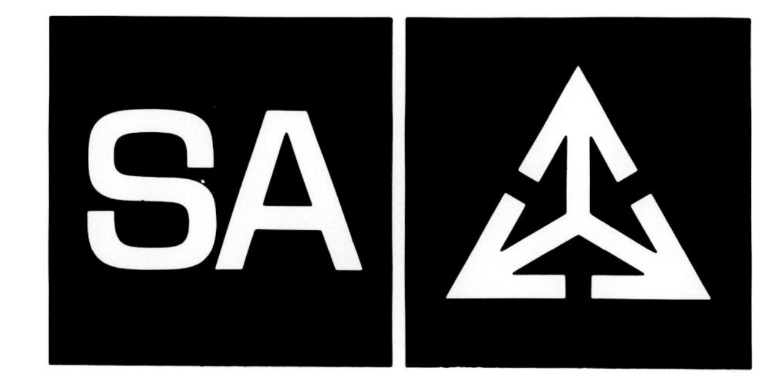

982

Mobil

971 Brentwood Sportswear
New York City

972 American Can Co.
New York City

973 North Carolina Mutual Life Insurance Co.
Durham, North Carolina

974 Deposit Guaranty National Bank
Jackson, Mississippi

975 Rand McNally & Co.
Chicago

976 The Hamm Brewing Co.
St. Paul, Minnesota

977 PPG Industries
Pittsburgh

978 Hercules Incorporated
Wilmington, Delaware

979 FMR Corporation
West Haven, Connecticut

980 Xerox Corporation
Rochester, New York

981 Sanders Associates
Nashua, New Hampshire

982 Mobil Oil Corp.
New York City

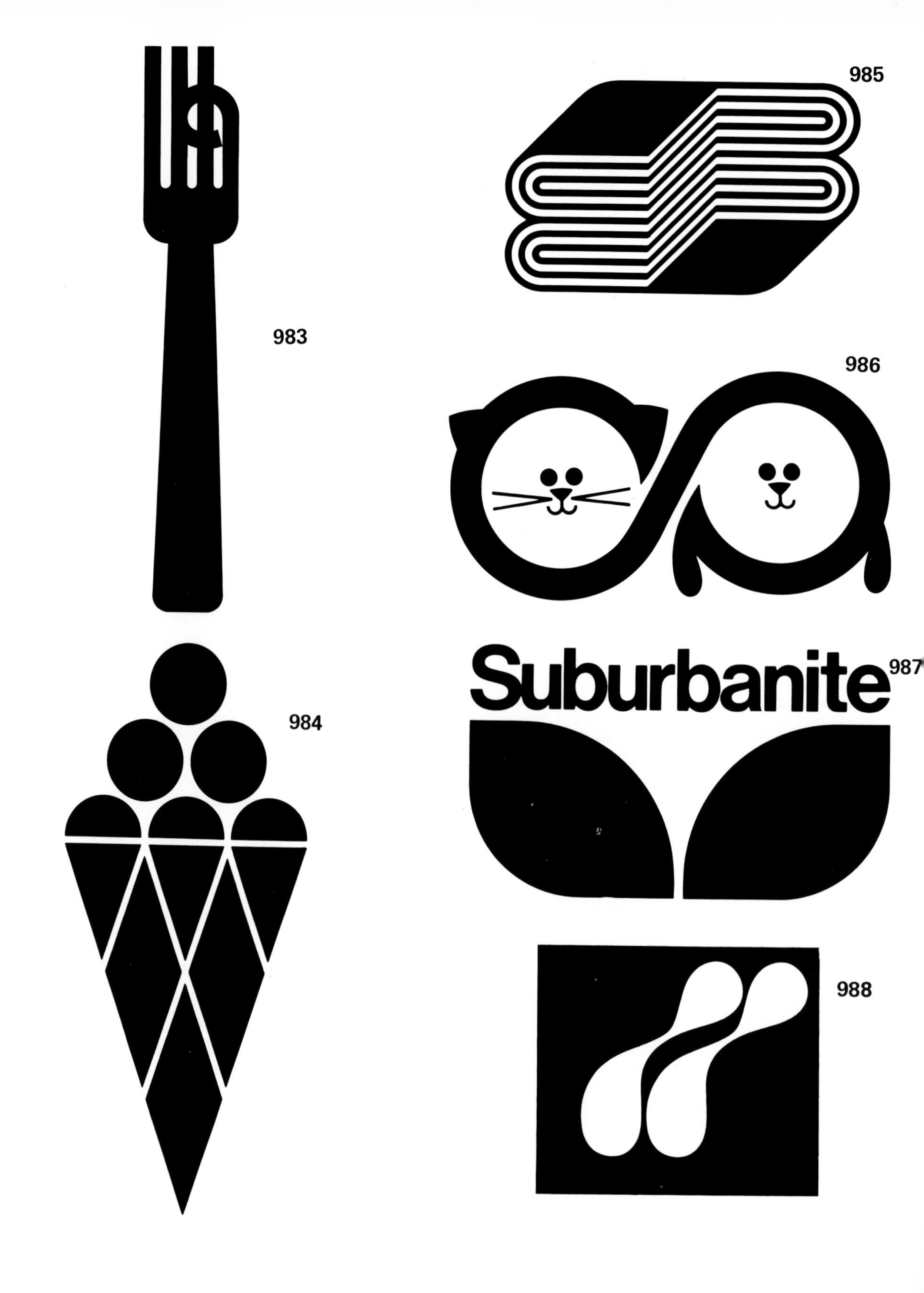

983

984

985

986

987

988

989

990

991

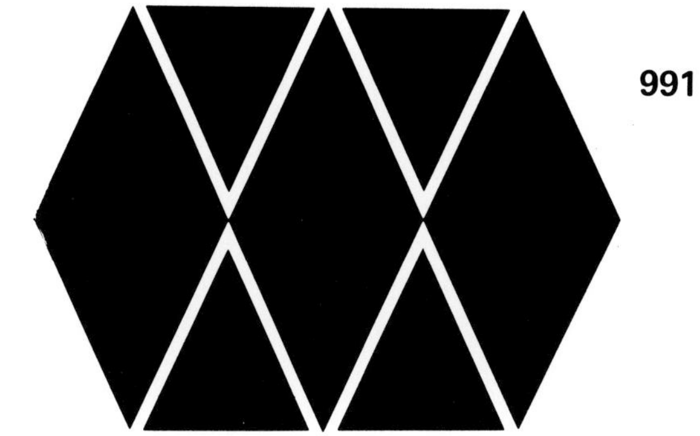

992

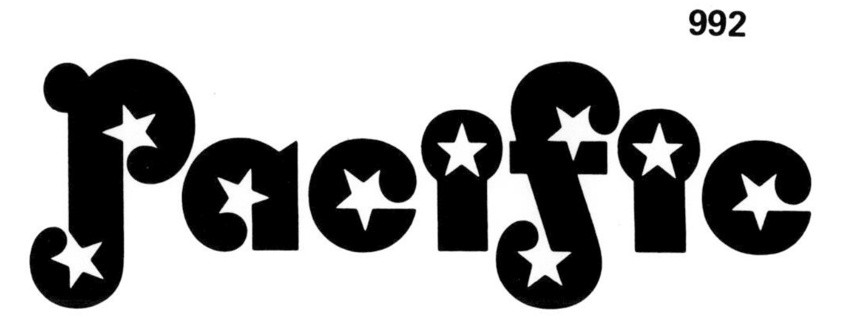

983 9 Muses Restaurant
Los Angeles

984 James McManus Corp.
(ice cream manufacturer)
Quincy, Massachusetts

985 Brown University Press
Providence, Rhode Island

986 Animal Rescue League
Boston

987 Suburbanite Mop Co.
Brookline, Massachusetts

988 Price Pfister Brass Mfg. Co.
Los Angeles

989 Kenroy Inc.
Skokie, Illinois

990 American Actuaries, Inc.
Chicago

991 Kings Lafayette Bank
Brooklyn

992 Pacific Theatres
Los Angeles

Index

Index of Designers

Adrian Loos Design Studio, 2000 Stadium Way, Los Angeles 90026; 24, 62, 677, 729, 737, 839, 983

Robert K. McDonald, 2659 Knob View Rd. New Albany, Indiana, 47150; 255, 777

Alver W. Napper, Jr., 46 Johnstown Road, Albany, New York, 12203; 58, 698

Page, Arbitrio & Resen, Ltd., 595 Madison Avenue, New York City 10022; 368, 710, 843

Parkhurst & Associates, 8032 W. Third St., Los Angeles 90048; 193, 194, 267, 430, 714, 784, 842, 846, 847, 872, 873, 925

Robert Pease & Company, 1636 Bush St., San Francisco 94109; 3, 712, 824, 825, 826

Alan Peckolick Graphic Design; 118 E. 59 Street, New York City 10022; 307, 354, 429, 769

Remington Advertising, Inc., 140 Chestnut Street, Springfield, Massachusetts 01103; 139, 285

Robert Miles Runyan & Associates, 6800 Vista Del Mar, Playa del Rey, California 90291; 66, 67, 80, 83, 97, 164, 239, 241, 732, 801, 832, 967

Salesvertising Art Int., 645 Grant Street, Denver 80203; 4, 82

Selame Design, 2330 Washington Street, Newton Lower Falls, Massachusetts 02162, 143, 197, 200, 220, 240, 302, 303, 346, 348, 349, 361, 612, 675, 676, 814, 901, 906, 939, 987

G. Dean Smith, 633 Battery Street, San Francisco; 477, 478, 479, 480, 481, 482, 483, 484, 525, 527, 528, 529, 530, 531, 532, 533, 534, 535, 536, 537, 538, 539, 540, 541, 542, 543, 544, 545, 546, 547, 548, 772

Stone Associates, 101 Park Avenue, New York City 10017; 35, 105, 215, 259, 260, 419

David Strong Design Group, 30640 Pacific Highway South, Federal Way, Washington, 98002; 441, 442, 443, 444, 445, 446, 492, 493, 494

Howard York Design, 244 E. 58 Street, New York City 10022; 176, 756

Bibliography

BOOKS

Corporate Design Programs, by Olle Eksell, Reinhold Publishing Corporation, 1967

The Corporate Search for Visual Identity, by Ben Rosen, Van Nostrant Reinhold Co., 1970.

Packaging Power, by Walter P. Margulies, World Publishing Co., 1970

The Principles in the Design of Trademarks, by Carlo Vivarelli, Neue Graphik, Switzerland, 1960.

Signet/Signal/Symbol, by Walter J. Diethelm, Hastings House, 1971.

Trademarks/USA, Society of Typographic Arts, 1968.

Trademarks — A Handbook of International Designs, by Peter Wildbur, Reinhold Publishing Co., 1966

Trademarks and Symbols, by Walter Herdeg, Graphis Press, Zurich, 1948

Trademarks and Symbols of the World, by Yusako Kamekura, Litton Educational Publishing Co., 1965

MAGAZINES

The Game of the Name, Life Magazine, November 7, 1969, Volume 67, No. 19, pp. 57-62

NEWSLETTERS

Corporate Identity, published 18 times yearly, 207 E. 37 Street, New York City 10016

BOOKLETS

Reflections (3 volumes) by Leo Burnett, privately printed by the Leo Burnett Co., Chicago, 1969-70

About the Editor

David E. Carter is the designer of a number of corporate symbols, and he taught advertising and design at two universities.

He is a graduate of the University of Kentucky, and holds a master's degree in advertising from Ohio University. His articles have been published in a number of journals, including Journalism Quarterly, The Journal of Typographic Research, The Journal of Advertising Research, and Direct Marketing.

Presently Director of Advertising/Communications at Kentucky Electric Steel Company, Mr. Carter has won more than 120 awards for his creative work in advertising, and his work has been shown in many national exhibits.

His biography appears in the Second Edition of Who's Who in Advertising.